SHARING
— OUR —
EXPERIE

Edited and with an introduction by Arun Mukherjee

Canadian
Advisory Council
on the Status of Women

Conseil
consultatif canadien
sur la situation de la femme

Prepared for the
Canadian Advisory Council on the Status of Women
P.O. Box 1541, Station B
Ottawa, Ontario
KlP 5R5

This book was commissioned by the CACSW. This document does not necessarily represent the official policy of the CACSW.

Available free of charge from the Canadian Advisory Council on the Status of Women by quoting no. 93–G–200.
(The CACSW reserves the right to limit quantities.)

Design & Illustration: Emerging Design
Typography: WordWise
Printed by Mutual Press
© Canadian Advisory Council on the Status of Women 1993

CANADIAN CATALOGUING IN PUBLICATION DATA

Canadian Advisory Council on the Status of Women

Main entry under title:
Sharing our experience
Issued also in French under title: Des expériences à partager.

ISBN 0–662–21090–5

DSS Cat. no LW31–41/1993E

1.   Minority women — Canada.
2.   Women — Canada — Social conditions.
I.   Canadian Advisory Council on the Status of Women.

HQ1233.S42 1993   305.4'0971   C09-099706-9

TABLE OF CONTENTS

COME FROM AWAY

TAKING A STANCE

FOR THE RECORD

FOREWORD

Here we are, a CACSW book that speaks to the diverse experience of racial minority and Aboriginal women. It is designed to bring to the attention of the public the unique experience of women whose lives have not been the blueprint for the theories of feminism, womanism, and other schools of thought that purport to speak on behalf of all women. In *Sharing Our Experience*, the voices of the contributors ring out to me, telling me how much we have in common, how much our lives overlap, and how profoundly our experience as Aboriginal and racial minority women crosses geographical, class, and cultural boundaries. The divisions created by different historical heritage pale against this symphony of voices, speaking about joy, bitterness, dreams, yearnings, abuses, anger, discrimination, hardship, successes, and triumphs. My ears are full of these voices, my mind is preoccupied with these stories. My heart goes out to meet these women. I do not want them to stop, because their stories are my stories, their happiness my happiness, and their pain my pain. In this communal act of sharing experience, I feel uplifted. I feel at once a confirmation of myself, and an expansion of my being.

Experience is the realm where differences and commonalities are worked out. Without hearing women's own account of our perceptions, thoughts, and feelings, all discussions of commonality and difference are abstract, unreal, and unrealized.

Women's difference is a difficult theme. However, our experience of being marginalized as women has shown that, in ignoring difference, we run the risk of creating unique forces of oppression. We run the risk of being forced to see ourselves as similar, as "visible minority women". On the other hand, stressing differences can be dangerous in that we may play into the hands of oppressive forces that encourage divisions that fracture rather than unite.

That is why we should share our experience, apart from the sheer pleasure of doing it. Sharing our experience enables us to identify with one another. We come to understand that we are all similarly affected by forces that bind us. Although it is true that the "essence of womanhood" does not exist, and that our being women neither makes us all the same nor gives us the same problems, as women we are all on a continuum, albeit some of us occupy more privileged places. Because racial and sexual oppression work in diverse and devious ways, we need to find out about the lives of other women. Because we see different bits and aspects of the world, we need to tell one another what we see in order to form a common front.

i

We have come from different racial and cultural backgrounds and many of us do have stereotypes and ideas about one another. Like other members of the general public, some of us imbibe distorted images and concepts. We are often influenced by them unknowingly. Those of us who, like me, are racial minority immigrants brought a lot of baggage with us from different areas of the world in terms of our relationships with one another. First Nations women, growing up in this land, on reserves and in towns and cities, have similar burdens to carry. These burdens can translate into relations which are not always good and exemplify how generally accepted images can oppress and isolate. Sharing our experience enables us to shed our perceptions of one another which derive from these images. Exploring alternative images gives us access to the social realities lived by other women. In fulfilling our yearning to create new images from our unique vantage points, we also eliminate the isolating effect of prevailing images.

In its presentation of the lives of racial minority and Aboriginal women, this book is unique because we at the CACSW have avoided the "institutional" approach, both in conceptualizing the project and in its final production. We do not provide statistics. There are no repetitions of well-worn and hackneyed comments on "visible minorities". The reader is spared many prevailing stereotypical platitudes and falsities. Here our approach to exemplify the lived realities of Aboriginal and racial minority women is via these women's own subjectivities, not via answers to questionnaires. Heeding the advice we received from our national consultation, we have adopted an approach anchored on the plane of imagination. This novel approach fulfils the CACSW's mandate no less than other approaches. Here we aim to gather information concerning women's equality status as a step towards informing the federal government.

The result is this locus which brings together the complex realities of our individual lives as women at the present time. Yes, it is a history book, if history is an account of the present as well as the past. We contend that history should not only be about superstars and great achievements. It should also be about the political reality that keeps so many women disenfranchised in this society. History should highlight the roots of inequality and oppression. It should illustrate that these roots are very different for women belonging to different groups. Life histories shed light on the multiple ways in which women are oppressed. They can play a significant role in the decolonization of our minds and institutions.

One aspect of the CACSW's mandate is to gather information concerning the status of women. This project, by providing a forum where women from non-dominant cultures can speak, facilitates the gathering of such information. At this forum, all of us at the CACSW keep our ears open, and our minds alert. And what do we hear? We hear voices with a variety of timbre, tonality, individuality, pitch levels, modulation, and accents. Each voice is unique. Each evokes association of a specific cultural and linguistic community. Each expresses the perspective of the speaker, as an individual, and as a woman who lives her life in her cultural milieu and derives her being from it.

A forum by its nature provides the space for a variety of views. The forum itself is neutral. It does not generate or affect the substance of what is spoken. The writers of both the Introduction and the letters featured in this anthology speak for themselves and express their own opinions. They do not speak for the CACSW. Neither does the CACSW speak for them. Although the CACSW may, on occasion, with proper consultations and research, speak on behalf of specific groups of women, this is not one of those occasions. In short, the CACSW steps aside at this forum. It gives centre stage and primacy to the speakers. Metaphorically, we just pay for the rental of the hall and the microphones. We take notes, knowing full well that women's experience is the basis for developing analyses and strategies to shape our direction and guide our work in the future.

Glenda P. Simms, Ph.D.
President

NOTE TO THE READER

Throughout the twenty years of its existence, the Canadian Advisory Council on the Status of Women (CACSW) has produced hundreds of publications, but there has never been one quite like *Sharing Our Experience*. The book's uniqueness is the result of how it was created, its content, and its format which reflect the many viewpoints of women whose identities have been racialized as minorities. Under the auspices of the CACSW, and its President Glenda Simms, a national consultation was conducted and an external advisory-editorial committee was struck. One member of this committee, Arun Mukherjee, became the book's external editor and wrote the Introduction.

It was wonderful to receive the outpouring of mail from women who sent us their letters from across Canada, in response to our calls for contributions. The CACSW is grateful to all those who responded and to those who participated in the national consultation. We also want to thank all those who spent time responding to us and sending us their valuable suggestions. The selection session, chaired by President Glenda Simms, was particularly helpful. Comments from all members of the Editorial Advisory Group — Maryse Alcindor, Hilda L. Ching, Marie Marule, Arun Mukherjee, Midi Onodera, Joanne St. Lewis, and Maxine Tynes — were extremely useful. We relied on their sensitivity and thoroughness in the process of reading and selecting the contributions for publication. Because they came from different communities, they were particularly helpful in terms of achieving a balance of viewpoints. Our outreach efforts were enhanced by their ideas and their help. This book represents the collective efforts of many people.

Words are not adequate for expressing our appreciation of the women who sent us their created works — the contributed letters and, in some cases, photographs and drawings. It is as if they have sent us portions of their lives, inviting us to share the sense of achievement, humiliation, pain, bewilderment, hope, triumph, enlightenment, and vision. We feel very honoured by their confidence; we are very grateful for their support. We wish we had the resources to publish all of them.

The efforts of Arun Mukherjee were very special and indispensable to this book. At a crucial stage of the project, gaps needed to be filled by personally inviting people to write letters; and the know-how of an expert on literary merit and on editorial strategies was needed to preserve the styles and voices of Aboriginal and racial minority women. Arun Mukherjee's commitment and labour enabled the birth of this book.

The primary aim of this project was and is to provide a forum for women whose voices have been under-represented. No specific themes were prescribed at the outset. After much discussion, the arrangement we chose is primarily aesthetic; the letters fall into five clusters with certain internal themes. Many of the letters have more than one theme, and many of them could fit into several categories.

The first cluster is about this land and this society we call Canada. It contains letters which talk about the terrain, the vegetation, and the social setting. There is variety in the feelings, attitudes, and judgements of the contributors, some of whom were born here, some of whom were born outside of Canada.

The second cluster contains letters which speak about the past, and which express the pain of growing up, of specific events, abuses, indignities, and unhappiness. The span of feeling is impressive, plumbing the depth of the darker emotions or expressing the bittersweet flavour of memories. This cluster is about identity, and about the role others play in identity formation. It explores the function of culture in the complex process of attaining self-knowledge. Mothers feature prominently in most of these letters.

The third cluster is a partial selection of letters describing immigrant experience, by those Canadians who have "come from away", to use a Newfoundland expression. Additional letters by immigrants are clustered in the other divisions, because they harmonize or contrast well with letters in the other clusters.

The fourth cluster is about taking a stance. The ways in which racial minority and Aboriginal women express their chosen positions reflect the variety of life situations they find themselves in; this diversity pricks the bubble of the homogenized stereotypes of minority women. This cluster features letters which express anger, or which describe their writers' activism on specific issues such as sex selection technology, or which convey the writer's vision of the divine. It features self-determination in the private sphere, such as a decision to celebrate Chinese New Year, seen as a political decision in the personal realm. The letters in this cluster also feature persistence in the public sphere, such as in academia and the media.

The last cluster contains letters which do two things. Some attempt to draw lessons from different types of struggles, such as making a living, pursuing a career, or forging a cultural identity. Others record events, either public or private, which have implications for others, especially younger people, either in one's culture or profession, for the women's movement, or for the world. This section is meant to be a record of the living, personal histories as well as meaningful lessons learned by racial minority and Aboriginal women. They link the past to the present, and they look forward to the future.

This book features the voices of many women who hold different opinions about many things. This is their book. The viewpoints are theirs. The CACSW is listening and taking notice.

Yuen-Ting Lai

Research Analyst

ACKNOWLEDGEMENTS

Many people have helped with my various tasks as editor of this anthology. I am deeply grateful to them for their material and spiritual help without which I would not have survived. Yuen-Ting Lai, CACSW Research Analyst, has sustained me throughout this period by facilitating my work in various ways. I have also benefited enormously from my discussions with her about our vision of the project. Next, I would like to thank my son, Gautam, who typed many of the letters and helped with the materials in French. And I would like to thank my husband, Alok, for patiently reading through my drafts and making helpful suggestions.

I cannot express fully my debt to Glenda Simms, President of the CACSW, and the members of the Editorial Advisory Group. Working with them on this project has made me think in new ways. Their dynamic personalities, their experience of working with Canadian women in various walks of life, their refreshing and original analyses have impinged on me in multiple ways and their influence is etched all over this volume.

My heartfelt thanks go to Alootook Ipellie who took a stranger's plea seriously and supplied me with the addresses of several wonderful Inuit women.

I would like to thank all my friends at York University who listened to my half-baked ideas and my considerable anxieties and made thoughtful suggestions which have benefited me. I would especially like to mention Leslie Sanders and Marlene Kadar.

Finally, I wish to thank all the contributors I worked with in my editorial capacity. We have shared laughter, ideas, letters, and gossip, and I hope that all these intangibles are somehow reflected in the book.

Arun Mukherjee

INTRODUCTION

The contributions anthologized in this collection powerfully communicate the life experiences of Canadian women of Aboriginal, African, Asian, Caribbean, and Middle Eastern descent. Each contribution, written in letter form, articulates the perspective of its author and tells a unique story that she has chosen to share with the readers of this volume. These stories, told honestly and simply, are directly accessible to the reader and do not require the mediating voice of the interpreter to bring out their significance.

However, the story of the coming together of these stories within the pages of this volume needs to be told. When individual voices come to us through a selection process and are arranged in a particular sequence and according to certain categories, they can no longer be said to have come directly from the author to the reader. The subtle transformations of meaning that occur through the interventions of editors bringing together contributions and arranging them in super-imposed categories is often glossed over and presented as natural. It is here that undeclared assumptions do their work of excluding, including, highlighting, foregrounding, and ventriloquizing, i.e., subjecting the authors' agendas to those of the editor's.

The editor, thus, fulfils an important but invisible role in the process of knowledge production. S/he has the power of including or excluding, valorizing or negating, arranging and/or distorting other people's work and/or experiences, a power that is too seldom acknowledged or questioned.

As a woman of colour who teaches in a university setting, I have become extremely aware of the power of editors. They control what I can or cannot teach by deciding who will or will not be included in the anthologies that are used as texts and that communicate messages to students about who writes literature and who makes knowledge. A teacher is often out of luck if s/he wants to teach an inclusionary curriculum, i.e., a curriculum that does not focus only on a very limited set of white male authors, philosophers, artists, and scientists, but gives equal representation to those who are not white and/or male. That goes for Women's Studies as well, a discipline where one would expect greater equity. However, the unavailability of materials produced by and about racial minority and Aboriginal women in Canada persists after more than two decades of second wave feminism, and their lives and aspirations remain marginalized and often misrepresented. *The Issue is 'ism: Women of*

Colour Speak Out,[1] remains the only comprehensive resource to date on Canadian racial minority and Aboriginal women. I hope that *Sharing Our Experience* will help rectify the current marginalization of these voices in our country.

Having suffered under the dictatorial powers of editors and anthologists who convey a hidden message to their readers that few racial minority and Aboriginal persons create knowledge and art when they systematically exclude them from their collections or grant them only token representation, I believe it is imperative that I make the processes of selection and categorization used in this volume visible to the reader since I occupy the editor's seat here. For what knowledge will be produced, and for whom, is profoundly determined by those editorial decisions that operate like the hand of God in their invisible yet ubiquitous presence.

To make the editorial process visible, I must begin at the very beginning, with the genesis of the project that has culminated in this volume now in your hands. I must then recount its progress through conception, gestation, and birth. And continuing with the maternal metaphor, I must also recount the hopes, expectations, and visions of all the women who have contributed to its coming into being. It is a collective story and I hope that I can tell it right without falling into the editorial hubris of exclusion and erasure.

Because it is a collective project, I have resorted to more than one voice. When speaking in the first person as editor, I have used the first person singular. I have used "we" both to refer to the Editorial Advisory Group and to the collective experience of racial minority and Aboriginal women.

THE GENESIS OF THE VOLUME

The project entitled "Sharing Our Experience" has been developed by the Canadian Advisory Council on the Status of Women (CACSW), under the auspices of the Social Development Committee, which is one of three CACSW research committees. The original conception was that of providing a forum "in which the voices of under-represented groups of women will be heard", as the original call for letters stated. The forum was to be a volume of letters which the contributors might have written to people to whom they would like to say something, but for some reason, did not. The anthology was going to contain "the living personal history of many women who, because of their ethnicity or racial origin, believe it important to share their thoughts and feelings." The generality of the project's conception was intentional, and it reflected the outcome of the discussions of the Social Development Committee. It was expected that a sharper focus would emerge as the process unfolded.

A national consultation by mail in the spring of 1990, based on a draft call for contributions to this anthology, resulted in an overwhelmingly positive response. The following quotes from the consultation suggest that many women in Canada feel they have been absent from the overall picture.

- "It puts together the situation of immigrant women into graphic terms which, if expressed in a light form such as a letter, can put points across simply and plainly."

- "The anthology will be a forum for women from all walks of life and different ethnocultural communities."

- "We feel that the voices of immigrant women have either been neglected for too long or others have been speaking on their behalf."

- "Only they can understand their experiences and they do have the ability to share their stories with others."

- "It will create awareness of women's issues."

- "It will perhaps reduce/eliminate discrimination and racism if there is a wide distribution of the material."

The respondents also made suggestions for broadening the framework of the project, many of which were incorporated into the project's design and process. Other suggestions, such as the one to provide "translation service for those women who would like to participate but cannot write in either English or French", poignantly remind those of us who are proficient in either of our two official languages that the skill we take for granted in our day-to-day existence is actually a privilege. And it is a salutary reminder that the voices of those who could not express themselves in English or French are largely absent from the collection, except in the case of Ann Haney's letter which is the outcome of a daughter's attempt to give voice to her non-English-writing mother's experience. Following are some of the other suggestions received by the CACSW from the spring 1990 national consultation:

- "Make clear that elderly immigrant women are included."

- "Adopt more than one format such as essay, poem and play in addition to letter."

- "Add a section on the expertise, values and resources immigrant women come with to Canada; let immigrant women tell what they do and what they contribute to this society."

- Talk about "how women survived their challenges"; depict "women's strength, and their role as agents of change".

- "A planning committee should be struck to think collectively."

- "Fair representation and cross-section of issues (must be) addressed."

The respondents also suggested topics that the letters should focus on. The topics suggested were: immigrant women's labour market experience; experience of single mothers in the paid labour force; double shift work; stress caused by double shift work and isolation; cultural gaps between mothers and daughters; access to the health-care system; access to training programs; and the diversity of history, culture, and traditions of women in Canada.

The subsequent CACSW nation-wide call for submissions was in total harmony with the views expressed by the respondents. Widely distributed through women's networks as well as advertising, the call was addressed to "racial or ethnic minority women" and invited them to share their "thoughts and feelings about the difficulties and pleasures of living and working in Canada." The call spelt out in detail the possible topics that prospective letter writers could choose to write on. The guidelines were extremely flexible and left a lot of room for individual interpretation.

The CACSW received ninety letters in response to the call. Now the task was to determine the criteria for selection and to choose the letters for publication. The Social Development Committee decided that an external advisory cum editorial committee would be ideal for undertaking this important task. The idea was to have an impartial committee, made up of women who are respected members of their communities. The CACSW chose women who were familiar with the issues raised in the contributions, and who could select the letters with sensitivity and understanding.

Members of the Editorial Advisory Group (EAG) met on March 24, 1991 for a full day, and they consulted again a few weeks later at a conference call on April 11. Apart from comparing the selections each member had made previously, they were presented with a number of possible issues to consider. One issue pertained to the question of whether the focus of the anthology should be exclusively on racial minority and Aboriginal women. The question had to be answered because of the perceived ambiguity of the term "ethnic minority women". During the time in which the call for contributions was in effect, the public enquiries about the project and the contributions received made it clear that some women understood the call to be for women of colour only, and other women perceived it to be for all women.

A passage from "Possible Issues" — a document prepared by Yuen-Ting Lai (CACSW Research Analyst) and distributed to the EAG members — clarifies the dilemma:

> Another question is whether we should distinguish clearly between "racial minorities" and "ethnic minorities". We have contributions from Polish, German, Dutch, Italian, and Jewish women, and their communities are supposed to be "ethnic minorities", not "visible minorities". **The question is whether we should equate "racial minorities" with "visible minorities"**[2] (emphasis added). One point to keep in mind is that these women, by virtue of having responded to our call for contributions, have already self-identified themselves as belonging to racial and ethnic minorities.

The excerpt gives some indication of the definitional problems faced by the CACSW at this time. A number of women had read the call to imply an equivalence between the terms "racial" and "ethnic". The respondents' comments quoted earlier had not only considered these two terms synonymous, they had also used the term "immigrant" as though the three terms were equivalent.

The respondents, who thought of these terms as interchangeable, were following the prevalent definitions. However, using these terms as interchangeable is quite problematic. Because everyone except the Aboriginal peoples has entered Canada as an immigrant, the category "immigrant women" ought to apply to all non-Aboriginal women in Canada. However, as the comments of the respondents suggest, it often refers to racial minority and/or ethnic minority women. For example, I was once invited, along with another woman of colour, to speak to a Women's Studies class on "Racism and Immigrant Women". Both of us felt that the topic was a good example of unconscious racism because it assumed that all women of colour are immigrants. It implies that only women of colour are "new" arrivals and that those excluded from the category are the "real" Canadians. The fact is that many racial minority women are nth-generation Canadians. Whereas ignorant people continue to ask them about where they are from, thus implying that only whites are "real" Canadians, white immigrant women usually are asked that question only if they speak with an accent. It is also important to remember that second or third generation white immigrant women, once they no longer speak with an accent, do not face the kind of systemic discrimination that remains the lot of immigrant women of colour, no matter which generation they belong to.

Using the terms "racial minority" and "ethnic minority" as though they were synonymous poses similar problems because such usage suggests that only racial minorities have ethnicity. Somehow, the ethnicity of white Canadians is seldom acknowledged; they are considered "just Canadians". In fact, white Canadians are as much ethnic as Canadians of colour.

In a recent trend, some white ethnic groups have begun to identify themselves as "ethnic minorities" to denote their difference from dominant anglophone and francophone groups. While they have every right to define themselves this way, such usage has caused problems for racial minorities. According to Norman Buchignani, the "mainline white ethnic groups'" concern with "such things as symbolic cultural preservation, *group cultural rights*, and the promotion of greater and more positive awareness of their group in Canadian society at large" has led to a subordination of racial minorities' "issue of their *individual rights* of access to jobs, advancement, housing and the like." He goes on to suggest that "This split in ethnic group interests is quite consequential, for unless it is actively overcome, it robs the political drive to eliminate racism of the important (and perhaps crucial) support of these mainline white ethnic groups".[3] In the light of this new usage of the term "ethnic minority", we must be doubly vigilant about terminological confusion.

Unfortunately, these terms continue to be used imprecisely in government documents, consultants' reports, and feminist analyses. By using the categories of "immigrant women", "racial minority women", and "ethnic minority women" interchangeably, these discourses deny the specific oppression that racial minority women experience in Canadian society. Most important, these categories, when used interchangeably, make it impossible for us to take into account the racial oppression of Aboriginal women, since it is caused by institutionalized racism and not immigration.

The following passages from Dionne Brand, an African-Canadian woman, and Kari Dehli, a Scandinavian-Canadian woman, spell out the need to keep these categories separate if we want our investigations to tell us the truth:

> Basically, I really did not think of myself as an immigrant *per se*. Yes, I came from another country, but I didn't think that the worlds were that far apart, and I knew that the problems I would have would not stem from my being an immigrant, but would stem from my being black. If I had been white, within a generation my family would have been assimilated. I could escape being an immigrant, but along with the black people who have lived in this country for three centuries, I would not escape my race at any point. Racism was the focus of my encounter with Canada, not immigrancy.[4]

6

As an immigrant from one of the Scandinavian countries entering university, my experience of being an immigrant in Canada has been quite different than what is often presumed within the discourses on immigrant women. Indeed, it is quite rare for me to be positioned as an immigrant woman by, for example, having to answer the question: "Where are you from?" or more consequentially for employment, "Do you have Canadian experience?" The practices of state agencies, employers and university admissions departments (to mention some) which tie together skin-colour and "accents" with being an immigrant, thus producing racist discrimination and exclusion for many, produce a kind of invisibility and erasure for me. In contrast to many immigrant women, these assumptions provide a whole range of advantages for me: I am included as a "Canadian" as a matter of course.[5]

The two excerpts suggest that racial minority women and white ethnic minority women have distinct experiences and identities, and ignoring these distinctions only means an erasure of the fact that the two groups do not enjoy a level playing field.

The document entitled "Possible Issues", quoted earlier, gives some indication of the dilemmas faced by the CACSW vis-à-vis definitions and their implications. The Editorial Advisory Group recommended that the CACSW produce a book devoted entirely to letters by racial minority and Aboriginal women. The EAG's recommendation was based on the realization that the experiences articulated by Aboriginal women and women of colour were very different from those articulated by women who self-identified themselves as ethnic minority women and mixing the two up might result in once again marginalizing the voices of Aboriginal and racial minority women.

The decision by the Social Development Committee to accept the EAG's advice to devote this book exclusively to racial minority and Aboriginal women is a momentous decision. It implies a recognition of the fact that the voices of Aboriginal women and women of colour have been marginalized, not only in the larger arena of Canadian society but also in the domain of feminist theory. It is only very recently that white feminists have become aware of the invisible racism of their own categories of analysis and modes of institutional behaviour. This awareness has been brought about by the struggles waged by Aboriginal women and women of colour to have themselves included in feminism's agenda.

Racial minority and Aboriginal women were marginalized by some theorists of second wave feminism when the latter identified women's biological difference from men as the primary source of their oppression.

These theorists explained patriarchy through this biological difference between the sexes, and all other oppressions were declared to have arisen from this institution. Gender oppression was said to have emanated from women's reproductive capacities, which were responsible for their confinement to the private sphere. These theories were, of course, produced by white feminists and did not take into account such historical facts as slavery and colonialism and their parenting of present-day racism. By focusing so obsessively on sexual difference, these feminists produced an "essential" woman who was the same all over the globe and whose oppressions were produced by her gender.[6] After stipulating a "common oppression", these theorists then postulated a sisterhood that all women experienced due to the similarity of their experience. They wrote about "women's oppression", "women's experience", "women's literature", "women's history", and "women's work", in a universalizing vocabulary which suggested that women across the globe were not differentiated by such factors as history, culture, race, class, ethnicity, and nationality, and had similar destinies because they shared the same biological features.

While this vocabulary of "women's experience" claimed to be universal, the inclusion of only white women's writings in the Women's Studies courses and anthologies showed that only white women's experience was being talked about. Thus, on the one hand, these feminist theorists spoke of a common oppression and a universal sisterhood; on the other, they excluded the experiences of racial minority and Aboriginal women by failing to acknowledge their differences.

As a result, much of the feminist theory produced, taught, and practised since the beginning of second wave feminism is of no relevance to Aboriginal women and women of colour. Himani Bannerji articulates the alienation of women of colour thus:

> Controversies over International Women's Day, which I celebrated with fervour, conveyed to me the astounding revelation that "imperialism" was not a "women's issue." Readings informed me that class and gender struggles were to be separately conceived and waged, that women were "class-less," a "caste" perhaps, and patriarchy was an "autonomous" power system....Racism was not even mentioned as a real issue by the "Canadian Women's Movement." Our lives, our labour remained unmentioned, and intellectual/cultural production unsolicited, in the annals of publications of the (Canadian) Women's Press. We were at best a separate category of sub-women — "immigrant," "visible minority," "ethnic," "black," later "women of colour."[7]

As Bannerji suggests, issues of utmost concern to her as a South Asian woman were denied validation by her white colleagues. It happened because of the fundamental assumptions at the heart of feminist theory I mentioned earlier: that women share a common oppression and that it is rooted in their biology. It leads to a feminism that does not think that racism and colonialism are women's issues. In a 1991 newspaper article, Patricia Bishop expressed the view of such feminists: "Women who have joined together as feminists have identified the oppression of women as women as the central reason for their coming together."[8]

Such a view implies that racial minority and Aboriginal women have detachable parts of identity that can be added or taken out at will. However, as many of them have reiterated again and again, and do once again in these letters, they are women and Aboriginal, women and Black, women and Asian at the same time, and not separately. And their oppressions are related to being both non-white **and** women, and have to be addressed simultaneously.

It is hard for me, as a woman of colour, to understand why it is so difficult for many white women to see our differences. And yet, I know that there are deep rifts and tensions within the women's movement today around the issue of race. White women have been called privileged because, in the eyes of many racial minority and Aboriginal women, not only do they not have to bear the brunt of racism, but, in fact, they get certain advantages because of their skin colour. That race is felt as the foremost oppression by non-white women is evidenced by the fact that it has also provoked disagreements in the lesbian community even though both white and non-white lesbians must struggle against homophobia and heterosexism.

Racial minority and Aboriginal women have also challenged the theorists who foreground class at the expense of race. It is too often the case that Marxist and socialist feminists create a unitary class oppression and class solidarity despite the fact that the past working-class struggles in the Western world did not only not protect the rights of non-white workers but also supported racist governmental policies. Hence, those of us who are not white cannot accept analyses proposing that working-class solidarity will overcome racism automatically.

Thus, we are saying that women cannot be constituted as a unitary category for the purpose of analysis simply on the basis of their sexual difference from men, and when feminist theory constructs its universal woman, thus erasing our differences, we suffer. Perhaps no one else has defined this difference, as clearly as Lee Maracle. When she overheard a white woman at a conference say, "Hey wait a minute. We're all women, we're all equal, so what if you're a different colour?", she wrote:

No, we are not equal. We live half as long, are unemployed, impoverished as a people. No youth should ever have to attend the funerals of thirty-seven young relatives and friends, grow up to watch her children weep with hunger, search for work and be told "the position is filled" by employers who continue to advertise, or be told that she is "not qualified to be trained," as I and now my children and the majority of Native women are told over and over again. Half of the women in our community are single, near-destitute mothers. Half of the children apprehended each year by the Ministry of Human Resources are our children. No, we are not equal and I don't believe the woman who said that is blind. I believe she is uncaring.[9]

These words say it all. In a world scarred by racism, colonialism, imperialism, heterosexism, and ablism, all women are not equal, and cannot be equal unless we change the world. And these words warn me, who criticizes white feminists for erasing the differences between white women and women of colour, not to turn around and erase the very distinct oppressions of Aboriginal women by assuming that all racial minority women are similar or equally oppressed.

In order to ensure that Aboriginal women and women of colour are not rendered invisible in the cogitations of feminist theory, it will have to admit our inequality and our difference from white women and not lump all of us under the category "women". As Elizabeth Spelman has pointed out:

> [T]he focus on women 'as women' has addressed only one group of women — namely, white middle-class women of Western industrialized countries. So the solution has not been to talk about what women have in common as women; it has been to conflate the condition of one group of women with the condition of all and to treat the differences of white middle-class women from all other women as if they were not differences.[10]

The publication of this book under the auspices of the CACSW suggests to me that the Council has undergone a salutary process of soul-searching. For, like other institutional bodies, it too has operated in the past from the theoretical premise that the category "women" is a unitary category and can take into account the experiences of all Canadian women. *Sharing Our Experience* is the concrete evidence of this reconceptualization. The title connotes that our experiences as women are different and we need to listen to each other in order to understand each other rather than assume similarity of all women at the outset. This way of thinking does not assume an absolute difference but suggests that dialogue can lead to a shared understanding. We must all pay heed to Minnie Aodla Freeman's words: "We do not sit with each other long enough to understand each other. We do not educate each other enough to understand each other's cultures." I hope that *Sharing Our Experience* will begin this process among our diverse communities in Canada.

THE SELECTION PROCESS

The CACSW decided that "the participation of an external group in this project would be beneficial".[11] Maryse Alcindor, Hilda Ching, Marie Marule, Midi Onodera, Joanne St. Lewis, Maxine Tynes, and myself were invited to be part of the Editorial Advisory Group (EAG). The CACSW sent all of us the submitted letters without disclosing the names and addresses of the writers; as a result, I think the EAG members had a very different reading experience from the one that the reader of the published volume will have. In my own experience, each letter started as a mystery, and yet, after I had read the whole pile, I found myself arranging them in sub-groups, so clearly did the messages of the authors' ethnic and racial identity come through to me.

The reading of many of these letters was one of the most profound experiences of my life. These words were about real pains and pleasures, by women who were writing about their day-to-day experiences of surviving in a racist, sexist, classist, and heterosexist world. The texts they had made out of their life experiences hit me with a force I had seldom experienced before. As a person who makes her living by teaching literature to university students, I felt that the letters' "aura" of authenticity was not just a textual effect but "true" in a most profound sense. I began to question the way our society privileges literature and literary writers and believes that only writers have the ability to give voice to our realities. The success of these women, most of whom are not professional writers, in drawing me into their worlds has forced me to rethink all the definitions of art and artist that circulate in our society. I strongly believe that the "truth" of these autobiographical accounts hits with a far stronger force than the "truth" of art where one is always conscious of the fictionality of art and the artistry of the artist. (I write these words despite the possibility of my being considered naive by poststructuralists who will perhaps find these letters as textual as works of art.) As I read these accounts by women who inhabit this land called Canada with me, I had a profound sense of sharing the bittersweet experiences of flesh and blood women, women who walk the streets of Canada, women who work at jobs, women who shop and cook, women who raise children, women who go through life persecuted by racial and sexual oppression, and women who resist these oppressions with all their power.

While the "artifice" of these accounts is not to be denied — the writers were instructed to use the epistolary (letter) form and have thus produced a text and entered the realm of textuality — the lived experience of the writers demands that we respond to these texts differently from the way we respond to fiction or other literary genres. These texts are testimonials, or what Marlene Kadar has termed "life writing".[12] While I am not claiming that they are transparent representations of the writers' sentiments, for they all use narrative and literary devices and are aware of a larger reading public beyond the addressee (who is at times fictional), as "life-writing" they demand from the readers an acknowledgement of the writer's truth-claims. They **are** about the writer's own life and they **are** about communicating the truth of that life.

These writings also alerted me, once again, to how far academic feminism has travelled from the lives and experiences of the majority of women. Most of the works taught in Women's Studies courses are either by literary writers or academic theorists whose concerns as well as language seldom reflect those of ordinary women. Most personal narratives of second wave feminism are by celebrity women. Grassroots women's stories remain untold except for works such as *I, Rigoberta Menchú: An Indian Woman in Guatemala*; *Jin Guo: Voices of Chinese Canadian Women*; Makeda Silvera's *Silenced*; and Dionne Brand's *No Burden to Carry*. There is a great need for personal narratives, both oral and written, that can communicate to us the diverse experiences of women in Canada. This volume, with voices of Aboriginal women and women of colour from all parts of Canada, and spanning many generations, fills a large gap by allowing us to hear the voices of women who have been denied a hearing thus far.

Having had such a strong response to most of the letters, I found it extremely difficult to make a selection on my own. As I was to discover, other women in the Editorial Advisory Group had a similar response. It was reassuring to know that I did not have to make such important decisions in the isolation of my own study, and that my personal biases would be balanced by other voices in the Group.

The members of the Editorial Advisory Group, except for Maxine Tynes, met in Ottawa on March 24, 1991 to make the final selection. According to the letter we received on January 25, 1991 from Yuen-Ting Lai, Research Analyst for the CACSW's Social Development Committee, our mandate and functions were as follows:

- To ensure comprehensiveness in the choice of themes;

- To suggest racial, regional, and ethnic balance of the content;

- To suggest a concrete structure for the anthology;

- To clarify principles for selections;

- To select 22–27 contributions;

- To suggest a framework for a non-racist and non-sexist understanding of the experience recounted in the letters which may be articulated in an introduction;

- To identify possible gaps in the collection of letters chosen and, if necessary, to suggest the names of possible persons whom we might invite to write additional letters to fill these gaps.

As we sat huddled together for a whole day, starting at 9 a.m. sharp and ending at 5 p.m., with lunch and coffee breaks, in the daunting Committee Room of the Government Conference Centre in Ottawa, we developed our procedures as we went along, by trial and error. Meeting the members of the Editorial Advisory Group as well as Glenda Simms, CACSW President, and Yuen-Ting Lai, was an electrifying experience for me. Most of us had never met one another before. Glenda Simms made the welcoming address and conveyed to us the momentousness of our task. She told us that "in order to really know what Canadian feminism is, we have to have feminism instructed by all our experiences." She hoped that this volume would "put the face on the unique kind of oppression Aboriginal women and women of colour face in this country and also bring out their unique perspective."

I had a feeling of being at a crossroads when Glenda Simms said: "What we are doing here today is unique. It is the first time that the Council has called together a [working] committee of people from different backgrounds. This is part of the process of change and we wanted to make sure that we had people representing different groups around this table."[13] During our conversations and discussions, we became aware that all of us around the table have had first-hand experience of our own marginalization and exclusion as well as the marginalization and exclusion of our communities. We were all seasoned fighters and that's perhaps why we had ended up seated around that table, deciding which voices would be included in this historic volume.

As we started on the task of selecting the letters, we speculated on our role as judges. As one member said, "Part of me felt incredibly uncomfortable at attempting to evaluate someone else's experience." This view was shared by all of us around the table. Throughout the day, we kept coming back to this basic question and examining our own biases and preferences. I do believe that our collective wisdom has done a fair selection. We chose letters in terms of giving fair representation to various geographical regions, the diverse ethnic communities and, finally, the diversity of themes and issues.

During this meeting, we often changed our individual minds through hearing the views of others on the committee. While it was easier to change a "maybe" to a "yes", it was very difficult to say "no", especially to a letter that we had all liked and that had an interesting story to tell. Yet, we had to say "no" because we couldn't take too many letters on the same theme, or from the same region, or from the same community.

By the end of the day, we had selected a number of definite "yes" letters, deferred decisions on several others pending further information or revision, and made up our minds about the definite "no's" as well. As we had gone through our task, we had also identified several gaps in terms of issues and representation that we felt needed to be filled. Then we went home.

The Editorial Advisory Group had a teleconference on April 11, 1991 to tie up the loose ends. At this meeting we advised the CACSW to send out a limited call for submissions to fill the gaps we had identified. We also decided that the CACSW as well as the EAG would solicit from individuals and communities on a person-to-person basis. We made a strong recommendation that the solicitations be made to "profiled individuals" only as a last resort.

THE FINAL SELECTION

As editor, I can by no means claim that we were successful in filling all the gaps that we had identified. However, the volume does indicate that we tried, and can claim a reasonable, if not total, success in our effort to represent the diversity of experiences encountered by racial minority and Aboriginal women of Canada. Along with the widely distributed first and second printed calls, we also resorted to word-of-mouth networks in our attempts to fill the gaps.

This word-of-mouth search also indicated to me how the printed call itself might have been a barrier for many women, particularly women who use English or French as a second language. As a group, we became acutely aware of that barrier during our March 24, 1991 meeting when we went through a pile of letters from a Centre for Job Re-entry that had been written as a classroom assignment for English as a Second Language students. We felt they couldn't go in as they were because they were very descriptive and very short and quite similar. However, that made us feel that these women's voices were being excluded because of a built-in barrier. We ended up putting many of the letters from this class in the "maybe" pile. Many of the letters in the book are from women whose first language is not an official language of Canada and who have attained varying levels of fluency in their second language. And finally, Ann Haney's letter reminds us of women who are not in this volume because they cannot write in English or French. Also excluded are women who cannot write. For even though the CACSW had invited voice tapes, it did not receive any.

It is no less a matter of regret that we received no submissions from physically challenged racial minority and Aboriginal women. As with the other "isms", ablism affects racial minority and Aboriginal women in particular ways. We would have liked very much to have the specificity of these experiences included in this book.

A voice that is under-represented here is that of racial minority and Aboriginal lesbians. We wish we could have generated more responses from this community. As Asein's letter in this book suggests, homophobia and heterosexism, barriers enough on their own, become lethal when combined with racism. Her words remind us of the necessity to make connections among sexism, racism, and homophobia — and of the importance of challenging all of them.

These are gaps that, I hope, will be filled in future projects undertaken by the CACSW.

THE EDITING AND THE EDITOR

The CACSW approached me in September 1991 to take on the responsibility of editing the collection and writing an introduction. Although I regarded it a great honour to have been considered suitable for the task, I also felt some trepidation in terms of the awesome responsibility it implied. For I knew that neither my experience of producing academic literary criticism nor academic feminist theory was going to help me articulate the importance of this project. Indeed, the letters as testimony of the lived experience of these diverse Canadian women, as acts of bearing witness, are beyond the grasp of academic theories.

Much too often, Women's Studies courses give the message that women's experience is universal by simply choosing and arbitrarily mixing materials from the United States, Britain, France, and Canada. I have felt acutely uncomfortable teaching these courses because they negated my experience as a woman of colour. This volume, I hope, will make us aware that Canadian women's experiences as a whole are different from those of women in these other First World countries on the one hand, and, on the other, that there is considerable diversity within Canada as well. We therefore need to think of our own experiences and our own theories rather than importing them from New York, London, and Paris.

For me, the past several months — which I spent reading these letters, and speaking and writing to several contributors across Canada — have been a period of intense speculation and re-education. Some of the letters I received from contributors in response to my queries were so forceful that I wished they could be published as well. Every time I spoke to a contributor, I wished the conversation had been taped, so enthused and empowered we both felt as we talked. Many of our conversations, full of humour and sorrow, intimacy and laughter, will remain etched in my mind for years to come. What writing for this anthology has meant to the contributors came alive to me when I read the following words of Evelyn Hamdon: "Once again thank you for including my experience in the book. It has given me a tremendous feeling of empowerment. For my thoughts of so many years to have a voice is more than I ever dreamed." (quoted with permission of the author)

While it would be physically impossible to share all the letters I received from the contributors, I still would like the reader to get a sense of my interchange with them. I quote below from a letter that Thao P.T. Vo wrote me after I had written to her, informing her that the Editorial Advisory Group was not sure if she had had her letter translated by someone into English after writing it in Vietnamese because, although the letter complained of the writer's problems with the English language, the writer's command of the language suggested otherwise:

> Your letter also stroke [sic] me more surprisingly than ever. You are suspecting that I had written my letter in Vietnamese language and I had it translated by some one!! You said if I could write such a beautiful letter like "mine" why I failed in applying to Nursing Assistant program in 1990???
>
> Dear Ms. Mukherjee, would you please listen to my words once and for all. The letter that you are having in your hands is my own work. I wrote it myself without receiving any help from the outsider. Is it very clear to you Ms. Mukherjee? ...In 1990, I applied to the Nursing Assistant [Programme] of ... College and failed miserably!! You know the reason why? Because I had no idea of how to write aptitude tests and how to write Multiple choice tests!! I still remember the horrible feeling when I saw aptitude tests for the first time in the Test Center Room of ... College. This happened to me as if the earth had cracked under my feet. (quoted with the permission of the author)

I also learned from Thao P.T. Vo's letter to me that she was a pharmacist in Vietnam but had started working in Canada as a sewing machine operator three weeks after her arrival, details that are not given in her letter to the CACSW. Her letter also told me that after a two and a half year stint as a sewing machine operator, at age forty, she is now about to graduate as a Nursing Assistant. What is not in Thao P.T. Vo's published letter reminds us that the letter is a present-oriented form and, while it reveals and highlights some aspects of the letter writer's life, it leaves a lot to the reader's empathetic imagination to fill in.

I believe I should also tell the reader that some of us in the Advisory Group had felt that Thao P.T. Vo's letter was a bit "sentimental" when she talked about being buried in the beautiful land of Canada. That is when we started speculating that the letter might not have been written in English but Vietnamese! Some of us had talked about how translations at times sound "flowery" and "sentimental" while others said that our response reflected a certain kind of cultural conditioning. I will let Thao P.T. Vo herself be the judge:

> How did they know that my feeling about Canada is insincere effusion? They can't feel about this country in the same way as I do because they are not in my shoes at all. Have they ever burst into tears, tears of glorious joy, when their feet touched the cold icy ground of Canada in the winter night when landed on the new land with two empty hands? Have they ever been waiting for 14 years in [a] hopeless situation in order to seek for a chance to come to a new land like I did?

> No, I am afraid they haven't.

You are right, Thao P.T. Vo and you have taught us a lesson.

As editor, then, I have worked with the contributors whose letters were in the "maybe" pile and the contributors whose letters were solicited. Some of my suggestions were gladly received and others turned down. Ultimately, the letters belong to the contributors themselves and represent their experiences, in their words. I have corrected grammar or spelling errors and dotted the i's and crossed the t's, sometimes at the explicit request of the authors, but that is as far as I have gone, bearing in mind the Editorial Advisory Group's March 24, 1991 stipulation that "the letters should not be processed or perfected, and the ideas and the feelings expressed should not be filtered."

ARRANGEMENT OF THE LETTERS

From the beginning of our involvement in the project, the Editorial Advisory Group was concerned about the ordering and categorizing of the letters. We discussed ordering according to themes, regions, ethnicities, age group, and type of work; however, no final decision was reached by the group on that score. My preference is to categorize the letters according to the group identification of the writers. I feel that a large part of the experiences described in these letters are predicated on whether the writer was an Aboriginal or an African-Canadian or an Arab or a Chinese or a Japanese or a South Asian woman in Canada. There are many statements in the book like this one from Anna Woo: "I live today because of my past experiences; how I act at work, at home, with friends, all my hopes and expectations have been shaped because of my experiences as a Chinese woman." All the writers spoke about their racial and ethnic identities, and as members of the Advisory Group noted, we knew which group the writers belonged to even though we had been given the letters with the names removed. Also, the Canadian state has treated each group differently by specifically targeted legislation. Thus, there is the *Indian Act* for the Aboriginal peoples. And there were the Head Tax for the Chinese, the internment camps for people of Japanese descent, and the "continuous journey" clause for South Asians and other groups from the Third World. Our encounter with this country, then, is heavily determined by our racial minority status on the one hand and our ethnicities on the other. This fact, however, is seldom acknowledged. I have yet to see a feminist history which acknowledges that not all Canadian women got the vote in 1918; in fact, Aboriginal peoples, the Chinese, the Japanese, and the South Asians did not get the right to vote until the end of World War II.

Racial identity is not essential, or genetic, but socially constructed. We have a racial identity because a racist society characterizes people according to their skin colour and physical features. I have often heard many white people deny this fact and claim that they do not see my colour when they see me. However, given the fact that they said such things to me when I was protesting against being turned down for employment, I took their answer to mean that they refused to acknowledge my racial oppression. As Allan Hutchinson writes: "Put bluntly, it is the privilege of the white establishment to pretend that race is not important and that it does not contribute heavily to the kind of lives that people live and, therefore, the values and perceptions that they develop on the shape and experience of social justice."[14]

Despite the importance given to race in our society, categorizing according to racial identity may also mislead. Some readers might not remember that categorizations are not cast in stone and that general categories such as

Aboriginal women or South Asian women do not exhaust the diversities within the groups. The general category Aboriginal may make us disregard the existence of categories such as Haida, Inuit, and Métis. The final decision reflects the agreement that the experience of each contributor should not be mediated by preconceptions about the group she identifies with.

WHAT THE LETTERS SAY

Taken together, these letters span three generations, and in terms of memories of the writers, go back even farther. Written by grandmother to grandchildren and grandchild to grandmother, mother to daughter and daughter to mother, sister to sister and friend to friend, they map the joys and pains of life in Canada in the realm of the personal and the public. There are also letters by a devotee to the Virgin Mary, by a constituent to a government minister, by a world citizen to the leaders of the world, and by a seeker of employment to the prospective employer. There are letters by an American Express gold card holder, and by a woman making a subsistence wage. And there are letters by university degree holders and by those who are self-educated. They encompass a wide swath of Canadian life as it is being lived in the last decade of the twentieth century by those on the other side of the colour line that W.E.B. Du Bois had identified in 1901 as the problem of the twentieth century.

They are letters by survivors. They are about the pain of rejection and facing closed doors. They are also about the sheer joy of achievement against all odds. These letters will take the reader on a roller coaster of intense pain and sheer laughter, anguish and exhilaration. Ultimately, I believe, they empower the reader and strengthen her in her resolve to fight for justice for herself and for others.

While unique as individual creations are, the letters also map out a common ground. The commonalities of experiences are based on the writers' status as racial minority or Aboriginal women. It is as racial minority or Aboriginal women that they find their aspirations thwarted and their physical and emotional well-being invaded. They experience sexist racism and racist sexism simultaneously and separating them as two separate oppressions fails to deal with the complexity of their experience. Often, the literature on Aboriginal and racial minority women identifies their oppression in terms of "double jeopardy". I think it would be more correct to call it multiple jeopardies. For example, a racial minority man who comes home after having experienced racist denials of his humanity might take out his anger on the women in his family. And the women who have come home having experienced similar racist assaults on their own dignity might experience the sexism of their men as a further addition to their burdens.

Hence, I suggest that we move beyond the additive approach to oppressions and think about the lives of racial minority and Aboriginal women as beset by multiple jeopardies. However, before that can happen, the dominant group will have to acknowledge that Canada is a racist society. There has been a lot of denial about racism. As Rosemary Brown puts it, "If I were to write a book about Canada and its people, the title would be 'Let's pretend, Let's deny'. The first line would read, 'Canadians are a tolerant and compassionate people . . . at least that is what they tell me.' I might then recall the ways in which we discriminate against each other because of dislikes based on a person's sex, race, disability, age, sexual orientation, religion, culture, or class."[15]

We in the Editorial Advisory Group envision that this anthology will give a human face to the cold statistics about the lives of Aboriginal and racial minority women. We hope that these powerful autobiographical accounts will produce a shift from denial to an admission that there **is** a problem. For once we admit that there is a problem, we can, then, take steps to solve it. Because there **is** denial, I would like to highlight some of the important themes that came up again and again in these letters.

THE SITES OF RACIAL MINORITY AND ABORIGINAL WOMEN'S OPPRESSION

(a) The Playground

A dominant motif in this book is the playground, the site where the child first experienced racial hatred. Letter after letter records that searing pain of rejection that the child suffered and could not fathom. Minnie Peters tells us about her experience in the schoolyard in 1934: "Some school children stoned me, chased me off the grounds, beat me, made fun of me, called me names, and laughed at me." The increased racism directed against Arab-Canadians during the Gulf War revived similar painful memories for Evelyn Hamdon: "All at once I was seven again; cornered against the school portable by most of my grade two class, while they taunted me with 'Look at you, you look like a 'nigger' in the (class) picture.' That sea of little white faces hating me, scorning me because of my dark skin, large nose, coarse black hair." Experiences like these lead to self-denial and desire to become a white person. Sharda Vaidyanath describes how her son, Rahul, "who was then barely four years of age, stood in our family room in the basement with an entire can of talcum powder smeared on his body from head to toe. He . . . said, 'Mom, you should do it too; it will make your hair golden!'" Haruko Okano recalls how "Following the example of the blonde girl in summer camp, I tried peroxide only to end up with a carrot orange patch, ridiculously visible against my own colour." Obviously, the message given to these children was that they were less valuable than white children, that white was beautiful and other colours were ugly. Such emotional traumas of childhood cause a great deal of suffering for the victim and produce a profound alienation. Irshad Manji's letter captures the pain such alienation causes within the family when the second generation begins to look down on its elders because they don't speak or behave as a "Canadian" is supposed to. Many writers recall the painful memories of how they denigrated their heritage culture and how they now feel a great loss. The lessons learned in the playground, thus, leave lasting scars. If future generations of Canadians are to escape the traumas so movingly portrayed in these letters, then it is imperative that multiculturalism and anti-racism become operative in the playground.

(b) The Teachers

Many letters record the writers' bafflement that their childhood teachers did nothing to protect them. Writing to the Minister of Education, Althea Samuels asks: "Where does a four-year-old learn the racial slurs and hate-filled language this child used against me everyday? It is one of the few memories I have of that age. One of the others is of the kind, sweet teacher who never did anything about it." Lee Maracle writes of "Hands that didn't pat me on the head at school for a job well done."

The children, thus, not only got verbally and physically abused by their peers, but they also experienced the disappointment of not being protected by authority figures. Instead, Beryl Tsang's teacher read a racist book in class and ridiculed her when she protested. Many contributors have written about how unloved and abandoned they felt in school.

One of the major complaints against Canadian teachers has been that they "stream" racial minority children towards special education classes. Asein writes about how she was classified as a "slow" learner. Heather Crichlow describes the teachers' lower expectations regarding her son and their unwillingness to recommend him for the enrichment program.

As a 1992 newspaper story — "System fails our youth, black parents testify"[16] — suggests, things haven't changed much since the childhood experiences of the writers recorded here. The school remains a site of multiple oppressions, racism being one of the most prominent. And teachers have to accept responsibility for that. Instead of guiding these children towards self-actualization and intellectual and financial achievement, they have turned out to be one of the strongest barriers in their way. This is where systemic issues are deeply connected to the shaping of individual destinies. Systemic racism has ensured that the school system hires few minority teachers who can bring empathy and expertise as well as serve as role models.

(c) The Curriculum

In addition to the absolute need to institute anti-racist training for teachers, to make them aware of their unconscious racism and their responsibilities to minority children, the curriculum must also simultaneously change its Eurocentric focus. Marcia Crosby's words point out the shameful absence of Aboriginal cultures in the curriculum: "There's nothing in the textbooks that say anything about who we are. I mean, gram, we go to school to learn about them and when they think we can think like them and speak like them, then we get a degree." And Mayann Francis informs her dead father: "In school, I did not study about Black people. I remember very well the story about Betty and Tom, Flip, Pony, mom, and dad. None of them looked like me. I only remember little black Sambo. I did not know that Black people were scientists and inventors." It is poignant to read about Maya's futile search for images that would give her a positive black image: "There were virtually no positive reflections of my image anywhere around me. (Well, it's true that one day we discovered a picture of a young girl who looked exactly like me in the pages of a Christian/Misssionary magazine. A twin sister — her face was my face — born possibly at the same time, but obviously a different time and place.)" And as Anita Wong reports, the omission of racial minorities from the curriculum suggested to her that the whole community was stigmatized: "And this is where I feel most cheated by the school system. I do know Canada's history inside out, but what roles do the Chinese-Canadians play in our history? Like the native Canadians who disappear from the history texts after the fur trade, the Chinese-Canadians disappear after stories of the many who worked on the railroads in British Columbia."

The dominant sections of the society must ponder what messages are being given by this kind of education. I hope that the Ministers of Education will read the letter that Althea Samuels has addressed to them. She demands: "I want the educational system to change. It has to, or racism will just keep increasing and increasing. I want the truth to be taught in our schools, Ms. Minister. And not the white man's version of the truth, but the truth."

If a person comes to believe that educational institutions are telling her lies, then alienation, anger, and cynicism are bound to set in. Dolores Gabriel is so enraged that she can only express her feelings by capitalizing, by repeating, and by exclamation marks: "I GET ANGRY! I GET ANGRY! I GET ANGRY! I GET ANGRY! I GET ANGRY!" Her anger burns on the page. And while Camille Hernández-Ramdwar does not use such dramatic methods, she is equally angry: "My life experiences have made me in many ways an angry woman. To some people this anger is unacceptable and offensive. To me it is justified. Fortunately, I have learned that I am not alone in my anger, and my friends are a great source of support to me."

Some writers can write about these same experiences with a dose of humour. It is their way of coping with the pain. Whether expressed in terms of anger or laughter, it is a serious message and must be heeded. Camille Hernández-Ramdwar speaks for many of us when she expresses her sense of alienation thus: "The experience of being labelled at so young an age has deeply affected my feelings of being a Canadian, of 'belonging'. My general feeling has been that I do not feel like a Canadian (despite being born and raised here) because I am not accepted as one at face value."

(d) The University

It is true that unpleasant experiences at school do much more harm to the psychic core of the self because they happen at a very young age, and that when individuals go to university they are older and more mature and therefore can handle the onslaughts of exclusion and direct mistreatment by distancing themselves. Nevertheless, the university is another major site of racial minority and Aboriginal women's oppression because the better paying and intellectually satisfying jobs in our society are reserved for people with higher education. The university hampers the desire for higher education on the part of racial and Aboriginal minority students through its admission, hiring, and curriculum selection procedures. Its callous disregard for minority students is described effectively by Mila who struggled unsuccessfully for eight years just to get into a Ph.D. program. And Jaya Chauhan's letter illustrates one aspect of the difficulties confronting racial minority women whose qualifications and experience are not readily accepted at face value. At best, they are required to provide further validation. At worst they are shut out altogether. The universities hit Aboriginal and racial minority women with a double whammy: on the one hand, the women face a chilly classroom climate; on the other, they have to overcome additional hurdles when seeking employment as academics — hurdles which often result in their being excluded altogether.

I believe that the university has become a means of propagating and justifying the ideologies of racism which, if left unchallenged, get dignified as science and objective truth. These theories have exacted a heavy price from people of racial minorities in the past who demand protection from them in the name of their inviolable human rights. It enrages me to think that universities continue to allow certain individuals to teach and propagate their racist views in the name of academic freedom.

(e) Employment

In a society structured by racism and patriarchy, racial and Aboriginal minority women's aspirations for suitable employment continue to be thwarted. The writers of these letters have had doors shut on them again and again. They have been the last hired and the first fired. They have watched helplessly as less qualified candidates got precedence over them. The letters paint a dismal portrait of the Canadian workplace.

Chanthala Phomtavong was a teacher in Laos. She has been in Canada for thirteen years and has yet to find steady employment. It is incredible to read that she was not hired for a housekeeping job in a nursing home even after taking ten weeks' training, just because the employer found her pace slow. I wondered as I read her letter how they decided upon the right time it takes to clean a washroom. And why could it not be that Chanthala's higher standard of cleanliness was responsible for her "slower" speed. It seems absurd.

Pham thi Quê describes her experience in a Montreal sweatshop where new immigrants, mostly racial minorities, work long hours in an unhealthy environment: "You barely earn enough to live on. This is why the whole family — father, mother, and children — works. Only those under eighteen go to school. The salary is even lower than the minimum wage in France, and raises are so slight that the difference between the authorized minimum wage and that of a worker with one year of seniority is approximately thirty cents an hour." The situation she describes is a perfect catch-22: "As long as orders are pouring in, you work non-stop up to the last minute. Eight hours of concentration and mental stress tied to the work table are enough to put you on edge. And when the orders are slow, you are plagued with thoughts of being laid off or unemployed." Ironies of ironies, after ten weeks of work, she was laid off, without becoming eligible for unemployment insurance.

Jobs such as the ones described by Chanthala Phomtavong, Pham thi Quê as well as Lee Maracle nourish neither the body nor the soul. In the era of free trade and global restructuring, this type of work threatens to become the lot of racial minority and Aboriginal women in Canada. These non-unionized jobs, whose pay is below the minimum wage, are a mockery of the aspirations encoded in the *Canadian Charter of Rights and Freedoms*.

The situation of racial minority immigrant women is even more precarious in those parts of the country where unemployment is chronically high. Grace writes: "My options are very limited since employment is scarce and seasonal.... I was always told that I don't have a Canadian experience — that whatever experiences I carried from home or from other places were not acceptable here. My education was not enough and my credentials without substance."

24

"Canadian experience" is a code word for discrimination as far as racial minority immigrant women are concerned. As people who have had this excuse used against them, they ask, how can one have Canadian experience without being given the chance to work in Canada? It is a conundrum whose answer I do not know.

Another hindrance in the path of racial minority women is the evaluation of their credentials, as Grace found out. While some people may think that it is not a racial problem, the fact is that the degrees earned in Third World countries are evaluated as much lower in value than those earned in the First World because of an erroneous perception that education received in a Third World country is inferior. Those of us who have come to Canada as racial minorities from other countries have had to struggle for several years to earn Canadian qualifications while we saw our white fellow immigrants go on to better things after a simple refresher course or an examination. This is a built-in inequality that is painful on the individual level and a waste of potential that would have been beneficial to the larger society.

And then there is exclusion based openly on perceptions of race. Racial minority women are denied jobs in the media, advertising, and the arts because they do not fit the prevailing image of Canadians as whites. Asein found that her degree in dance was no guarantee of success: "I was the only Black person in the company, a token. It seems that I was re-experiencing my childhood; ... I decided that my health and well-being would suffer if I continued to stay and work...". Beryl Tsang was told that "it was too unbelievable to have a Chinese in a Shakespearean or any other 'Western' production." Camille Hernández-Ramdwar writes about the "all-white Canadian face in advertising and television shows". While this all-white image causes a psychic wound through erasure, it also ensures that minorities will not find employment in these enterprises.

(f) Media

The media not only exclude us by projecting an "all white" image of Canadian society, they also refuse to hire minorities. Evelyn Hamdon and Naïma Bendris poignantly remind us that the stereotypes of Arabs in the dominant media continue to fan the flames of hatred against this group. Beatrice Watson's and Rosemary Eng's letters describe their lives on the margins of Canadian media. While the blocking of their potential is itself a tragedy, as Rosemary Eng's letter underlines so well, there are larger implications. The media are uninterested in covering news in the minority communities. Her recounting of how the media turned down her story on the Congress of Black Women's national meeting was painful to read. It was obviously not important for the dominant media to report that "[t]he women were angry. They were sick of bottom-level jobs. They were fed up with how they were represented in the media. They had had it with taking the emotional brunt of the frustration felt by their men in this society."

25

However, these are our realities and I am glad that this book is finally bringing out the truth that was suppressed.

(g) Health Care

A large number of contributors mention the shattered state of their physical and mental health caused by their hostile reception in Canadian society. They speak about anger, hurt, and depression that they have suffered in the past and continue to suffer in their day-to-day life.

However, I wonder if Canada's mental health establishment, operating from Eurocentric frameworks, has not ignored the pathologies produced by living in a society structured by racism. Nor is psychotherapy easily accessible to racial minority and Aboriginal women. What is needed are culturally sensitive mental health workers who work in community clinics that are premised on the preventive model.

When it comes to the care of our bodies, barriers and prejudices exist in plenty, even though Canada's universal health-care system makes us so much better off than our neighbour to the south. However, as Sunera Thobani's letter suggests, medical practitioners harbour many cultural stereotypes about racial minority communities. Her letter detailing the targeting of South Asian women by a sex selection clinic forewarns us about the brave new world attitudes operating in the field of reproductive technologies. And as she points out, these highly expensive technologies are geared primarily toward middle-class white women and take precious health dollars away from poor and racial minority women's needs.

The news story about northern women undergoing therapeutic abortions without anaesthetic in Yellowknife's only hospital is also very disturbing. One wonders if such a practice would have gone unnoticed for so long in the south. While none of the media stories mentioned the race issue, one does not need to be a genius to figure out that such a policy would predominantly affect Aboriginal women because Aboriginal people are the majority population group in the north.

(h) Family

Ideally, family should provide a refuge from the onslaughts of the world. However, it too has been battered and distorted by the multiple pressures of colonialism, racism, sexism, poverty, and homophobia. Aruna Papp's letter recounts the physical abuse suffered by a disabled South Asian woman at the hands of her husband which may have caused her death. Similar stories appear in the media about Aboriginal women. Marcia Crosby's powerful words relive the double anguish of incest and its denial. While some branches of feminism would attribute such behaviour to male biology, Crosby attributes it to the cultural genocide suffered by her people: "Speak Haida grandpa. Speak the language they told you not

26

to speak in residential school.... If you speak Haida grandpa will the silence of abuse be over?"

The oppression suffered in the bosom of the family is, perhaps, the most insidious. For where does one go for help? The intense anguish and tremendous courage of Crosby's words left me speechless. Her courage, let us hope, will end the denial around rape, incest, and sexual abuse so that healing can begin.

Asein's letter to her estranged mother poignantly reminds us of the unacknowledged homophobia in our communities. Again, the pain of rejection by one's own flesh and blood goes much deeper than anything the outside world can visit on a person. Often, it has been hard for racial minority and Aboriginal women to speak against the oppression visited on them within the intimate space of the family. As Evelyn Hamdon says, Arab women are vulnerable to being triply marginalized. She is "an Arab within Canadian society, a woman within Canadian society, and a woman within the Arab-Canadian society". Sunera Thobani pinpoints the reasons for this marginalization when she refers to the "reluctance" South Asian women feel to raise their voice against the sexism of their men lest it "become yet another stick to beat the whole community with".

This reluctance has often been misinterpreted in the past by the dominant feminist movement, and racial minority women have been labelled as male-defined. Their different approach to women's rights struggles, which is necessitated by the racist nature of the society in which they live, has been perceived as not feminist enough and they have been shut out of jobs and funding allocated for Women's Studies and women's issues as defined by white feminist scholars. Exclusionary feminist theory, thus, locks racial minority women out of another familial space, the much-touted sisterhood.

(i) The Government Agencies

While many letters refer to the racial discrimination practised against the Aboriginal, the African-Canadian, the Middle Eastern, the Chinese, the Japanese, and the South Asian communities by the various levels of government, and the erasure of this history of racism from Canadian history books, and while those wounds have still not healed, I would like to focus here on current inequities about which governments can do something.

As all the letters by Aboriginal women strongly underline, the relationship of the Aboriginal people with the Canadian State continues to be colonial. Perhaps we can call it progress that Rhoda Tagaq is no longer #E5-1661 to the Canadian government and that Aboriginal children are no longer being "kidnapped" and taken to residential schools as were Minnie Aodla

Freeman and Minnie Peters. But what kind of progress is it when Aboriginal peoples earn the lowest per capita income in Canada? When Canadian jails have disproportionately large numbers of Aboriginal men? When Aboriginal children have the highest school drop-out rate?

Both preservation of culture and control over their land remain priority issues for Aboriginal peoples. All the letters by Aboriginal women speak forcefully about the issue. Some of them, for example, Minnie Peters' letter, which recounts how her language came back to her after years of residential school, give us reason to celebrate. However, other letters, particularly those written by Minnie Aodla Freeman and Mary Cousins, remind us that things are indeed dismal. Mary Cousins writes: "It may not be important to some people, but it has bothered me that my land has been dug-up, scraped, and bulldozed; that the scarce topsoil has been destroyed; that the little plant life has been devastated; that streams have been diverted; that rocks have been dynamited. This violation of the land is irreversible."

The present time is a crucial one in the struggle of Aboriginal peoples to improve their status. Rhoda Tagaq's words capture the high drama of this phase in the nation's life: "Today we are on the verge of a land claim agreement. Inuit are holding their breath at this history-in-the-making event." I wish I had a crystal ball and could look into the future.

While Aboriginal women have a special relationship with the government and need specific safeguards targeted towards Aboriginal peoples, we all need mandatory employment equity legislation which has been a long time coming and has yet not arrived. In fact, as various studies demonstrate, the federal government itself has a poor record in terms of hiring and promoting racial minorities and Aboriginal persons. Legislation with some teeth is urgently needed or else we will continue to be victimized by discrimination in the workplace.

Governments need to take a close look at the racism as well as the other "isms" in educational institutions. For too long these institutions have worn the fig leaf of academic freedom to cover up their exclusionary curriculum and discriminatory hiring practices. For too long they have tolerated the racism expressed by the educators, both inside and outside the classroom.

Governments must look at the justice system and policing and how they particularly single out Aboriginal and African-Canadian communities for differential treatment. And we need better protection against hate-mongers who attack us through hate messages on the telephone, in the print media, and in face-to-face verbal abuse. There is much that governments can do by demanding mandatory compliance in the name of our human rights and by putting their own house in order.

In the area of service delivery, governments need to look at the current practices of assessing unemployment benefits and access to retraining. As several letters in the book point out, racial minority immigrant women's access to unemployment benefits as well as second-language training classes is inadequate and often nonexistent. Nor are they properly evaluated in terms of their credentials.

The letters by Maya and Haruko Okano on their experiences as adopted children underline the need on the part of welfare agencies to take a closer look at cross-racial adoptions of racial minority and Aboriginal children.

Minnie Aodla Freeman's letter reminds us that war is a women's issue and we must demand that our leaders work to prevent it. Read against accounts of "surgical strikes" and "ethnic cleansing", her words acquire a deep resonance: "[A]t the present time, we need world peace. You, the leaders of the world, are given that opportunity by us, the people, to lead us into a peaceful world." I hope our leaders will take Freeman's words to heart.

While the government cannot legislate individual attitudes, it can certainly ensure that institutional practices are bias-free and equitable. Unfortunate as it is, we do realize that racism expressed and experienced at the personal level will not go away overnight. However, life for Aboriginal and racial minority women will improve considerably if they are provided adequate protection against systemic racism which can be tackled through legislation.

CONCLUSION

These letters, written from the heart, are intimate revelations of what it means to live one's life as a racial minority or Aboriginal woman in present-day Canada. They challenge the dominant community's smugness about so-called Canadian equality and tolerance. They implore people in the seats of power to look at the truth in front of our eyes and not deny it. From these writers' perspective, change seems too slow and a long time coming. Mayann Francis speaks for many of us when she reports to her dead father that "there [is] very little change. Slavery no longer exists in the way known to Sojourner and Harriet. Systemic discrimination and institutionalized racism inherent in our social systems replaced slavery of the 1700s."

The letters, which convey a deep disappointment with the institutions of the Canadian State and the social order, bring out the heavy price paid by racial minority and Aboriginal women for being who they are. It is up to the dominant community to listen and resolve to bring about change. I hope that this book will impel people to work for change.

The letters also register a protest against the dominant versions of feminist theory and feminist agendas for having failed to include Aboriginal and racial minority women. Again, I hope that the book will create a bridge of understanding between white women and Aboriginal women and women of colour on the one hand, and between women of different minority communities on the other. We know so little about each other. I hope that the book will help us learn about each other and contribute to the building of a unified feminist movement which will include the voices of all women.

The letters report about awful hurts and palpable pain. They report about cycles of inequity that have existed for generations and do not seem to be on the verge of disappearing. To that extent, the book is not your average bedtime reading. It is a tough book and will cause pain and anger. It does not yet have a happy ending, for as Marcia Crosby says, "I guess it's not really good-bye because it's not over." The same refusal of closure is voiced by Dolores Gabriel when she rewrites the old song of hope: "I've not overcome, but I've survived."

It will take all of us working together to give this book a happy ending. Despite all their disappointments, the women who wrote these letters have not given up hope. Despite thirteen years of unsuccessful searching for a suitable employment, Chanthala Phomtavong's spirit is not broken: "I never give up. My dream is to have a good job, with good pay, in the day time." The words of Beatrice Watson are equally courageous: "Nothing worthwhile has ever come easy. I still have faith in people and in the Government and people of Canada to do the right thing." Rajani Alexander has a similar message of hope for her three-year-old daughter: "There is hope here, and that is why we will stay and why we belong."

Yes, we belong to Canada and Canada belongs to us, as much as it belongs to anybody else. And the making of Canada is an ongoing project. If we heed Minnie Aodla Freeman's words and "learn something out of each wrong that we have done to the world and especially to each other", we can make the building of a future Canada such an exciting project that it might allow us to let go of the past. It is up to all of us to write a happy ending for this book. I hope we can. I hope we will.

Arun Mukherjee

Editor

EDITOR'S BIOGRAPHICAL NOTE

Arun Prabha Mukherjee was born in 1946 in Lahore, India. After the 1947 partition of the country, her parents fled to India and she was raised and educated in Tikamgarh, Madhya Pradesh. After doing graduate work in English at the University of Saugar, India, she came to Canada as a Commonwealth Scholar to do graduate work at the University of Toronto. She has taught at several universities in Canada, and is currently employed as an Associate Professor at York University, Toronto, where she teaches courses in Postcolonial Literature and Women's Studies. The mother of a sixteen-year-old son, Gautam, she is also the author of *The Gospel of Wealth in the American Novel: The Rhetoric of Dreiser and His Contemporaries* (1987), and *Towards an Aesthetic of Opposition: Essays on Literature, Criticism and Cultural Imperialism* (1988).

ENDNOTES

1. Nila Gupta and Makeda Silvera, Managing Editors, *The Issue is 'ism: Women of Colour Speak Out* (Toronto: Sister Vision Press, 1989), originally published as Issue 16 of *Fireweed, A Feminist Quarterly* (1983).

2. The Canadian Advisory Council on the Status of Women has passed a motion not to use the phrase "visible minority". The CACSW's decision indicates its awareness that many racial minority Canadians disapprove of the term "visible minority", seeing it as a negative expression.

3. Norman Buchignani, "Some Comments on the Elimination of Racism in Canada", in *Racism in Canada*, ed. Ormond McKague (Saskatoon: Fifth House Publishers, 1991), p. 200.

4. Dionne Brand, interview by Dagmar Novak, in *Other Solitudes: Canadian Multicultural Fictions*, ed. Linda Hutcheon and Marion Richmond (Toronto: Oxford University Press, 1990), p. 272.

5. Kari Dehli, "Leaving the Comfort of Home: Working Through Feminisms", in Himani Bannerji *et al.*, *Unsettling Relations: The University as a Site of Feminist Struggles* (Toronto: Women's Press, 1991), pp. 61–62.

6. Chandra Talpade Mohanty, "Under Western Eyes: Feminist Scholarship and Colonial Discourses", in *Third World Women and the Politics of Feminism*, ed. Chandra Talpade Mohanty, Ann Russo, and Lourdes Torres *et al.* (Bloomington: Indiana University Press, 1991).

7. Himani Bannerji, "But Who Speaks for Us? Experience and Agency in Conventional Feminist Paradigms", in Himani Bannerji *et al.*, *Unsettling Relations: The University as a Site of Feminist Struggles* (Toronto: Women's Press, 1991), p. 71.

8. Patricia Bishop, "Let's not lose sight of the true cause", *The Globe and Mail*, June 18, 1991.

9. Lee Maracle, "Ramparts Hanging in the Air", In *Telling It: Women and Language Across Cultures, The Transformation of a Conference*, ed. The Telling It Book Collective: Sky Lee *et al.* (Vancouver: Press Gang Publishers, 1990), p. 165.

10. Elizabeth V. Spelman, *Inessential Woman: Problems of Exclusion in Feminist Thought* (Boston: Beacon Press, 1988), p. 3.

11. Letter from the CACSW to members of the Editorial Advisory Group, January 25, 1991.

12. Marlene Kadar, "Coming to Terms: Life Writing — from Genre to Critical Practice", in *Essays on Life Writing: From Genre to Critical Practice*, ed. Marlene Kadar (Toronto: University of Toronto Press, 1992), pp. 3–16.

13. The statement refers to a working committee of this type. The CACSW, of course, has brought together people from different backgrounds many times before, the most visible of these events being the various national symposia held over the years.

14. Allan Hutchinson, "Why Juries Must Mirror Ethnic Reality", *The Toronto Sun*, May 14, 1992.

15. Rosemary Brown, "Overcoming Sexism and Racism — How?", in *Racism in Canada*, ed. Ormond McKague (Saskatoon: Fifth House Publishers, 1991), p. 168.

16. "System fails our youth, black parents testify", *The Toronto Star*, May 14, 1992.

BIBLIOGRAPHY

Bannerji, Himani. "But Who Speaks for Us? Experience and Agency in Conventional Feminist Paradigms". In Himani Bannerji *et al. Unsettling Relations: The University as a Site of Feminist Struggles*. Toronto: Women's Press, 1991.

Bishop, Patricia. "Let's not lose sight of the true cause". *The Globe and Mail*, June 18, 1991.

Brand, Dionne. Interview by Dagmar Novak. In *Other Solitudes: Canadian Multicultural Fictions*. Ed. Linda Hutcheon and Marion Richmond. Toronto: Oxford University Press, 1990.

Brand, Dionne. *No Burden to Carry: Narratives of Black Working Women in Ontario 1920s–1950s*. Toronto: Women's Press, 1991.

Brown, Rosemary. "Overcoming Sexism and Racism — How?" In *Racism in Canada*. Ed. Ormond McKague. Saskatoon: Fifth House Publishers, 1991.

Buchignani, Norman. "Some Comments on the Elimination of Racism in Canada". In *Racism in Canada*. Ed. Ormond McKague. Saskatoon: Fifth House Publishers, 1991.

Chinese Canadian National Council. Women's Book Committee. *Jin Guo: Voices of Chinese Canadian Women*. Toronto: Women's Press, 1992.

Dehli, Kari. "Leaving the Comfort of Home: Working through Feminisms". In Himani Bannerji *et al. Unsettling Relations: The University as a Site of Feminist Struggles*. Toronto: Women's Press, 1991.

Du Bois, W.E.B. *The Souls of Black Folk*. Millwood, N.Y.: Kraus-Thomson Organization Limited, 1973.

Gupta, Nila and Makeda Silvera. Managing Editors. *The Issue is 'ism: Women of Colour Speak Out*. Toronto: Sister Vision Press, 1989. Originally published as Issue 16 of *Fireweed, A Feminist Quarterly*, 1983.

Hutchinson, Allan. "Why Juries Must Mirror Ethnic Reality". *The Toronto Star*, May 14, 1992.

Kadar, Marlene. "Coming to Terms: Life Writing — from Genre to Critical Practice". In *Essays on Life Writing: From Genre to Critical Practice*. Ed. Marlene Kadar. Toronto: University of Toronto Press, 1992.

Maracle, Lee. "Ramparts Hanging in the Air". In *Telling It: Women and Language Across Cultures, The Transformation of a Conference*. Ed. The Telling It Book Collective: Sky Lee *et al*. Vancouver: Press Gang Publishers, 1990.

Menchú, Rigoberta. *I, Rigoberta Menchú: An Indian Woman in Guatemala*. London: Verso, 1984.

Mohanty, Chandra Talpade. "Under Western Eyes: Feminist Scholarship and Colonial Discourses". In *Third World Women and the Politics of Feminism*. Ed. Chandra Talpade Mohanty, Ann Russo, and Lourdes Torres. Bloomington: Indiana University Press, 1991.

Silvera, Makeda. *Silenced: Talks with working class Caribbean women about their lives and struggles as Domestic Workers in Canada*. Toronto: Sister Vision Press, 1989.

Spelman, Elizabeth V. *Inessential Woman: Problems of Exclusion in Feminist Thought*. Boston: Beacon Press, 1988.

THIS LAND

Thao P.T. Vo
Nipisha Lau Bracken
Mary Panegoosho Cousins
Rhoda Tagaq
Camille Hernández-Ramdwar
Beatrice Archer Watson
Grace

THAO P.T. VO

Green Pines

My Friends:

I call you "friends," even though I have never met you in real life before, for I believe that you are the people who have the same feeling and the same love as mine toward Canada, our country.

Well, I had better tell you a little bit about myself. I came here last year [1989] in February, and now I am working as a sewing-machine operator. I must confess that I feel so hesitant to write this letter, because English is not my first language. I am afraid I don't have enough talent to express well what I want to tell you, my friends. However, deeply in my heart, something constantly persuades me to write, write my feeling about Canada, the country I consider as my second-mother country.

I do love Canada, the beautiful country of peace, of real freedom; the promised land that I will be living in for the rest of my life — when I die my body will return to the ground here, to fertilize the soil to help the trees grow up and grow green.

My friends, have you ever had the feeling of sheer happiness when you see a glorious red sun rising from the horizon, while you are walking heavily and slowly on the path covered with white thick ice? A feeling of reviving, you still see the beautiful sun shining in the winter blue sky, and our shining sun is smiling at you; the land, the trees, the sun and you are the one — you are not alone on your way, anymore.

How wonderful it is to feel that you are close to something or someone you love; on the other hand, you would feel uncomfortable, unhappy, and hurt if you catch the look of somebody who looks at you as if you were a leper living among the healthy people.

I have received several looks like that in my life since the day I came here.

Who are they? People who have a bad look for a human being? And why do they look at me like that?

Most of them came from backgrounds different from mine. I still remember I was bitterly sad, and I tortured myself furiously when I received their scornful looks.

They have no right to look at me like that when I speak English with a foreign pronunciation, when I mispronounce some words, when I feel confused about the new ways of doing something, or when I wear shabby clothes!!

What a child I was!! Why do I waste my breath, my time, my energy to be angry with them or to be hurt deeply about it?

There are always a lot of people like them in the world, not only in Canada.

I should take pity on them, people who have never understood the warm splendid feeling of real communication between people with different backgrounds.

I remember one proverb in my old country: "you can't say the whole sugar cane is spoiled if you see some decayed areas on its body."

How nervous I was when I came into the office of Mr. Plant Engineer in my work place to ask for his advice, because I met some problems in my work. He is in the executive staff, and I am a poor worker, a landed immigrant who might not speak English fluently. But, his broad, warm smile had given me a new strength to talk, and how surprised I was to see that I was treated in a friendly manner, as a human being by a human being. And Mrs. Manager, a handsome lady who always say Hello. Or Mr. Director, a white-haired respectable gentleman, who always calls me "dear". What a sweet word for me!

Who are these people? They are also the people who have different backgrounds from me.

My friends, I don't intend to make a lecture to recommend some people in my work place. Not at all! I just want to tell you there are still more and more good and broad-minded people who came from different countries, who are from different races and backgrounds. But their hands always reach out to you anyway. They will be your good friends some day. The good will defeat the bad. The discriminating line among different races will be wiped off completely some day.

It might not happen for the rest of my life or in the life of my next generation or many later generations; but it must happen because all of us are living in Canada; we share the destiny of our country. And who are we? We are Canadians. Sometimes I think of the day I will get the Canadian citizenship. I definitely have the country in my heart, and I love my new country as much as I did love my old mother country.

I wonder if the true love in my heart can help me to learn English better.

I remember I was in a great shock when I had been informed that my English level wasn't strong enough to qualify for the full-time program of Nursing Assistant.

My eyes welled up with tears, and I wept bitterly like a child who was beaten. I didn't want to do anything any more. How could I be better in English? English is like a deep jungle that I can't find the way out. Today, I learn some words, tomorrow, I begin to forget what I have learned.

The more I learn, the more I wonder myself if it is possible for me to make myself master of speaking, of writing, and of understanding English some day. And if my English level hasn't got better, how can I go ahead to be trained to be a nurse as I wish?

I want to be a useful person; I want to do the job I love and contribute my small part to the prosperity and welfare of Canada; I want to understand the new knowledge of life in Canada.

"Do I want too much?" Sometimes I ask myself. "And how can I achieve what I want?" "No", as I see it, I don't think what I want is "overweight", but the way to reach my goal is very far for me.

One of my beloved friends, often tells me: "Don't lose your hope — Don't give up — Work hard in English again. Next year you shall pass your examination." I don't want to make my parents as well as my dear friend disappointed because of my failure again. I do want to learn nursing and what a great joy if I can use English fluently to communicate with the people around me.

So, I find only one way for myself — making the most of my free time to learn English; going to school on weekends to learn English, and praying for God's help. Some day I may get a good reward for my studying hard.

My friends, it seems that I tell you a lot about myself. I must have made you feel bored with my story of learning English.

So I should talk about something else. About time? Perhaps?

One year is nearly ended. We are going to be older and I hope the older we grow, the wiser we are. We are wiser for we learn more by our own experience the lessons of our lives.

I have learned my own lessons of the new life in Canada, the bitter as well as the happy, and I know that I will remember them as clearly as ever.

I have tried to learn the song "A lonesome pine" by heart from a film on television but I forgot all the words, afterward. I only remember the picture of a tall green pine standing alone on the top of the hill.

I admire the great strength of these everlasting green pines in Canada. They always stand somewhere, straight with their heads looking up the sky, and smile down at the pedestrians who are hurrying on their way.

THAO P.T. VO

I was born on January 10, 1952 and grew up in a middle-class family. In my old country, I was a pharmacist. My life had been full of hope, progress, and peace before 1975, the year that South Vietnam was taken over by the communists from North Vietnam. In February 1989, my parent, my sister, and I landed in Canada as immigrants. I became a sewing-machine operator in Warner's Ltd. for almost three years. After that, I studied at a community college to be a nursing assistant. I graduated in 1992 and I am looking for a position. I need to earn my own living first. Someday, I hope my life will be more stable financially. And at that time, I can start writing again what I have been longing to write for a long time in my heart.

Nipisha Lau Bracken

Up North, Down South

Dear Cécile:

Nothing really exciting happened today. Took the two kids I'm looking after for a friend to the nearby park. I asked my next door neighbour, Tabitha, if she'd like to join us with her two kids. Two more little girls joined us. Yep, all eight of us trotted along to the park. They played and we watched while we gossiped a bit and talked about the upcoming summer and that pool we were sitting nearby. Once in a while Tab would join them. She has a two-year-old little cutie whom we call Jullienne, so she kept close to him. Soon, it was lunch time and we fed the kids right there at the park. Tab had brought some dried caribou meat so we ate that. They were small and thin pieces so they were tasty. Perfect snack on a perfect sunny day (I thought).

Watching those kids back at play, I thought of those times when I was one of those kids and busy playing doll with my relatives in a summer camp, back home. The same perfectly sunny day with a light breeze blowing all around us and we'd feel it because it was kind of a hot-warm day. Instead of playground swings and slides we see today down south here, we played on rocks and moss, sometimes sand. We'd gather tins and such garbage we could think of that would look good in "our little playhouse". Which of course was a small surrounding where a rock looked like a good little table, another that looked like a couch, a chair, adjacent to bedrooms. We'd pretend to cook food and take care of our babies which were rocks as well. But we had amautis*. Our mothers took time to sew our amautis in between taking care of sealskins and caribou skins. Dads were barely around when there was food needed around the camp. But we were happy. What we saw our mothers do and how they did things with everything they touched was the main part of the fun we used to enjoy the most. We would make do with only tin can tops that were cut with a can opener and

---

* "Amautis" refers to Inuit mothers' parkas that have pouches on the back to hold babies.

fold them to make them look like ulus*. Of course, our mothers would give us some seal flippers' skins to practice on. Naw, they weren't as good enough to practice on, but they gave us the idea. But the real pleasure and a real good result of those skins were our new kamiks** and new parkas our mothers made with pleasure because they were sewing together and telling good and funny stories. I think you could only imagine what they were talking about! If you're a housewife, it only makes a lot of sense to be able to. I've heard a few of their stories, but I'm not telling you! Not till we meet anyway.

During those times, I was always with my step-grandmother. And everywhere she went I went. I still picture this scene in my mind when I think of her. All dads were out hunting as usual and all of us kids and mothers were left behind to look after our camp. Well, one of my aunts had a piece of seal meat to cook. All three of my aunts were already in that tent waiting for my step-grandma. We kneeled down to get in the tent. As we were entering through that little tent-way, one of my aunts noticed some dogs smelling around our tent. Soon as she said they were entering our tent, my grandma turned around and shouted: "taikani!."[1] I looked around to see what my aunts' reactions were all at the same time. And they were all snickering. Trying hard as they could to muffle their laughter. Grandma turned around and just as fast as she looked out the tent's little entrance, she saw all of her step-daughters' faces and started laughing. All of us started laughing right along with her.

What she said was not really the right thing to say at the time. To err is human. I learned that point at that time and I had fun getting it. If you were ever in the same situation, I'm pretty sure you would understand, but you know what? If you weren't, you wouldn't get it. You just had to be there.

Since I've been living down here, a lot of people have had a lot of influence on me. I am now a mother myself. I have three wonderful boys, ages eight, eleven, and twelve. And, a perfect and loving husband. All of us adore him almost to the point where he is pleasantly not wanting to leave us for any one and anything. He is our life and our main man of the house. No, we don't have a marriage made in heaven either, but we get by in spite of a lot of financial problems. We all handle things together, and we work them out. We also have some things which are hard to handle, but we do count on each other, just as a family would in these hard times. You see, we have each other. And I think that if we all can pull together,

---

*   "Ulus" refers to women's knives used for cutting meat and skinning.
** "Kamiks" refers to sealskin boots.
1   Editor's note: "taikani" means "over here". Instead of telling the dogs to get out of the tent, grandma seemed to be inviting the dogs in.

we can make a difference. In what way, I don't know. But each and everyone of us could make a difference. As a loving mother, I wouldn't know what to do if any one of my kids were abducted by a desperate stranger who absolutely had to make money and to make it fast. Or perhaps he didn't need money, but he needed to take his anger out. I'd worry if I knew anyone like that in our neighbourhood. But then who knows why anyone needs to take their anger out on anyone they didn't even know. He, she, no one, has any idea whether it'd be a neighbour or someone who came from a larger city. Nowadays anyway.

What do I think of living down south? Well, being an Inuk, and coming from the cold harsh country of Northwest Territories, I have to say that I do find it hot in the middle of summer and not as cold in the winter. And of course the TREES! No such things back home. In my opinion, I think they're great, but I heard that they're in the way of most things that would be visible had they not been there. True, Inuit hunters would agree. But what I'm saying is that these are only visible to the human eye. What I also think of human beings seeing others as different colours is that it's prejudice. Mind you there weren't that many Negroes, Italians, Mexicans, or other people from other countries living in Iqaluit, Northwest Territories. And I have three sons. The older two were just beginning to talk and able to have conversations with us (Mom and Dad). We went shopping one particular day on a Saturday back home. As we pulled up to the parking lot area, Lionel Jones[2] came out of The Bay. My younger son Tommy asked: "Why is he brown colour, Dad?" Francis and I looked at each other and smiled. No, we laughed. We were not used to the colour brown. Now, I'm an Inuk and my husband is white. And Lionel was a good person we knew briefly and he lived across the hall from us when we lived in the eight-story highrise as a young couple. But that day, we happened to run into him as a married couple **with** children. Well, Dad answered Tommy: "That's because he's from another country and they are born like that. Just as mommy is from here and I'm from down south." Of course, Tommy wasn't listening that well because he was busy trying to get off the truck and this went on while we were getting off the truck. And Lionel heard. Francis told him what Tommy asked and why, and that he was just answering Tommy's question. Lionel laughed and patted both our boys' heads as they ran into the store.

We chatted for a bit and said our "see ya laters".

But down here, we notice that a lot of people are obviously rude when they notice you're native. My three sons have had to put up with kids their own age who will either call them "chinks" or "welfare case". I've

---

2 Editor's note: Lionel Jones was an American who first came up as one of the army troops, but settled there.

been told by a young Jamaican kid to "go back to your country" because I told him to go home when he was fighting with my kids. He had just run over one of my kids' friends with his bicycle and this kid was on his own bicycle as well.

I am a full-blooded Inuk (Eskimo). Sometimes I am mistaken for a native Indian by "white people". For instance, when we first moved to Waterloo, Ontario, we used to shop at this Towers store which was right across the street from where we lived. Of the few times we'd shop there, none of the cashiers had ever asked me for my "band number". Until one day. (This was in the summer and I had tanned very nicely.) I think this cashier was a new employee. She asked me for my "band number" but I asked her instead: "What's a 'band number'?" She then answered/asked: "Oh, you're not Indian?" I said: "I'm an Inuk." She then turned red. (Aren't Indians labelled "red" by the white people?)

I do find it really annoying when I'm told to "go back to your country". (Because this has happened more than once.) I consider myself one of the cousins of those who inhabited the Arctic before it was called CANADA. And it is my home. I'm married to a "whiteman" (and proud of it) for thirteen years now.

Living in the southern part of Canada, I feel, has its good and bad days. The only difference between here and up north (back home) are trees, many tall buildings, lots of different races of people, vehicles and, of course, the hot and humid weather we get in the summers. Shorter winters and dirtier snow. Yeah, and the pollution. Back home there are no trees although there are some willows that grow up to six or seven feet tall in between Iqaluit and Lake Harbour (South Baffin). But they're in only one area and most of us wonder why they're there. Perhaps they are leftovers from the days of dinosaurs? Who knows, maybe some explorer tried to plant some trees and they turned out like that as a result of cold weather. But we experience quite a few winter storms and it gets really cold in the winter. (Sorry, I'm not good at telling temperatures.) I wrote this short presentation which I read as a speech when I was in Iqaluit in January as a participant in a training course called Communications 1 for a week. It goes like this:

"Home"

I like coming home. It's always good to see friends and relatives. The air is clean, crisp, and cold in the winter, the land is quite beautiful in the summer. Any season I come home, it always makes me want to move back. People smile as you walk past them on the roads. Every one is so welcoming when you visit with them in their homes. (I think I usually gain a lot of weight when I come here!)

Snow, lots of it as usual. I used to like walking in a light snow storm. I still do that down south but it's not the same. The snow here is usually dirty and sticky. That's south. But then it's not always that bad. I like the south too. But I'm not going to grow old down there. I am going to grow old here and watch my grandchildren grow up.

I don't think that I'm that great a writer. I usually write what I think and how I think about things going on around me. This letter is how I feel about living down south in general. I hope that you are enjoying learning about my culture as an Inuk, too.

We are proud people. We are proud of what we have accomplished so far. And they are not many things. I know some carvers who are very proud that they can do such animals as a caribou with miniature antlers out of real caribou antlers. A narwhale with a real walrus tusk as its ivory tusk. And so on with carvers. I also know some people who do drawings of what they imagine as they draw what they picture in their minds. Some of these are real famous artists now. They have gone to different countries in the world to show their work and do their work there. There are hunters who have stood in the freezing temperatures waiting for a seal to come up for air for hours and hours at a time in the winter. And when it finally comes up for air, he'd spear it with his harpoon and fight with it to pull it up on the ice. And when he finally wins the struggle, he'd put it on his qamotik* and head off home on either his ski-doo or qimutsiq** with his reliable dog team. His family will not be hungry for a while and he has earned himself a pair of kamiks*** once he has caught a bearded seal as his wife will need that bearded sealskin for the foot part of the kamik. Few women are talented now. Even I can't make any patterns of sealskin. Few young girls are better than I will ever be. I can't even make a caribou parka. And they are very warm in the winter. Get a manufactured one next to it and you still prefer the caribou parka. Kamiks are very warm too. They can also be made to be waterproof. It takes a couple of days to a week for a pair. For a woman's pair, there are black strips (about two inches thick) and white strips that go around the shin part of the leg. For men, the black strip goes straight down in the front of the shin. The rest of the skin being white around the leg.

They usually come with duffle socks which may be decorated with embroidery thread. The foot parts are usually yellowish colour and that is of a bearded sealskin except the fur part is scraped off. They are usually chewed to make them softer and easier to sew by hand. They also have braided laces to tie around the leg below the knee and are usually

---

* "Qamotik" refers to dog sled.
** "Qimutsiq" refers to dog team.
*** "Kamiks" refers to sealskin boots.

decorated with a "bell" at the tips. The waterproof ones are usually without any fur at all. All the fur on the skin is scraped off so that they are plain-looking and almost resemble leather. All the work done in preparing the skins before they are made into either kamiks or parkas is just as hard. My grandmother, as I remember, would take her ulu, a triangular piece of wood (made by grandpa), and scrape the skins with a fast and perfect motion, and without tearing the skin. The blubber would easily (I thought it was easy) slide off. Once that was done, the second layer of blubber was then scraped off more slowly and carefully as that part was the thinner blubber next to the skin. Next, the skin is done perfectly without a cut or slit and it's tied to a wood (again made by grandpa, but some women do make their own sometimes) and left outside to dry in the sun. Once dry, it gets tough and stiff so that it has to be stepped on and on until it is easier to work with. This takes approximately four to five hours depending upon how large or small the skin is. It is then scraped again but this time with a U-shaped piece of metal with a wooden handle. Once it is soft and leather-like, it is then ready to use to make things to wear.

If you're financially well off, I'd recommend a short trip up north to the Baffin Island area. There are thirteen surrounding communities there. People there, both Inuit and non-Inuit, will ensure you enjoy your trip there. There are various tour guides who will take you either on dog team rides or canoe rides around the beautiful land. There are interpreters who will assist you in communicating with the elders. There are also long-time residents who are originally from other countries but who have lived there for many years. They will tell you how and what got them there in the first place and why they decided to stay and live there. One Scottish man even has his own little farm and he lives in Iqaluit. (Iqaluit is the main point to land by jet, and other communities are reached by smaller planes such as twin otters.) Bill MacKenzie has a pig and egg-laying hens in his little farm. He lives in Apex, a small settlement three miles from Iqaluit, where Inuit moved to get away from the main U.S. Army base, at first called Frobisher Bay. There is also an elder from England who lives in between Apex and Iqaluit. Bryan Pearson has been in Iqaluit since the early fifties. (Correct me, if I'm wrong, Bryan.) He will tell you how the town of Iqaluit was formed. But if you want or need information about how the Inuit have survived for so many years in the Arctic, talk to any elder. They have many interesting stories to tell and will talk to anyone willing to listen. I hope that you will talk to them. I'd highly recommend that you talk with them. I always like talking with them whenever I get the chance and when I'm lucky enough to have made a free trip there. Should you need an interpreter, please ask me to go with you. Of course, you'd have to pay for my trip as well. Place to stay is no problem for me. I have many friends and relatives there.

Speaking of relatives, I have one special and favourite cousin here living in Vanier, Ontario. Only she doesn't have that much time. She has lung and liver cancer. Martha and I have become close friends and confidantes. Before she found out she had cancer, we'd enjoy each other's company in my home working on jigsaw puzzles and just plain getting to know each other better. You see, we are, and have been, related but did not know each other that well. We have just begun to share sentimental feelings toward each other as cousins. And now, she is slowly fading away. I have never seen anyone looking so sickly since my aunt who passed away last August. Martha is a strong lady and she is still able to keep me and other visitors smiling. You see, she has turned yellow all over as a result of her liver being swamped with cancer. The whites of her eyes are now yellow as well. All that is left of her is her skin and bones. Her stomach is swelled up. In spite of it all, she has her wit. I am very proud of her for that. But it still makes me want to cry when I'm there with her. I tell myself to be strong for her and I'm okay. If she has courage enough to still talk of her past full of ups and downs and still come out smiling about them anyway, then I have learned from that. A lot too. There is someone more powerful than any of us on this earth. And it is up to Him to let her live a little longer or to let her go when He needs her. I know that He needs her and I think that she knows it too. I cannot really be angry at Him for that. Because I have gotten to know her better and she with me. She has given me more confidence than anyone ever has and that is a whole lot better than nothing at all. I hope that I have given her as much in return.[3]

She will not be the last friend and relative who I have gotten close to. But she has really made a difference in my life. All of us will go at one time or another, either by illness or by other ways. My own mother and brother were murdered in one night by my brother's own childhood friend with an eight-inch blade knife. Those two friends (with my mother) were celebrating my brother's twenty-first birthday in a local bar where they were both working as waiters. They had gone to my mother's home with a cake made by one of the cooks at the hotel where they both worked after the bar closed. They smoked hashish and played crib until they passed out. When he woke up, we heard in court, he had this urge to kill. And so my brother was first because he was right there in the room. He had gotten that knife from the kitchen downstairs where my mother was passed out on the living room couch. But he did my brother first. Once he had stabbed my brother many times, he took a shower and changed. Then on his way out, my mother coughed a couple of times and he thought that she will not like to find her own son dead; so, he did her in too. What we heard in court was that the knife was left in my mother's rectum and she was in a pool of her own blood. This scene was later discovered by my

---

[3] Editor's note: Martha died on Monday, May 18, 1992 in the arms of her boyfriend. Nipisha Lau Bracken has requested me to append this note.

own little sister at approximately three o'clock in the morning. She had just come home from the local poolhall. And she had seen him there. Quuyuq had this eerie sense because of the way he was staring at her that night at the poolhall. What she later discovered was the answer she got as to why he was looking at her that way. What I heard and saw of the evidence in court was nothing compared to what my sister experienced. And I saw my own mother's and brother's blood-stained clothes they were wearing that night. I also heard how many stab wounds they both had to their bodies. They were many.

I was adopted by my grandparents because they felt my mother was too young to raise me. (She was only sixteen.) So, they actually took me away from her and made an agreement with her and my dad, that I was to be taken back by themselves when and if my grandparents passed away. Sure enough, when my grandfather passed away in 1977 (I was twenty years old), and an Inuvialuk from Aklavik was taking last names of Inuit (I was in Yellowknife then) when he entered my parent's home to take their selected last name, they claimed me back then. So, later on that year and the following years up until my mother and brother were slain, my own mother and I were just beginning a mother and daughter relationship which we never had all through the years I was growing up! Unfortunately, it wasn't meant to be. Sure, I was very angry at God. And I never used to be able to tell this story without weeping. But now, I am beginning to understand that life is and always will be very precious to all of us. We must absolutely take advantage of it.

But I don't think that we should forget others and only think of our immediate surroundings. I wasn't given any more time to spend with my mother and brother; nor were they allowed any more time to live as long as time allowed them. But the kid who cut their lives short is spending time in a prison now. He has lots of time though, but alone. Alone with his thoughts and regrets of what he has done during his young life. He probably lived his life full of ups and downs like all of us. But he is going to live it full of downs because he can't walk around freely like the rest of us. Unlike my mom, Martha was given at least some time, very precious time, to let me know how she feels about me and my family here. To give me advice, to give me her ears so I could say whatever I think, and to love us. I give myself credit for having gotten to know her and have her with me. But then, she might not live long enough to see her grandchildren being born and grow up with her. I have been given that chance and I will not take total advantage of it either.

My friend, you must by now wonder if I am still with you. Well, I am very much so. I thought I'd let you know how I've felt about all that I have written here. But now I'll let you go back to whatever you were doing because I'm going out for lunch with Tabitha. She is treating me today. After that I'm visiting Martha at the hospital for the rest of the day. I hope that you have enjoyed reading my letter and sharing our experience.

NIPISHA LAU BRACKEN

My full name is Nipisha Lau Bracken (née Ejetsiak). I was born in a family camp, around the area of Markham Bay on southern Baffin Island and adopted by my grandparents, some thirty-odd years ago. I grew up in Iqaluit, which is in the southern part of Baffin Island. I got married some fourteen years ago to Francis J. Bracken and we have three sons, Iola Aoupaloutaq, Thomas Mickijuk, and Michael Davidee. We moved to Waterloo, Ontario, in 1989 from Iqaluit, Northwest Territories. We have since moved to Ottawa, Ontario, and are liking it so far.

MARY
PANEGOOSHO COUSINS

A Circumpolar Inuk Speaks

Dear Arun P. Mukherjee:

Well, here it is, the fifth decade of my life and I've lived four of them in the Arctic. I survived the 1950s and 1960s in southern Canada.

My real home is here on Baffin Island, but I have lived in northern Saskatchewan, northern Ontario, Hamilton, and Ottawa. I have had the opportunity to travel to all parts of Canada, parts of the U.S.A. (including Alaska), Europe (including Greenland), and even West Africa.

I'm a "circumpolar" Inuk. I'm also an artist, a poet, a mother, a teacher, a linguist, and a quiet philosopher. But in the fragmented life of an Inuk, I am mostly an observer. My mere "observer status" is balanced off somewhat by the fact that I come from a society and a family with strong cultural ties. As the mother of six children, I've learned to be a realist; this part of me is NOT mere "observer status".

I would like to tell you of some of my concerns.

I am concerned that Inuit, who have an amazing history of Arctic living, have been nationalized under the flags of the U.S.A., Canada, Denmark, and whatever country is across the Bering Sea from Alaska. We Canadian Inuit are then sub-divided by the borders of Labrador, Quebec, and the Northwest Territories.

The "outsiders" seem obsessed with drawing lines on maps, and they really believe these lines appear on the earth. What strange thinking! However, by making maps with political boundaries, the "outsiders" have had an adverse effect on Inuit. These boundaries are the first signs that the "outsiders" decided to dominate, operate, control, and generally run people called Inuit.

I am concerned with the aggressive nature of the "outsiders" who have found it necessary to recreate their society in MY land. They searched and found us scattered in hundreds of little enclaves (sometimes called camps) throughout the circumpolar north. The "outsiders" were not happy with our decentralized settlement pattern. It took some time, but we were soon the targets of coercion and enticement, and we were organized into towns and villages. The thinking was, "if it's good enough for Madoc, Ontario, or Denholm, Saskatchewan, it must be good enough for the semi-nomadic people of the Arctic." It's NOT good enough for me!

I am concerned because the aggressive nature of the "outsiders" has led to serious anti-nature behaviour that has affected my land. It may not be important to some people, but it has bothered me that my land has been dug up, scraped, and bulldozed; that the scarce topsoil has been destroyed; that the little plant life has been devastated; that streams have been diverted; that rocks have been dynamited. This violation of the land is irreversible. This may be good enough for Leduc, Alberta, and Montague, Prince Edward Island, but it's not good enough for me.

I am concerned that these well-meaning but misguided "outsiders" did more than mess up the land. They also occupied much of the land in all these artificial communities they created. Once again, they drew lines on townsite plans telling us where to live and where not to trespass. Our little "gift-towns" were marked up with signs like "Land Reserved", "Commercial Only", and other such foreign remarks. Unfortunately, some Inuit have become convinced that these rules of the "outsiders" are necessary for our society. I'm not convinced that this is good for us "New-Found" Canadians.

I am concerned that the hopes, dreams, and aspirations of the Inuit are being lost and now replaced with the objectives of the "outsiders". Sociologists probably understand what is going on and what is happening to the Inuit, and they probably understand the harmful effect. The problem is that someone seems to be taking advice from some of the less enlightened scientists. I'm not a scientist but I am a serious student of the Inuit society and I'm not happy with the "second hand" ideas and conceptions that are being applied systematically to our people.

Inuit and "outsiders" do not communicate very well and this is of concern to me. This lack of communication is understandable because we are on two, totally different wave-lengths. The "outsiders" expect that we will learn from them and act like them. We never will; I will never think like an "outsider". If Aboriginal people are to achieve progress, people who come to live and work with us must understand this.

High levels of organization, ownership of land, accumulation of money, high levels of competition. Does someone really believe that Inuit have these things as priorities in life? I suppose that the "outsiders" think northern Aboriginal groups will some day become like the folks who live in Fogo, Newfoundland, or Thurso, Quebec.

There are very few developments in my society to be optimistic about. Maybe, just maybe, the day will come when my society will be able to evolve without all the negative influences we endure. There is really nothing wrong for one society to "borrow" from another. It is most important that my minority society has the right and opportunity to decide what its future will be.

Let me tell you a little bit about our formal education in the Northwest Territories, which was nonexistent until thirty years ago. It was during the Second World War that the American military raised the question of why Canada was doing nothing to educate Inuit of the Eastern Arctic.

An education system was almost completely absent in those days. In 1944, only four residential schools existed in the whole of the Northwest Territories — all in the Western Arctic. The government did not want to get involved with education of natives in the north.

Soon the Roman Catholic and Anglican churches and missionaries were running some schooling or classes in many small settlements. The churches also operated the few residential schools. In addition to the Americans, the Anglican church was critical of the government's lack of initiative in northern education. Government grants were called "hopelessly inadequate". The Canadian government argued that the problem of northern education was "very complex". Their excuses included the thinly scattered population, the transportation difficulties, the nomadic habits of the Inuit, and the linguistic questions. All these were considered serious obstacles to the development of an education system.

Also, there was considerable difference of opinion amongst white people (most in the north) regarding the type of education necessary for Inuit and how it should be provided. The missionaries insisted that schools should be operated by the churches. Some people wanted government schools. Others felt that Inuit should not be given much education because they could not support schools with their small income from their fur trade. Some insisted that the Inuit "would have a hard time competing with whites outside".

Supporters of education stated that a school system would provide an opportunity to tackle health problems in the north. Schools could teach children an elementary knowledge of hygiene. Without this, doctors said that natives "will always be susceptible to recurring epidemics and the spread of communicable diseases".

Other views of education "emphasized that any education system in the north had to take into account the nomadic character of the Inuit". Some said "Eskimo children cannot follow a fixed school term as white children do." It was assumed that if native people were denied the opportunity of southern education, they would remain illiterate and backward by southern standards.

It appears that little or no Inuit involvement was considered by churches and government regarding decisions on future education plans for the Arctic.

In the 1950s and 1960s, "Day Schools" were established in the north. Perhaps this means non-residential schools. Until the late 1950s, Iqaluit (potentially the most important settlement in the Eastern Arctic) was without any education facilities — federal or missionary. The government administration "note[d] this lack in 1952". Organization of Arctic education was so weak at this time that new educational officials had to follow the D.E.W. Line[1] looking for Inuit children and their parents.

Beginning Arctic education had major problems (not counting Inuit's problems). Instead of organizing classes for Inuit children during the four to six months the culture would allow, schools demanded full year attendance, or much longer than southern schools. This had already proved a failure in southern and western areas in the Arctic and in Greenland. Their policies (like those being introduced in Canada) "... failed because it did not manage to make Greenlanders, as a people, bilingual, but rather produced a generation of people who were semi-lingual" (meaning unable to speak either Danish or Greenlandic).

In the Eastern Arctic no Inuktitut was used in education for the first many years of Inuit education. Later, elementary Inuit teachers taught and used Inuktitut — but for three years only. After this period, no Inuktitut was and is required for Inuit pupils.

---

[1] Editor's note: The Distant Early Warning Line, extending from Alaska to Greenland, is a surveillance system set up by the United States to detect threats of air attack to the North American continent.

Also in the Eastern Arctic, a great number of Inuit were sent to a government residential school in Churchill, Manitoba. From the 1960s to 1970s, Inuit attended the Churchill Vocational Centre for further education. Graduates of this school did not become experts or competent in any culture, southern or northern.

Thank you.

Mary Cousins

MARY PANEGOOSHO COUSINS

I am a Canadian Inuk born in Pond Inlet, North Baffin Island of the Northwest Territories. I am one of the ten children of Letia and Lazarus Kyak. My father has been a special RCMP constable for thirty years. I was raised by my grandmother, and one childhood memory was that of travelling on the RCMP schooner, St. Roch, through the Northwest Passage.

RHODA TAGAQ

We Don't Live
in Snow Houses Anymore

Dear Friend:

We don't live in snow houses anymore. In fact, most of our younger generation don't know how to build a snowhouse (Igloo).

Land meat is still our main food, but we don't eat it raw, as some people think we do. We eat our foods cooked, roasted, stewed, fried, dried, and frozen. Today we add store-bought food to our land food.

Inuit don't eat large amounts of blubber. Blubber's main use today is in the Kudlik (oil lamp), which is still used to heat the ladies' work houses in which the skins are prepared and sewed.

Living in the north is very expensive. Food, clothing, fuel, and hardware are much more expensive than in southern Canada; so it still remains very important to us to use the animals around us, and to share amongst ourselves.

The land is an essential part of our lives. It not only provides us with food, but also with an inner well-being.

We don't fully understand modern education. It is still new to us. However, it has become an everyday part of our lives.

We are aware of the rest of the world, through radio, television, and newspaper.

Modern technology has come to the north. Because of the way our language works, we have easily adopted English terms like plane, snowmobile, medicine, etc., to accommodate it.

There are few privately owned houses. The large part of the population rents houses from the North West Territories

Housing Corporation. The monthly rates are from $32.00 to $535.00, depending on what kind of house it is, how many people live in it, and your income.

The main transportation in the north is the snowmobile. Dog teaming is coming back, but they're not used as they used to be long ago.

Couple of years ago, I hosted foreigners from other countries visiting our little above the Arctic Circle town, and found out how little we, as Inuit, are known to the rest of the world and Canada. Living up in the north all my life, any other way of living was non-existent to me. So, some of the visitors' questions shocked me and made me think of my life and where I was going. Where am I going?

Right now I see my people in a limbo, fast forgetting our language, traditional principles and values, and yet not moving towards any new goals or a way of life. Sure, land claim talks are progressing well; so is self-government. Education is worked on to fit in more with Inuit life. But where is the value and self-esteem within the Inuit going? These are my negative fears, I know.

I must congratulate the Inuit on how well they have managed to adapt to the fast change of life in the past sixty years. They have moved from living out in the land with primitive tools to modern-day life, using modern technology.

Today we are on the verge of a land claim agreement. Inuit are holding their breath at this history-in-the-making event.

I grew up in an outpost camp, moving from hunting ground to hunting ground. All my clothes were made of caribou or seal skins. I was called by my Inuk name Tagaq, but to the government I was #E5-1661, a little tag with a crown on one side and a number on the other side. I still keep the little tag, but as a souvenir.

When I turned nine years of age, Grandpa sent me to school and ordered the rest of the clan to move into town, where there was a Health Centre, a store, and a school. Like most of the Inuit in town, we lived in a tent that first year. The next year we moved to a real house. My, it was so huge, bright, and warm!

I was one of the unfortunate children whose parents wouldn't send us for higher schooling. Therefore, I've got a low education. Whatever else I have learnt, I had to learn on my own or on the job.

Being the eldest among my siblings, I had to hunt for my father. Therefore, I was considered an improper female. That title gave me the courage to try out any job I wanted to try out, and find a job I liked, to organize community festival events, and to participate in any recreational activities which were so new and exciting for me.

All the excitement and participation didn't come easy. Nor did the jobs I pursued. I found out women are secondary to men in society's life and work force.

Years have passed quickly. Today I'm married with four children,[1] and have a full-time job.

Today we are well up-to-date with world events and get news from radio and television and newspapers and news magazines.

My children learn to use the computer, which I've never touched.

Today I also get weekly fresh fruits and vegetables. One apple costs $1.15!

We don't have the government tags anymore. We now have full names and social insurance numbers.

Today I can be seen pretty well caught up with the modern world, physically. Mentally, I'm still struggling to catch up and am very confused as to where I really am.

Our elders, compared to my age group (20-40), are so ready to give support and help others in need while we, as a younger generation, are only thinking of ourselves and how to have the best of the earthly materials, before we give a hand to the next person in need. That is what I see in my settlement today: lack of concern for fellow humans other than family.

That is a fact of life today whether we like it or not. The new generation is changing, learning to live in the money-operated world where, very often, human feelings are secondary to profit.

Above the Arctic Circle

Rhoda Qumituq

---

1 Editor's note: Rhoda Tagaq adopted two children on August 4, 1993.

RHODA TAGAQ

I was born on an island called Kapuivik, on November 6, 1959. I now live in Igloolik. Today I work full-time at a health centre as a clerk interpreter, raising six children: Jane, Adam, Philip, Benjamin and the twins, Joey and Jeffrey. I like sewing, reading, organizing events, relaxing, writing, and listening to music.

CAMILLE
HERNÁNDEZ-RAMDWAR

Once I Wanted
to Run Away from Canada

To the Canadian Advisory Council on the Status of Women:

I would like to write to you about some of my experiences growing up and living in Canada.

I was born in Winnipeg, Manitoba, in 1965. I am a woman of mixed heritage, i.e., I cannot conveniently be put into any one racial or ethnic category. My mother was of Ukrainian-Canadian heritage, and my father is from Trinidad, of many heritages. Unfortunately, my parents did not give me a strong sense of identity while growing up (perhaps because they were dealing with their own feelings of alienation in Canada), and I was exposed to a lot of racism at school. It was the other children (I lived in an all-white neighbourhood) who attacked me. I was called almost every racial slur imaginable: "nigger", "paki", "injun", "boggan" (slur for a Native person), "chink", "spic".

The experience of being labelled at so young an age has deeply affected my feelings of being a Canadian, of "belonging". My general feeling has been that I do not feel like a Canadian (despite being born and raised here) because I am not accepted as one at face value. People, upon meeting me, still open conversations with "And where are you from?" as if a person of my complexion could not possibly be born here. I blame a lot of these continued misperceptions on the media, who seem satisfied with presenting an all-white Canadian face in advertising and television shows. To be quite honest, I am fed up with this distortion of reality. I think it is very harmful. Firstly, it supports the ideology of Anglo-Canadian supremacy and domination, and does not open people's minds to change. Secondly, it does damage to young people and children of colour who are growing up in Canada looking for acceptance and identity. We continue to be excluded, and this attacks our self-esteem.

It has taken me years to forge my own identity, one that I finally feel comfortable with. In 1986, I moved to Toronto with my son (I am a sole support parent). My reasons for moving here were largely cultural. I realized how much more comfortable I felt in a cosmopolitan city like Toronto rather than a more homogeneous one like Winnipeg. I do not feel like such an outsider here; I do not feel so vulnerable to racism because I feel a sense of solidarity with the Black community and other communities of colour (although I would argue that racism is very evident in this city, only on a larger scale). My present situation has made me aware of the multiple discriminations I experience daily — not only racial/ethnic, but gender- and class-based. I have had trouble finding housing; I have been shunted into low-paying and menial jobs; I have been discouraged from attending university in this city — I would argue, on the basis of my sex, colour, and economic status. It was actually a government agency for sole support mothers that told me I would never be accepted into university, that it was a "fantasy", and that I should find a trade instead. Was I being streamlined due to my colour? Luckily, I did not take their advice, and graduated from university cum laude in 1991.

Even at university I experienced discrimination. My life experiences have made me in many ways an angry woman. To some people this anger is unacceptable and offensive. To me it is justified. Fortunately, I have learned that I am not alone in my anger, and my friends are a great source of support to me.

I feel a great sense of responsibility to young people of colour in Canada who are struggling to form a sense of identity, the way I did. I would eventually like to write a book for adolescents about growing up in Canada as a person of colour. I would like to be involved in the educational system to help address the issues of racism and sexism, and how they are perpetuated in the classroom — through school-books, attitudes, curricula, etc. In many ways, I am impatient for change. I feel most Euro-Canadians have not accepted that Canada has changed, and will change more. There will be more "mixed" marriages. There will be more "mixed" children. There will be more Sikhs in the Mounties, more people of colour in government, in business. The world is shrinking, and people must adapt.

I wonder what Canada holds in store for my son. I have already started to instil in him not the differences between people that are perceived, but the reality that we are all human beings. I teach him about racism, I teach him about his heritage(s). I take him travelling with me. I have friends from many backgrounds, of many colours and countries, and so does he. But I wonder if at some point he will be forced to choose one camp, and will be excluded from others. Will he feel like a Canadian?

I am glad I had the opportunity to write this letter. In a small way, it has released me — by publicly expressing my frustrations at being — yes — a Canadian for twenty-eight years. Once I wanted to run away from Canada. Now I feel an urge to claim it — I have a right to be here, to be happy.

Sincerely,

Camille Hernández-Ramdwar

CAMILLE HERNÁNDEZ-RAMDWAR

I have been writing about my experiences as a Canadian woman of colour for most of my life. Born and raised in the prairies, I currently live in Toronto with my son and infant daughter. Besides going through cycles of identity crises related to "the Canadian Experience", I tend to identify with and find strength in my Caribbean roots. I graduated from York University in 1991.

BEATRICE
ARCHER WATSON

Canadian Experience

Dear Zizi:

It is almost midnight and I am in the middle of doing one of my freelance articles for a major newspaper of my community which I do not think I will finish. I am so angry and frustrated. I have been freelancing for this newspaper for more than a year. I have stuck with it during its lowest period, sometimes submitting most of the copy from the community that provides local content, taking the pittance they offer for pay. I kept on working in the hope that when a position becomes available, I would be given due consideration. My record with this newspaper has been impeccable. They have published everything I wrote, with only a minimum amount of editing. To my surprise, not only was I not called for an interview when a vacancy arose due to the resignation of one reporter, but the job was given to a girl fresh out of a community college who has to drive in from a city nearby every morning. Here I am living in the community and have many contacts and am respected as a writer, and I was not called for an interview. I had a talk with the publisher who has always been respectful and encouraging to me. All he keeps saying is "be patient, I'm looking at it." I felt like spitting in his face. The editor said he recommended me, but his hands are tied.

I don't know, Zizi, whether to call this discrimination. It's something that I refuse to allow myself to believe. It is so easy to blame all our failures on discrimination. In this case, what else could it be? It is not sexism; he gave the job to a woman. I have Canadian experience. I can think of no other possibility than discrimination on account of my skin colour and being an immigrant. I have always buried my head in the sand so as not to recognize this ugly side in human nature. I like to think people are fair and broad-minded. I tell myself perhaps it was a relative, a friend's daughter, to ease the pain and humiliation. It was not so.

You know Zi, I also freelanced for the other paper of the same company last year, and when a position came up there, I was overlooked again. Before the vacancy arose, I had left my application with the editor expressing my interest in full-time work. But I was not called for an interview because I did not resubmit another application. That's the excuse the editor gave me. The people they choose are not even in my league. I am a darn good reporter. I have always been praised for my accuracy and clear and simple way of writing.

They can't say I do not have Canadian experience. I have written and published articles in many major newspapers in Canada, including the *Toronto Sun, Winnipeg Free Press, London Free Press,* and numerous small community papers. I was trained in journalism at one of Canada's best community colleges — Lambton College in Sarnia, Ontario. I am nearing completion of a degree in Arts and have years of experience and credentials to my credit, but getting a job in the media eludes me. It seems right within my grasp but as soon as I am about to grab it, it fades away. I have applied to many places, even in the government for Information Officer positions, and have never been called for an interview. This is enough to make one lose faith in oneself.

Yes, I do get paranoid sometimes and think there is a definite plot to keep visible minorities out of these positions. It saddens me because I feel I can contribute a lot to this society. You know I can handle it. I was the Senior Information Officer in the Public Services in Guyana, responsible for publication of government informational materials, sending out news releases, etc. I can do it. I have done it. I have proven myself, but somehow I cannot land a job. I am not given a fair chance.

Sure, the government is doing all it can to help change the situation. The multicultural promise is fine and idealistic, but it is people who have to implement the policy, and if these people still have their old mentalities, do you see how far we can go? Nowhere. You can't legislate the way people think.

I worked for a while in various term positions in the provincial government doing secretarial work, which is well below my capacity. I got tired of moving from place to place. So I accepted a job at an immigrant women's association, where I have been for the past three years. Working here has opened my eyes to the many injustices meted out to visible minority people across Canada. I began to understand the big picture. I am not alone. I have heard stories sadder than any I can tell.

Some people face prejudice when they go to look for an apartment. I have never faced any direct prejudice of this sort, and I do not know if it is because my spouse is Anglo-Saxon Canadian. I think that could make a difference.

My feminist views, as you know Zizi, are very strong, but here again feminism is geared to the white middle-class Anglo-Saxon woman. They don't have a clue what Black women face. We have to face discrimination because of our sex as well as our race.

I have digressed from my original intention of writing you, but writing down my frustrations has helped ease the pain. It is very painful living in a society where you are being marginalized. Where, whatever you do or say, does not count for much. Slowly one's pride is chipped away. In spite of the way I feel, I think I would have to finish the article and submit it because I need the money. Inflation is going up and it's getting harder to make ends meet. This is how many immigrant families survive, Zizi. They take whatever they can get and hope for the better, but that better never seems to come and they settle in their position and find that that's all they are going to get. It's sad.

You know me. I am a fighter, Zizi, and I intend to get where I want to go. I was quiet for a while but I am ready to fight my battle now.

Zizi, stay where you are. Your work is appreciated. You are building something and people recognize your contribution. Here there is no such recognition for an immigrant woman, and especially if you are a Black immigrant woman. Nothing worthwhile has ever come easy. I still have faith in people and in the government and people of Canada to do the right thing.

Best of wishes to you Zizi.

Your friend

Archer Watson

BEATRICE ARCHER WATSON

I was born in Guyana, South America, and came to Canada nine years ago. I studied radio, television, and journalism arts and have been a freelance writer for eight years. My first novel, *Poison of my Hate*, a bestseller, was published in 1978 by the National Educational Company of Zambia in Africa. My work has appeared in several newspapers in Canada including the *London Free Press*, *Toronto Sun, Winnipeg Free Press*, among others. Currently working at an immigrant women's association, I am continuing my university education, and aspire to be a feminist writer/anthropologist. In addition to writing, studying, and being a wife and mother of two daughters, I also paint and draw. My works have been featured in several group shows. I graduated in April with a B.A. in Anthropology and Women's Studies from the University of Manitoba.

GRACE

Discontent in a Verdant Province

Dear Carmina:

I apologize for the long silence on my end, but life here has not been as easy as I expected. This place is not cosmopolitan at all, it is somewhat bordering between an urban and a provincial setting. I would say very much laid back, and can be compared to one of the smaller cities in our country. The countryside, however, offers lush rolling hills and very quaint sceneries. One can appreciate the fact the island is very clean. We have fresh air, and pollution is totally nonexistent. Although I missed the usual hustle and bustle, the perennial traffic jams, and the rat race lifestyle, I must admit that this Atlantic province animates a healthy outlook.

I started scouting around for a job, which brings me nothing but a series of heartaches and frustrations. My options are very limited, since employment here is scarce and seasonal. I have made the rounds of all the broadcasting firms hoping I could be hired because of my educational background, but was never given a chance for an interview. There was an instance where a receptionist handed me an application form in the most obnoxious manner but was friendly with the local applicants. Yes, I have experienced being called last when I was the first to report for an interview. I have observed that whenever a local person was present, there was an obvious different treatment. The few interviews I was lucky to be called for were all nightmares. It has come to a point where thoughts of it send shivers to my spine. I was always told that I don't have a Canadian experience — that whatever experiences I carried from home or from other places were not acceptable here. My education was not enough and my credentials without substance. I seriously felt that being different was a stigma, and I am forever doomed to my situation.

I do not have any Canadian acquaintances, much less friends.... I circulate around with people coming from our own country. The few English people I got acquainted with

were not gratifying. I was never welcome in their midst, often pushed to a situation where questions asked mortified me. Sometimes, and I'd say in most cases, I was given strange stares as though I was coming from a different planet. The indifference existed in all areas, public places especially. Initially, I was under the impression that my accent made them behave the way they did but I was wrong. It goes far beyond the articulation of the English language. I am different, and it made a mark. I have never mentioned the word "discrimination", because all these times it never dawned on me I was getting the treatment. I have always adhered to this value that in this world nobody is above nor below you; reality has indeed taught me otherwise. I have never felt degraded and debased to the extent that I really questioned my own being. It appeared to me that coloured people are less and low — whatever the white people do is always justified because they are of the superior race, and, therefore, race is almost an implied rule of life here.

I'd like to relate an incident which occurred a few months back. I was hired to work as a clerk although originally the position advertised was for a supervisor.... Explanation to this was that my qualifications do not merit the position and I didn't have the Canadian experience. I accepted the job just the same with the realization that I have to start somewhere, and have to earn Canadian experience. I found out later that the position was offered to a local person who was inexperienced and just fresh from school. Again, the animosities of the other employees were all apparent in their behaviour.... The cold treatment was too much to bear. I would eat alone, and whenever a problem arose from work, I was left to grope in the dark. I have grown tougher with their attitudes so that I truly felt I was gaining strength to carry on. It has served to build formidable challenges to meet the daily unpleasant situations I was confronted with. I was never discouraged by this reality. In fact I persevered in my work and pretended the indifference did not exist.

All the time I was employed, the fears hovering over me turned into reality. The company laid me off after eight months, stating that business was low and had to be cut down. I was made to believe that my position was absorbed by another staff who had been with the firm for a long time. I discovered my position was offered to an immediate relative of a senior manager. It was a terribly unforgiving act. I had personally assessed my performance in terms of the sensitive work I was asked to do; tasks that have no clerical bearings but rather are ones only given to supervisors. I supported my judgement that I was competent in my job. Although nothing was said about my performance, I never got a complaint either. In that period of time I did what I had to do in a surrounding where indifference emanated from everybody. The loss of my job was the ultimate test of my endurance to survive in this province. I was a hapless victim of injustices with no one to turn to. What did you think I did? Yes, I confined myself at home and did some soul-searching. There were numerous questions, my heart bleeding for answers. I had a good and comfortable life, coming from a respectable family, and educated in a prestigious private school where the Christian doctrine was literally a way of life: love one another, forgive those who wronged us. The moral values instilled in my growing years were the concrete foundation I based my existence on. I know, and was prepared, that out there in the real world is a jungle where survival of the fittest is the rule. But should men really resort to such actions when men are only transient visitors in this material world?

I searched for that tiny truth which says man is basically good at heart because goodness comes from our Maker. They may go astray because of the factors that affect them in the process of living, but goodness is at the very core of their hearts. Yes, my beloved friend, I have no answers to my plight. I have reasoned and tried to find excuses for their attitudes, relating that I am different, with different cultures, customs, traditions, and colour.... But does it really matter? Where is the acceptance as a human being with a right to dignity and respect? Maybe I was not good enough and not perfect, but nobody gives me the chance.

I don't know what to say to you, but despite all these problems I am here to stay. I have made my decision to move here. I know going back home in the arms of my own country, people, friends, and family would be a sweet refuge, but I will never be free of these haunting thoughts and experiences. I will continually fight for my survival. I can move to another place but that would not guarantee I will not suffer the same treatment.

It took me a while to try and look for another job, but I am far more determined to live. Now, perhaps, I have Canadian experience in my bag, the situation would hopefully alter. If I have less faith in the people, I have greater faith in God. I am consoled with the thoughts that I have my friends from our country and I belong here. I realize that this fight is not over but I will try to make a difference.

In my most depressed moods I take a trip to the countryside which indeed has given the ultimate pleasure to my otherwise lonely life. There, amidst the serenity and beauty of the land, I commune with nature. It is a breathtaking sight: "beauty indeed has its own excuse for being".

I admit that this province is blessed with splendid verdant hills, gorgeous beaches, and immaculate surroundings. I do truly appreciate them and I am lucky to live in a place where crime is almost nil, and the open spaces certainly give a healthy life. I would want to raise my children here, but I will teach them the values of life that I know. I am not at all bitter about my circumstances despite what I went through and will go through. I have seen the positive sides of this place, and that is where I will concentrate. Someday, somehow, a change might take effect on the people, but right now I cannot change them. I can only change myself and continue to show goodness.

Please pray for me and everybody who is in the same situation wherever they are.... It is still a beautiful world. God bless!

Grace (pseudonym)

GRACE

I arrived in Canada in 1978 and became a Canadian citizen in early 1981. I have a Master's degree and was a university professor prior to coming to the United States, then Canada. I have been involved with volunteer organizations, especially those dealing with the status and literacy of women, and have received several community and citizenship awards. I live in Atlantic Canada.

SPEAKING THE PAST, FEELING THE PAIN

Monica Goulet
Haruko Okano
Maya
Anna Woo
Anita Jennifer Wong
Althea Samuels
Asein
Marcia Crosby

Monica Goulet

Kiam

Dear Mom:

I never had the opportunity to get to know you because you died when I was only five. Later on I was told how you had known ahead of time that you were dying, that you had made arrangements for Josie, your second eldest living daughter, to come home and look after us.

We're not quite sure how you died, at the tender age of thirty-nine.... All we know is that "Wetigo", a neighbour lady, heard you moaning in pain in our outhouse. She came to your aid.

Easter Monday.... Blue Monday.... I'll never forget.... That memory is permanently etched in my brain. Josie walked into the house. She gathered everyone around to tell us that you were gone. It was a bright, beautiful day.... Sunlight streamed in through the windows, yet everyone was crying. I couldn't comprehend the meaning of death but I was uncomfortable with everyone's tears. I started laughing, in an attempt to "lighten the mood", but it didn't work.

Mom, I wish you would have had more time to hold me. I remember one time when we were on the shore of some river waiting to leave by canoe. You sat on the grassy slope of the shore. I was cold and I told you that I was cold because I wanted you to hold me and warm me up. You told me to run around, that I would warm up that way. I did, but I was disappointed that you didn't hold me. Yet I never told you.

I sometimes wonder now what thoughts are going through my children's mind that they aren't articulating to me.

I remember another time when my little brother, Ordean, and I were sent to the store to buy some lard. You gave us a **whole dime** to spend so that we could buy ourselves a treat. We could hardly wait to divide up the dime into two nickels. I knew money was scarce. That's why that memory stands out.

I also remember you lying in your coffin.... You were wearing green.... An Auntie held me so that I could kiss you goodbye.

Mom, I wanted to hold you, to tell you that I love you, to bury my face in the hollow of your neck.

Mom, I wanted to tell you that you were a remarkable woman; a good, kind, strong woman; someone with a great capacity to love. But you were also a tired woman; a Roman Catholic, Métis woman who bore thirteen children. You were always working, baking for our cafeteria, washing clothes, tending to all the needs (or so it seemed) of your household of eleven children. Joseph and Marie died at birth. You were also a progressive woman: you were politically involved with the CCF, the forerunner to the NDP. You obviously recognized the inequities that existed, especially for Aboriginal women, and you were committed to changing things.

Mom, I want you to know that most of your children are formally educated, and are carrying on the tradition of commitment for change. You would be quite proud and excited by what's happening.

There's one story I heard about you that seems to capture the essence of your being. One day, a neighbour woman, who shall remain unnamed, walked by our house and saw you outside with all your children. She snidely commented that you looked just like a schoolteacher with all your schoolchildren gathered around you. Rather than retaliate, you chose to utter a Cree word, "Kiam", which loosely translated means "let it be", "it's okay", "it doesn't matter".

But I know that "Kiam" can also mean you pick and choose your battles; you save your strength to fight against the oppressor, not against others oppressed; you forgive and you continue on in the struggle for equality for all.

Mom, Veronique Marie Carriere, I admire your courage, your strength, all that you were.

You never had the opportunity for a formal post-secondary education, but you were far more educated in other ways. Yet I know you would've liked the challenge.

I wish you were still alive to meet your grandchildren, Joshua and Sasha. They are both beautiful children. My hope for them is that I can raise them to be caring, loving human beings.

Mom, I feel your spirit close by from time to time, guiding me and giving me strength.

I am who I am because of the cultural, economic, racial, and other sociologically defined realities I was born into. But, most of all, I am who I am because I was shaped in your womb, and in your likeness. That gives me a sense of power and a sense of completeness. Thank you Mother for carrying me into this world.

I Love You
I Miss You

Monica

MONICA GOULET

I am a Métis woman of Cree, Saulteaux, and French ancestry originating from the settlement of Cumberland House, Saskatchewan. I am also the proud mother of Joshua (7) and Sasha (4). As the Curriculum Resource Coordinator for the Northern Division of Saskatchewan Education based out of La Ronge, my primary responsibility is researching and compiling appropriate non-biased Aboriginal and multicultural resource material for the Mistasinihk Place Resource Centre. I also have the exciting challenge of co-ordinating an annual Elders Gathering. As well, I am the president-elect of CRIAW (Canadian Research Institute for the Advancement of Women).

HARUKO OKANO

Spring is Here, Mama

Introduction

My mother, a Japanese-Canadian born in Haney, British Columbia, was raised in Japan and returned to Canada as a young woman of nineteen. She lived in Vancouver, then moved to Toronto and became a clothing designer. My strongest connection is with my mother.

My story begins in the last few years of my mother's life and is presented as a letter written to her spirit. It ends with me in my mid-forties. The story is divided into the seasons of the year, starting briefly with summer and traversing the annual cycle to spring. This is part of a written/visual project I have entitled "Come Spring".

Dear Mama:

Summer … those days of happiness were all too brief. Centre Island or the Riverdale Zoo; walking hand in hand bathed in the warmth and comfortable reassurance of just the two of us. You said I was a clingy, insecure child. I understand that now. The still tension of those war years shadowed the brightness of my little world. Your uncertainty and anxiety subtly charged the air around us, causing me to cling even tighter to your side. Tragedy stalked us like that grey wolf pacing its cage at the zoo. I miss my friend Wanda. I miss sharing carefree hours; playing house and selling freshie at 5¢ a glass. My first day of kindergarten was spent hanging onto Wanda's hand. Summer was too short a season, Mama.

Summer advanced into autumn with the destruction of the protective wall that you had so carefully built to defend me. I read its collapse in the terror and anger reflected in your eyes as you helplessly watched that older, white boy punch and kick me to the ground. Your face seemed to fill the entire scope of my vision. I watched your lips, pale and dry, shaping those words, "Hit him! Punch him back with your fist!" Everything seemed to slide into slow motion. There seemed to be no time to puzzle over how you had taught me never to fight. People were reasonable.... Neh? How do I make a fist? I felt the wind whoosh from my lungs as the pavement bit into the side of my face. Some part of me withdrew into a small room, deep within my body. I felt, from a distance, the fists and boots thud against my side and heard the dull snap of bone as he came down on my back. I'd never seen such hatred. I couldn't believe it was aimed at me by this perfect stranger. His face contorted with rage, he spat words that, in my dreams, never reached my ears as I curled up tighter in that dark, cool place within. Or so I thought.... Years later, while attending an Unlearning Racism workshop, I was stunned by the force of the anguished screams that rose from that forgotten place. My stomach heaved and blood vessels ruptured with the long-delayed release. When the storm had passed, I saw in my mind his face once again. This time his words rang crystal clear in my ears, "You dirty Jap, I hate you! You killed my father's brother! Why don't you go back to where you belong? I hate you, hate you! You dirty Jap!" Mama, you were so sick then, but even so I saw you chase him to his house where he scooted past his mother. I heard the brief exchange and the slam of the door. Rest now Mom, I made it.... I survived!

Not long after, I was trundled off to join Uncle's family in Coaldale, Alberta. That's where most of our family was evacuated to in 1942. Auntie Nan still has the last letter that Grandfather wrote from the beet farm in November 1946, just before he died.

Mama, I want to tell you that the long cold winter of my life began wrapped in the bleak hostility of the Alberta school system. A left-handed child in a right-handed world was not loved by teacher or God. My joyous flight into the alphabet, numbers, and crayoned images was brutally intercepted; the left wing clipped firmly behind the back or pinned to the desk seat. "There is a right way to use a pencil, a right way to behave in class", the teacher drilled. "Right is good! Left is evil!", the Principal lectured, as he jerked my offending left hand forward to receive its punishment for disobedience. I remember the shame rising up to colour my face; the humiliating alienation I felt as I peered through tears at the sea of faces in the auditorium. Mama, I spent two years struggling through grade one, using all of my attention to avoid the teacher's wooden pointer and laboriously coaxing my right hand to capture the expression silenced in my left. I remember the confusion, those blank moments of not knowing which hand to raise to request permission to use the washroom, and often the ensuing hopeless panic of praying, too late, for the strength to hold on till recess. Oh, how I missed the warmth of your reassurance as I dragged myself back to a family already burdened with the concerns of its own survival. One more mouth to feed, one more soul to nurture. One more too much. My tears for you eventually dried up in the arid prairie wind, my feelings numbed by the thundering hailstorms.

I held the memory of your face in my young mind. When the airplane finally deposited me at the Toronto airport, the changes that illness and worry had worked upon you made you a stranger to me. Surely the grey-haired woman, whose swollen body approached, aided by a walking cane, couldn't be my mother. How painful it must have been for you to witness the tragedy and withdrawal in that blank expression on your own child's face. For both of us, caught up in the circumstances, that moment was the harbinger of the end.

All hopes and dreams shrivel up in the heart of winter, in the foster home in Orange County. The announcement of your death came quietly, casually held in one sentence, "By the way, your mother's dead." No tears ... a sucking inward, deeper to places within, where my small, hurt animal self could crawl, to hibernate in the subconscious. I want to tell you the world became winter white, colours of brown and yellow only accented it here and there as bits of decay. I was stranded in an endless winter filled with violence, sexual abuse ... a place devoid of emotional nurturing. I was a case number, a commodity to some ... a burden to others. That was a significant year, Mama. I started wearing glasses; the first signs of suicidal tendencies sprang up in me and I began drawing, because art was a safe world of secret languages. No longer did my home reaffirm the beauty of who I might be. Instead, I set about saving my allowance towards operations on this flat-chested, slant-eyed person that I had to step out of. I made a brief attempt with bleach, secretly applied to my skin in hopes of that whiter than white look. Following the example of the blonde girl in summer camp, I tried peroxide only to end up with a carrot orange patch, ridiculously visible against my own colour. The messages stayed with me into adulthood; be white or at least Eurasian. Leave the traces of my first language, culture, and heritage behind like a snake discarding its skin.

In that landscape the role models of Suzy Wong and Madame Butterfly got mixed up with Cinderella, and I married my White Knight. Winter lasted eight years for me and somewhere in that darkness my Eurasian dreams became embodied in the birth of my two sons. As fairy tale turned into nightmare, the acid of self-hatred and sense of worthlessness ate away at me, until I gave myself up to the void that was left. I learnt that there's no winning, Mama. I came to believe that there would never be a place for me in this world. All my thoughts, my feelings, my gifts ... cultural, racial, and as a human being had been deemed without value.

Dry your eyes wherever you are, mother; spring comes late sometimes, but come it does. Somewhere in that seemingly endless winter, I understood. I had reached the bottom. To die, to go crazy would not benefit me or those I loved. I left my marriage, and as a result of the injustices of those circumstances, I lost touch with my children. In 1972 I went back to complete my art training. I reclaimed my Japanese name, "Haruko", and moved to B.C. I started a new life. I want you to know, Mama, that in the spring of my life, the artist in me remains my strongest gift. Racism, sexism, and discrimination are still here in the community and yes, it still hurts. It has taken many years of healing to empower myself, just to deal with today. Like the seeds in spring, the signs of new life start slowly, subtly. To return to B.C. meant completion, renewal, reclaiming hope for myself. With the Japanese Canadian Redress negotiations and the signing of the agreement in 1988, spring began in earnest. Denials of my Asian identity and the effects of racism had to be dealt with. My personal history needed to be reclaimed and Nikkei history understood. As I heal within, gaining in personal strength, I am turning my attention to the concerns of the larger community. I've become an activist, Mom. I'm out there working for change within this society. I am establishing personal connections and support with other Asian-Canadians and women of all colours.

Mama, in this spring, this season of my life, I know you would be proud of me. At the age of forty-six, my art has expanded into music, writing, theatre, and film. In the spring of my life, there are still tears. I wish you could see me now, to know that I have moved beyond just survival. I want you to know that I understand how hard it was for you as a single parent of Japanese ancestry, dealing with the war years and illness. I thank you. I want to tell you that I have gained a sense of the Japanese lineage within my very being and that I value that heritage and those sacrifices my people made for me. I thank my family. I catch a glimpse of the strength and endurance within myself, the seeds of hope that lay sleeping. I thank you for my potential to survive and grow. Mixed with tears of joy are moments of sorrow when images of my sons come to mind. In my bid for racial and cultural assimilation, there is the sad realization that circumstance has denied them half of their heritage. For them ... I pray. On this day, December 20th, the anniversary of your death, for you Fujie ... a candle burns. Goodbye Mama.

Love,

Haruko

HARUKO OKANO

I am a Sansei, third-generation Japanese-Canadian woman born in Toronto, Ontario, in 1945 at the end of World War II. My father, whom I never knew, came from Japan as a young man and moved to Toronto to further his university studies. From the age of nine, as a permanent ward of the Toronto Children's Aid Society, I was raised by Caucasians in foster homes and shelters in Ontario. At age 19, I married and had two children. This stormy relationship ended over a decade later and marks a major turning point in my life. I now live in Vancouver, British Columbia. I am a visual artist and have recently expanded into the areas of writing, performance, and music. In 1992 my essays and poetry were published in a book entitled *Come Spring: Journey of a Sansei* (Gallerie Publications); it is a visual and literary combination of an ongoing project of the same name. For all those who struggle with this deep longing to be ... Ganbata! ... be strong.

MAYA

Different Strokes in Real Life

Dear daughter:

The reason I became a ward of a Children's Aid agency and was given up for adoption at the age of one year will forever remain unknown to me. It was slightly before my memories of time. Of course, I can always conjecture as well as put together pieces of facts that I was given later. It's not hard to imagine that times were really very hard for my biological mother, a young unmarried Black woman in the late 1950s, living in Montreal. She had to help her mother with the responsibility of caring for her disabled and ailing grandmother who had multiple sclerosis. These representatives of three generations were already struggling through discrimination and hard times. My biological father, a young soldier from the United States, was only visiting Canada when he met the youngest of these three women. He was aware of the part he played in my imminent arrival, but he returned to his country. After my appearance on the scene, the fourth generation female, they named me Maya. They cared for me closely for over one year. It could have been that all three decided that four of us were a definite crowd. Or maybe my biological mother made this difficult decision on her own. I can imagine she tried her best and then decided that someone else could do a better job of bringing up her baby. Try as I might, I can't remember a thing about it. I like to imagine, though, that they would have given me the world on any kind of platter if they could have.

I do remember that my adoptive parents are people who are out of the ordinary. Who else would care for so many foster babies and then adopt a child of the Black race into their white Anglo-Saxon home? Being generous, kind-hearted Christians, they wanted to share their good fortune with others. To be particularly chosen to join a family is rare and something I've appreciated, to say the least. But you know that although babies and toddlers are incredibly cute at first, things are bound to change as one grows into an individual and complex person.

Was I at home in middle-class white suburbia? It certainly felt that way. I was too young to remember experiencing any hardship or dilemma that may well have preceded my biological mother's decision to put me into adoption approximately a year after my birth. My adoptive home was the only home I ever consciously knew. I was fostered by the same charitable family for ten years and was then asked if I wished to be their formally adopted child. Even then, I knew there could be worse places. I was happy most of the time, as my new parents and siblings made room for me and tried to treat me with no apparent difference. Quite content, I participated in the sharing of elemental things. There was much decency in the home, although not enough affection to go all around. It was occasionally around at arm's length — more so in my pre-school and elementary years.

Somehow, I did not lean all the way back with my feet up in that armchair called the "feeling of belonging". There was a scarcity of warmth and encouragement needed to nurture a positive sense of self-esteem and confidence. A more negative self-image developed. I internalized feelings of inadequacy in comparison to my peers — a growing idea that I possessed very little, if anything, to contribute to society. There were virtually no positive reflections of my image anywhere around me. (Well, it's true that one day we discovered a picture of a young girl who looked exactly like me in the pages of a Christian/Missionary magazine. A twin sister — her face was my face — born possibly at the same time, but obviously a different place.)

My parents purchased a guitar for me when I expressed an interest in learning to play it. But when I realized I would soon be called upon to play and sing in front of everyone, I knew I would be petrified with self-consciousness. It had happened before in grade five or six, when a teacher noticed my singing ability and suggested that I do a solo at church. The solo never came about, and the guitar was also left ignored and unlearned in the closet. No one likes to be singled out for criticism, but oddly enough I did not even want to be singled out in a positive manner. It seemed as if I had no desire then to make any kind of a name for myself.

At present it is interesting to note that people who do not risk that step seem to acquire a name for themselves anyway. "Miss Never-Finish-What-You-Start" seemed to be my suitable new moniker for a time. I did not express my fears of gigantic butterflies taking over the insides of my stomach and beating it to a pulp. In fact, I had nervous stomach problems resulting in painful cramps, especially during times of loud verbal complaints from my mother. I was told they were not real pains, just something I deserved for feeling upset (talking back was not allowed).

At some point, my mother became genuinely concerned about my having very little contact with people of my own race. She took me to a hair salon downtown to inquire about Black hair care, but discovered it was too expensive to follow that regimen. More importantly, she gave me a pamphlet and suggested I join a West Indian community group in the city to learn more about Black history. I declined the opportunity. Unfortunately, I elected to remain blissful in my ignorance, but it was not because of the subject matter. Quite literally, our closest and friendliest neighbours were a Black family from Trinidad. (Admittedly though, I had little social contact with them since the only child in that family was a boy at least seven or eight years older than myself.) Since I was a somewhat sheltered youngster, I felt in no way ready to jump into a brand new social arena. Especially going downtown which seemed far from my safe little suburb. (It was several years later that I even travelled on a bus into Montreal by myself at the age of fourteen.) So, at the tender age of twelve, I could not fathom that a cultural group was probably a good thing for me to experience at that time. I was shy and nervous, definitely. On a deeper level, it was probably my fear of being singled out mixed with fear of meeting the unknown social group. For that reason, I was glad when my parents did not ask me again.

It remained fairly easy to live with loads of rarely interrupted fun and laughter with siblings and friends. I usually preferred one or two close friends rather than hanging around with a group. But there was one group with whom I spent at least five years of enjoyable time from grades seven through eleven. That was the youth choir of our church, and I loved to sing with the group. I also spent a lot of time reading and unconsciously biting my nails while I read. My nail-biting had become a long-standing and unshakeable bad habit. It quite irritated my mother who was constant with firm reminders that there was nothing to be biting my nails about. I wondered how she was so sure. I had not shared with her my qualms about the future, and she did not share hers with me unless she was angry, and wanted to point out the undesirable character I might inevitably become.

I did babysitting jobs for neighbours and more neighbours. I saved my money and felt proud and responsible regarding these outside jobs. However, I did not feel appreciated at home for carrying out the same responsibilities which, in my mother's eyes, did not appear to have been done well enough. As I neared preparation time for the independence of young adulthood, I was unfortunately lacking in self-confidence. I was not ambitious and had no particular idea where my life would fit into the scheme of things. My friends had their goals and daydreams of what life would bring, but I did not. Outwardly, everything was almost fine as I easily finished high school, majored in office practices, and actively sought jobs. But I had to wait over four months longer than my white classmates who had lower grades, to get an offer of employment. Upon securing a position, it was soon apparent the company and I suited each other very well. I was promoted after only three months and was proud of my achievements.

Things seemed to be looking up, but I couldn't smell any roses due to the cold war at home that was on more than it was off. It froze out communication of any kind. Confusion abounded deep inside me during this time of transition from teen to young woman, and the depression was paralyzing. I wasn't sure I could get on top of everything that was expected of me, and I wasn't sure I even wanted to. I had always worked hard to please them before, but now I didn't care. I realized more than ever that I rarely felt appreciated or valued. So I made it a time of rebellion. I stayed out late drinking with acquaintances, making matters worse, and growing increasingly numb. Besides not having any idea of where my life was supposed to be heading, it was also unpleasant having to feel grateful for everything that was ever done for me but was naturally done for everyone else as a result of being part of a family — grateful for not having to jump around bare-breasted in the jungles of Africa (which, a teasing sibling had pointed out to me, was the place I should be).

My adoptive siblings have maintained that from their point of view, we were all treated similarly in the family dynamics. From a distance this is almost true. Most of them would fail to see that they could not have experienced the different reactions I did when I wished to, for instance, communicate my likes and dislikes as everyone else around me did so openly. I found that, for me, stating appreciation was fine, but expressing dislikes was a big no-no. "Don't be so ungrateful as to be dissatisfied", was not always said but often implied. They also did not experience being constantly accused of over-sensitivity as I was when others freely expressed their dissatisfaction with me. If they could see it and feel it from inside my shoes.... Similar treatment, yes, but definitely not the same.

Even though I was not outside of this family, neighbourhood, or country, maybe you can see how I often felt on the outside looking in. Feeling guilty for my resentfulness helped to keep me on the perimeter as well. How could I pay people back for their generosity; but then I would wonder why I should have to assume such a sizeable responsibility. These conflicting thoughts and feelings were basically at odds with each other in my head, never fully grasped at the time, and not at all expressed.

When I left home at seventeen, was I at home in New York, where many other Black people lived? I had learned from my adoptive family (besides having that natural inclination, anyway) to accept people for what they are regardless of race. I had not been searching for or trying to avoid people of either race. But my adoptive mother asked if it was nicer to be now among my own people. She did not know it was not by design but purely by chance that I found myself in Harlem. I had merely taken a bus, not choosing any destination, only trying to head away from my depression and jump into life from some other location.

Upon arrival there, it was NOT like suddenly belonging. My manner of speaking was so obviously different from the way the Black people of Manhattan were speaking. The first thing anyone would ask me was where I came from, and the next question, though not always asked aloud, was "why are you HERE?"

I had positive experiences with kind people from loving families who made their own healthy environments. But other times, I observed unhealthy and harmful milieux. I had no intention of joining in self-destructive activities at any point during my curious odyssey. Crossing the border between Canada and the United States was fairly uneventful. But, with or without a green card, I still felt like an illegal alien from another world. Although I was always easily understood, I did not easily understand my New York neighbours. It was more than speech differences which I found perplexing. Ironically, it was through some of these people that I saw how important it was to snap out of it and prepare for the future. I saw too many people, young and old, falling very low. They no longer believed in their own special talents and abilities. Too many were giving up and not caring anymore. They found it easier to remain numb and become something like the living dead. Some were still laughing — not yet aware of being deceived by substances into thinking they were in control. Why couldn't they see the tricks in devastation that were coming fast on the roller coaster ride of alcohol and drug addiction? There was no point in my staying to watch.

I finally realized it was up to me to go back to where I was born and try to get along with my family. I would have to heal my psyche and my soul in the place where they originated. Many have learned, as I did, that you can't run away from problems — especially when they are part of the puzzle that shapes your life. I had to piece mine together bit by bit, trying to make sense of it. Years later, those conflicting pieces of my life can still chase questions in my mind. But the road from childhood to adulthood has steep hills and valleys everyone can attest to, regardless of the reasons. My family's reasons for unconsciously making me feel on the margin and barely deserving of any privilege, are the same as much of society's reasons for treating non-white citizens as not entirely deserving as themselves.

Our relationship began with the best of intentions, but then insidious attitudes, not about me personally, but with regard to gender and race, crept in to keep me at a certain level. Acts of unfairness have not been easy to swallow, and painful memories are hard to forget. The best way to deal with it now is by refusing to agonize over preceding injustices and resentments. Constantly re-living painful events of the past only leads into a dark and bottomless pit with no way out.

To sever family ties would be like throwing the baby out with the bath water, and forgetting the really happy times. Instead, we have chosen to enjoy the benefits of amicable reconciliation based on respect for each other's trials and triumphs. People cannot pass on something they've never had themselves. Affectionate nurturing is not how my adoptive parents were treated, or their parents before them. Mistakes can be left in the past more easily when it is finally the distant past. We are not in touch with each other often. But at least we do occasionally talk about our most common prayers and concerns. That includes a better world for all of my parents' grandchildren.

The effects of inter-racial adoption may be simultaneously beneficial and deleterious; therefore not all good nor all bad. There have been many arguments against it within the social child-care agencies. But I think if these adoptees were the subject of a professional study, many different conclusions would have to be allowed to accommodate different personalities and family dynamics. People may have experienced similar situations but reacted differently. On the other hand, I also believe there are many who would understand how it feels to have only three-fourths of the opportunities. As for myself, I need to make the most out of those opportunities and try to help fellow human beings who know what it feels like. I also want to help change societal attitudes that discriminate against some of us because of race and/or gender.

It is apparent to me that my sisters, regardless of their colour, were not encouraged to "be all you can be" either. It was shown to us that our choices were fundamentally limited. We thought that however society is already functioning, you just have to accept it and be quiet. But all of us have learned a lot since that time. Thus, an imperfect past becomes the soil on which to plant my dreams for a better future. With this goal in mind, I can focus on the direction my life should take and will struggle to march forward triumphantly and not alone.

Maya (pseudonym)

MAYA

As a Black person born in a white community of Montreal in the early 1960s, I lived the life of a very "visible minority" long before the phrase was popular. But my life was generally more peaceful than that of Black people just across the border who were risking their lives for equal rights. I attribute my love of reading to the help received from books which discussed facts that were never really talked about. One of my favourite places was the high school library which was famous for being the largest in the province. I now live with my husband and three children and have been a resident of Toronto for ten years. I am a part-time writer and am also aspiring to become a literacy tutor to help share the excitement of reading. My favourite place is still the library where my daughters and I love to borrow books about people from near and far.

ANNA WOO

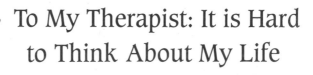

To My Therapist: It is Hard to Think About My Life

Dear M:

It is hard to think about my life: my childhood experiences. Yet I know in order to be free and to understand the way I became who I am now, I must try. I can feel it in my heart that I live today because of my past experiences; how I act at work, at home, with friends, all my hopes and expectations have been shaped because of my experiences as a Chinese woman.

I remember how painful it was to be different as a child. My mother could only say, "hi, hello, thank you" to our neighbours and friends. She came to Canada to marry my father in the late 1950s. Their marriage was arranged and she had never been overseas before. I imagine it was frightening for her to leave her home to live in a foreign land, where she did not speak or read the language, meet and marry a stranger, and live in a foreign environment with different-looking people! How she must have needed to cling dearly onto something which was familiar to her — the Chinese culture, of course.

My mother never tried to assimilate into the Canadian culture. She associated with Chinese people only. She did make attempts to learn the English language; she even attempted to work in a factory sewing car upholstery. She always claimed it was too difficult. I resented her failures. I could never understand what was so hard about learning English. In public, I shuddered with embarrassment whenever she tried to speak English. If I had to translate for her, I did so quickly and angrily. It is small wonder why she never learned English! Nobody supported her. When we the family did support her, we often ridiculed her efforts and hated having to tutor her.

I can see clearly now how the rift was formed between me and my mother, based solely on language. As soon as I had

Canadian friends, I abandoned the Chinese language. I tried **never** to speak it, even with other Chinese friends. I knew I looked different and I did not want to exaggerate this difference any further.

Yet try as I might, I could not hide my differences. Other kids were always making fun of me because I was Chinese. Songs and words haunted me. They would sing "Chinese, Japanese, dirty knees look at these!" or use words like "Chink" and "ah so". I learned to repress my anger and pain. I couldn't let people see how I felt or I was ridiculed even more. I felt victimized and helpless.

I remember with guilt about my Indian friends. We grew up as allies because we were outcasts. Yet I always felt relieved when they were picked on rather than me. "Thank God my skin isn't dark!", I thought. It gave me a sense of being the "same": being white. We were all trying not to be different. How terrible it was to repress words of defence in order to not be noticed by the bullies. Why did we have to suffer so much pain in silence?

I still do. I feel angry and resentful whenever co-workers, friends, or strangers imitate the Chinese language. There is always laughter which follows these profane imitations — LOUD laughter! I cannot laugh. I cannot smile. I am being ridiculed. Betrayal. I trusted you! Why do you hurt me so? And I still hide the pain. I still do not speak. Victimized, I am afraid to fight back. The anger that I feel boiling up inside, dying to erupt is SCREAMING! I struggle to put a lid on my emotions and paste on an expressionless face.

Differences. At times I take pride in being different, and at other times I wish I saw a different reflection. Gazing in my mirror, I wonder why my nose is so flat, why my hair is so straight, why my eyes are shaped differently. I am sure every woman must go through a similar identity crisis — always wishing to be something else, until we learn to accept who we are.

I feel lost as a Chinese-Canadian woman. I rejected my culture, yet I never felt totally accepted by the white Canadian culture. My parents laugh at my lack of ability to speak proper Chinese, though it hurts them deeply. To them I am not truly Chinese. I am a hybrid of two cultures known derogatively as "Jok Sing*". I believe they see the continuity of their culture lost in their children. How painful it is to struggle for words to express thoughts. Only a handful of Chinese words and phrases — which ones do I use? I feel as if I am grasping at thin air for words: I reach up high, and come back empty-handed.

---

* "Jok Sing" means bamboo pole. The metaphor is chosen because it is yellow outside, and hollow inside.

As a Canadian, I felt a little more accepted. But being Chinese or part of a minority culture always becomes an issue at some point. "Don't worry", they say. "You're different." "We don't mean you!" I feel a meek sense of victory as if I've won a hard-fought battle. Yet I also feel angry, resentful, and hurt. I AM one of THEM that you speak of!

It goes on: this pain of not knowing who I am or what I am being judged by. I want to find the strength in me to embrace my Chinese self and say to the world, "I am Chinese. I can love myself for who I am." I want to balance this need that I have to be white with being Chinese. Not to long for European features. To stop wanting to hide my identity behind my facade. To be whole.

You have helped me begin my journey. I no longer feel completely alone in my struggle. There is trust. All the tears, pain, and sadness that I feel will yield contentedness some day.

Sincerely,

Anna

ANNA WOO

I am the eldest daughter in a family of four. After graduating in psychology, I worked with adults with special needs. Currently, I am working in the field of accident rehabilitation.

ANITA JENNIFER WONG

Conversation
on a School Playground

Dear Trudy:

I still remember clearly that September morning when I first spoke to you. We were on the playground swings during recess, nervous about the beginning of a new school year, confident about being grown up and in grade two.

"Where are you from?", you had asked me innocently, sailing past on your swing, your braids flying in the air.

The question puzzled me somewhat. "From here", I had answered simply, referring to our home town in southern Alberta in which I had been born and raised for all of my seven years.

"No", you insisted. "You look different than us."

I wonder if you remember that conversation today. I recall it because that is when I was first truly aware that I "looked different" from my schoolmates. It was a distinction clearly affirmed by a cruel children's rhyme that started "Chinese, Japanese, dirty knees..." which teasingly synchronized words with gentle tugs on the eyelids to pull them into narrow slits. I don't think the children meant it viciously, but the feelings of powerlessness return too strongly when I think of living in a society which can produce such a rhyme.

From that day on I began to look in the mirror and compare my eyes with pictures in magazines to see if they really did look like the rhyme said they would. And I always wished for blonde hair or even brown hair, because I was the only person in my class with such a jet black colour. It singled me out, and I hated it. Magazines, television, and movies never ceased to aggravate that feeling either. The images always asserted that to be beautiful, one had to look like the models and actresses who appeared in the media — and they certainly were not Asian. I could never think of myself as beautiful.

Today, more than fifteen years later, I wonder about you, Trudy. We aren't entirely dissimilar. We followed similar paths. We both went to school and earned degrees, and had brilliant dreams about the future. But the years that it took us to get to this stage in our lives must have been marked by many disparate events.

I don't mean to sound as if I was accosted daily by accusations of "difference", because I wasn't. I grew up alongside everybody else the way my parents, who immigrated to Canada from China in 1950, wanted me to. I learned, I lived, I tried to get the most out of life. Nobody was literally preventing me. The boundaries of society, however, did appear occasionally, as if to remind me there were still lines and fences built up. Sometimes, something would happen which made me wonder how people truly felt. Sometimes, echoes of your statement, "You're different", emerged.

A person stopped me once when I was waiting for a bus and asked me a question. I didn't catch the words due to the noise — I think it might have been about time or bus routes. The person did not repeat the question but snapped at me in disgust: "If you're going to live here, why don't you learn the language?" I do know the language, thank you very much. I also speak French, will that make me a better person in your eyes?

In my apartment building, as recently as three months ago, I got on the elevator with an elderly lady. I made a comment about how it was nice to have a sunny day after the weeks of rain we'd had. She patted my hand. "Yes, dear, in this country we do have many different kinds of weather. You'll like it very much." Little did she know that I've been experiencing our weather for twenty-two years.

Situations like these have always made me want to blend into the rest of Canada, not wanting to look distinct at all. It is like I am transported back to the seven-year-old in the playground. Like you, Trudy, they noticed first of all how I looked.

Today, I am not so much angry as very sad. I have spent my life trying to be the same as everybody else. I wanted to be you. I learned what everyone else did, the capital cities of the provinces, our role in the world wars, our history, our language, our customs. I learned the words to the anthem, the players on the Toronto Maple Leafs, and all about Anne Murray too. I paid my dues. What I have, however, lost in the process is a part of myself, my true identity. At the same time I am still denied access to full acceptance in society.

My mother died when I was about eighteen, and that is when I first began to seriously consider the role my family and my heritage played in my life.

My overwhelming need to forget who I was because it made me distinct completely swallowed up any concern for my past, my ancestors. My mother, you see, was my bridge between being Chinese and being Canadian. She spoke to me in both languages. She wanted to know what I was learning at school, but she also educated me about China. She supplemented my formal education with her anecdotes on rituals and customs. Thus, with my mother gone, I feel a loss where my heritage is concerned. My only access to my past are my father and grandparents, but even today, my grasp of Chinese is not as precise as it used to be. I see the disappointment in my grandmother's eyes when I struggle to find the words to say something to her. My brothers and cousins are no better sources. They have been assimilated nearly as much as I.

And this is where I feel most cheated by the school system. I do know Canada's history inside out, but what roles do the Chinese-Canadians play in our history? Like the Native Canadians who disappear from the history texts after the fur trade, Chinese-Canadians disappear after stories of the many who worked on the railroads in British Columbia. We claim to be a mosaic, a multicultural society, but to fully benefit from the implications of such a term, should we not be sharing in each other's histories?

I hear about China in the news that the population is out of control and people are killing their babies. Or about the oppressive government that mercilessly fired on demonstrating students in Tiananmen Square. Why don't they also tell me about the good things that happen there? About the people? I took some Chinese history courses in university, and I know important dates and all about the different rulers, but this is rote information. I feel a great void in actually grasping and feeling what it means to be Chinese. I know that this could have been avoided; my family could have been more stringent on speaking Chinese at home and teaching us about our grandparents and great-grandparents. And I could have been more interested, but instead, I was falling for society's constructs and trying to be the same instead of different.

I was one of the first-generation Canadians in my family, and I feel this pain. I wonder what it will be like for the second generation, my nephews and nieces who are only about twelve years younger than I, and who cannot speak a word of Chinese. Will they also grow up wondering what our family is all about?

I have wasted much time. I have been embarrassed for so many years about my past, and I am ashamed that I ever have been. I used to cringe when a group of Hong Kong immigrants were near me at the university, talking and laughing in Chinese. I worried that people might think I was an immigrant too, instead of Canadian born.

How will it be for my nephews or nieces? Are they ashamed? I want to tell them not to be. There's much that can be done. I will put together my family history so that if they, or even my future children, ever wonder where we came from, they'll know. Otherwise it will all be lost. Much has already disappeared, but it is better to have some fragments of who we are than nothing. And, until society sorts itself out and multiculturalism truly does become accepted, encouraged, and part of our daily thinking — and I mean truly — and until the educational system helps us put our cultural groups into history, it is up to the people ourselves to sustain our unique identities.

I still feel alone in this struggle. It is a struggle between our cultural group and Canadian society, but as the boundaries become more clearly outlined, something may be done. More intangibly, there is a further struggle within my cultural group. My grandparents, for example, do not understand why I devote so much time to learning, and researching, and writing. I have one degree, why am I working for another? They keep asking me when I am getting married and giving them grandchildren. A marriage, they hope, will be with another Chinese person. In a way, there is a suffocating framework on that side too.

Marriage and children are definitely future plans, but for now the time is not right. I want first to establish who I am: in relation to the rest of Canada, and in relation to my family. That is the personal struggle that has to be worked through before I can get any further.

And that, Trudy, is what I've been immersed into since leaving school. As I said earlier, we're both at similar points in our lives, but I think underneath we're both radically different. You probably do not even remember our conversation that day. If you saw me today, however, would you still think I am different? I don't think that you ever meant anything harmful by that question at all. Don't get me wrong. It was natural seven-year-old curiosity. But if asked that question again, I would answer yes, I am different.

Anita Wong

ANITA JENNIFER WONG

I was born in 1969, in Lethbridge, Alberta. My grandfather first came to Canada from China in 1921, and my parents immigrated in 1950. Most of my family still lives in the southern Alberta area. I came to Carleton University in Ottawa in 1986, where I received a B.A. in 1990, and an M.A. in Canadian Studies (1992). My M.A. thesis, "Changing Images, Emerging Voices: Chinese Canadians in Canadian Literature", is focused on the cultural representation of Chinese-Canadians and the emergence of Chinese-Canadian writers and voices. I am now working with British Columbia Film in Vancouver.

ALTHEA SAMUELS

Full of Ideals

Dear Minister of Education:

When I was four I was a bright young girl full of dreams, ideals, and hope of what my new life as a student and my first step toward growing up would bring me. I don't remember being scared, just excited. I had my big brother to walk me to school in the morning and back home in the afternoon. Like most wide-eyed, innocent children, I was not prepared for the ugliness I encountered; nor did I understand it. It was only one little girl in the classroom, but her attitude toward me was terribly confusing because I didn't know her and had never done anything to make her hate me so much. I didn't understand it and I still don't. Where does a four-year-old learn the racial slurs and hate-filled language this child used against me every day? It is one of the few memories I have of that age. One of the others is of the kind, sweet teacher who never did anything about it.

The climax of this whole first year of school came in October. It was Halloween and I came from school to a house wonderfully decorated in the spirit. I was so excited that when I saw this girl walking by my house, I had to call out to her and show her what my mother had done. She answered me back with a fiery look of hatred on her face and said: "Shut up you F_ _ _ _ _ _ N _ _ _ _ _ ." It was a revelation to me because it was as if I finally realized what it was all about. I can't describe how I felt, but it was a combination of hurt and anger. This was the first and only time I ever yelled back at her. I don't remember what I said, but I do remember the feeling. It comes back every time I recall that incident.

We moved to another town after that year. I had to take a bus to school. I can remember being terrified that first day, even with my brother beside me. I can remember people on the bus saying I looked too small to be going to school.

This school was better though. There was no one here like the girl from my other school. Only the occasional incident such as having rotten fruit thrown at me, or a slur in passing by older boys. In grade five, I remember two boys who used to corner me in the far end of the playground and tell me I was all sorts of bad things because I was Black. On the advice of my mother, I spoke back to them. I can't remember what I said but it worked. They never bothered me again.

In grade six, an older boy decided it was his duty to inform me that all Blacks were nothing but slaves. All I did was look at him. What could I say? That's what he was taught. That's what I was taught. It's not true. But even if it was, why should I be ashamed? My ancestors did not invade another people's home and perform the inhumanities that his ancestors did. My ancestors did not kill babies, rip apart families, steal and destroy a people's way of life and culture for no reason except greed. What do I have to be ashamed of? My people are basically free except for the institutional racism that continues to drag us down. His people continue to destroy other people: Indians, the poor, women and children, as well as Blacks.

What I learned in school as history was a lie. I learned that when the white man "discovered" Africa, they were confronted by savages with black skin, flat noses, and thick lips. For weeks after that class I went around biting my lips to make them look thinner. It's ironic the fashion books now give make-up tips on how to make your lips fuller and more attractive. I was ashamed of how I looked because this teacher made my features and my race, the very essence of who I am, sound like an absurdity. That term was the worst of my school days.

I've been reading about my history and it makes me angry. It makes me angry because my teachers lied to me. The slave trade, something that is definitely a bad mark on the Europeans' record, was taught as if it was something to be proud of.

They told me that Black people were some strange people who were nothing until the white man "saved" them. They taught me that **my** people, **Black** people, were some thick-lipped, flat-nosed people who were discovered on a strange continent and simply brought over to **our** land, **their** land, to be used as slaves.

By the time I entered high school I had zero self-esteem. It was only after I started learning the true history that I slowly began to discover who I was and to like who I was.

I am writing this letter not to ask that Black history or the history of other races be included in the curriculum, but that the history that is taught be true and objective. No one benefits from the one-sided account of history that I received. Not only does this do harm to the youngsters on the negative side of this one-sidedness, it also breeds racists. (Did you know that the majority of white supremacist skinheads are below the age of twenty-five?) That is scary. And I don't fear for myself. I fear for my child and my children to come. I am mostly writing this out of concern for my daughter. I don't want her to go through what I went through. I want her to know the truth right from the beginning so no one will be able to take that away from her. No one will be able to take who she is away from her. I plan on teaching her myself but I want the other kids to know the truth too.

I want the educational system to change. It has to, or racism will just keep increasing and increasing. I want the truth to be taught in our schools, Ms. Minister. And not the white man's version of the truth, but the truth.

Sincerely,

ALTHEA SAMUELS

I was born in Ottawa, Ontario, of Jamaican parentage and grew up in a small town just outside of Ottawa. Over the years, I've been a volunteer in several community groups and organizations including CODE (Canadian Organization for Development Through Education), Interval House (a battered women's shelter), Council for the Multicultural Centre, the Canadian Rights and Liberties Federation, the Committee to Fight Racism in the Educational System, and the Jamaican (Ottawa) Community Association. A graduate of the Public Relations program at Algonquin College, I am currently establishing my own communications company and providing culturally sensitive child care in my home.

A SEIN

Breaking the Silence

Dear Mother:

There has been a lot of silence around the past, and this is why I have decided to write this letter to you. I have told you at times when I was hurt by children at school, the names they called me, but there are many more hardships I experienced over the years growing up in Canada that I kept to myself and that I am opening up to tell you now.

I wish to disclose to you, mother, some of my untold growing up experiences in Canada and my re-visit to Brazil to embrace the links in my life.

I remember living on Lawrence Avenue West in Toronto, an area we stayed in for at least a year before moving north of Toronto, to the country. This place in Toronto I liked mainly because of the vast park space. The park was, and sometimes still is, my favourite place to play. I remember visiting my friends who lived in the apartment building nearby. Anyway, this is all I really remember and then it was back and forth from Toronto to Tottenham (the country place north of Toronto) everyday when I went to nursery school.

I didn't really like the nursery school, and I remember being one out of two Black children in my class. The other Black child was male. So I adapted the best I could in my situation having to deal with racism in the classroom. Being treated poorly, and told things by teachers and children, caused me to become terrified of school, and not want to go there at all. I was told that this is where I must go in the day time, because both you and my father must work, and where else was I to go. So, hating it, I went. I was told to wash my mouth out with soap and water by the teacher I really despised, blamed for knocking the chalk off the desk, and it wasn't even me. The soap method was my punishment, but even at the age of four years, I found ways not to do what was asked of me, pretending I did what was put on me to do. I guess when thinking about it all now I had a really rough time adjusting and adapting, and just plain being. What I want to say clearly is that moving from one place to another where the percentage of Black children dropped so drastically, forced me as a child to learn some very tough lessons, just to survive.

Well, as I grew older, and also listened to you talk, mom, with my father, I remember it was like us breaking in new shoes. People in the village saw us around, saw us, building our house, just saw us, and we were the only Black family in the entire village. Eventually we met people. It was scary though. What I am seeming to ponder upon is that something affected another something, and if I was to stay with people in the village while my parents worked, and I went to school and returned to these strangers who looked after me, everything became like dominoes. Sometimes the people did not or could not look after me and then everything shifted and changed. There was pressure in our home as a result of this. No one to look after me caused worry as you could not afford to stay at home to look after me, and I could not stay by myself because I was too young. Anyway, things became sorted out and another place for me to stay was found. The stress on me of going from place to place to stay with some very awful people was just too much sometimes. I eventually took to the village streets, just finding myself here and there to make new friends as I came from school each afternoon.

School was the most awful experience. It was a horrible experience because, first of all, I was the only Black child in the entire school that year. Secondly, I was being confronted by a group of bigger kids, who usually surrounded me in a circle shouting "nigger, nigger" over and over until I was crying. It was very terrifying for me and I felt very trapped. I really don't remember how I got through that year at school, and I do not think I told you, mother, all that happened. When I think about it now, the experience brings tears to my eyes and I feel alone again. The children made fun of my skin colour and my lips by calling me "chocolate face" and "liver lips". They also associated me with the jungle by calling me "jungle bunny". One girl at the school hated me so much that she told me if she had a gun, she would shoot me.

The elementary school I had attended was convent-run at the time. A Roman Catholic school, with the church nearby, it was awful and I received more and more punishment for being the person I was and always will be. It hurts to be curious, explorative, unrestrained, and goofy. As this is me, I was told over and over again that I was bad, horrible, etc., etc. So, once again I found ways to get out of the punishment of going to the principal's office, but I could never get out of the punishment of getting my head hit, or my hand hit with a ruler and a red pen. I suppose the abuse I endured over the years affected me in my school work and in the development of my spirit.

I was still the only Black child at the school up until I was about nine years of age, and when Margaret, the new girl, came to school, I was becoming more hopeful that we might become good friends. She was also Black like me. Well, it turned out the opposite, and even though my parents gradually became friends with her parents, it didn't always help with my relationship with her. In this year, besides hoping that things would change for me at school, I was confronted by a very sexist and racist male teacher whom I had to put up with until I was thirteen. He was not my teacher for every year I went to that dreaded school, but there was much favouritism, as most of the teachers were related to some of the students. I became more and more frustrated and lost, bewildered, discouraged, and scared.

Well then, because of how I responded on tests, how I spoke (I was constantly corrected on how I would say words, especially the word "mirror" — my pronunciation worried my female teacher), and even how I held my pencil between my fingers (which was my way and evidently the "wrong way") led to concern. The last two corrections given to me were to change how I was, and, as a result, I was put into the "slow class". This class was a remedial class and being called the quoted, awful word by classmates was the most humiliating experience I have ever had. There were few students in this class, and we had to go to the library into a special room to do some of our subjects. Well, this label of "slow learner" stuck with me, and I was from then on treated in a certain way and was only expected to take certain classes at certain levels. I felt so stupid, angry, and hurt to see my friends moving up the ladder to higher education while I was being streamed to go to community college.

There was such a struggle going on and I became determined from then on to really give my all, and it showed once I got out of the combined class taught by the bigoted teacher and his cousin co-teacher, who had both suggested the "slow class" for me.

Science was my favourite and best subject, and I really enjoyed researching for my history project on Egypt. I eventually met up with some very inspiring teachers who encouraged me in my talents of singing, drama, and movement. As well as the weekly dance classes I took, I felt good about being me and expressing to everyone who I really was.

I eventually was given the responsibility of becoming bus patrol on our school bus and this added job was important for me as I worked with the bus driver in seeing that the students were safely brought home from school. I consider this my first work experience.

When I got my first real job at Canada's Wonderland at sixteen years old as a ticket taker, it was exciting and new because this amusement park had just begun operation for the spring and summer season. I met many people who later became my friends for the next couple of seasons. The managers were from the States, and I found them racist and, eventually, as each season passed, the friends I had started working with got promoted, but I stayed basically in the same job and even became demoted to parking attendant — the way I saw it. I experienced racial harassment that I believe many Black people and people of colour experience when they are timed for every minute activity they perform, treated as though they were school children again, needing a watchful eye and discipline. It reminded me of the slavery system, and of keeping one in line, should the oppressed person speak out of turn. I worked so hard but was treated as though I was unworthy of any job. The result was that I tried harder and harder until I gave 200% of my dedication to my work, but it did not seem to matter. I felt doomed, and I eventually found a better job, and I did not return there.

During the summers working at Canada's Wonderland, I really admired the artistic performers, especially in the area of dance, and having studied dance, I decided to make performing a career goal in the future. Eventually, after studying for four more years at university, and two years after graduation, I was performing and teaching in a dance company.

I needed to relocate and tried to adapt the best I could in a strange town in order to dance and teach creative movement to children. I experienced quite a bit of racism which included comments on my skin colour. This time one person whom I had been friends with at the university, made a comment about me not needing to worry about make-up because of the lightness of my skin, which is not true. She was trying to colour wash me, to deny that I was Black at all. I stared at her, angry and alarmed at what she of all people was saying. I was the only Black person in the company, a token. It seems that I was re-experiencing my childhood; the encounter about the skin colour and being the only Black person led me to be treated as a scapegoat. It was very despairing. I decided that my health and well-being would suffer if I continued to stay and work there. So I returned to Toronto. Upon returning to Toronto, I felt drawn, pulled towards the sound, the direction of Brazil.

I have always wanted to return to Brazil, even if it were for a short time, and so, with your help, mom, I went back. I left Toronto the first week of December, rushing around, getting everything together and was sad to hear of the shootings of the women in Montreal. This month was a horrendous one all over the world. Feeling imprisoned and trapped, I decided to seek freedom, not knowing exactly what I would find.

I ended up in a country after many hours of travelling where I could neither speak nor write the language, and I was really not too prepared for what I was about to face.

Well, my stay at my godparents can most probably be described as a prison sentence. So, wanting to flee from one entrapment, I landed in another. Why did I see the place where my godparents live as a prison? Well, the front of the house which also served as a garage was securely enclosed by metal barred doors reaching from floor to ceiling. I needed the key always whenever I needed to go. But when I was ready to go out on my own, wishing to explore everything in sight, that is when the trouble began. At twenty-five years of age, they seemed to see me as a child still, although it was explained to me that there was major concern about my coming into a country totally unknown to me and that I, becoming independent in such a short period of time, was bringing up my godparents' fears.

Besides the fear of facing homophobia in Brazil, I did not expect the contradictory experience of being a Black tourist in the country of my birth. One day I was travelling on a bus, and a man began to yell at me in Portuguese. He was accusing me of being a Bahia, a person from a particular part of Brazil who is seen as poor, low class, and dirty. Apparently, according to what he was saying, I looked like the people there; so I was picked on. Well, we got into a shouting fight because ever since I was a child, I learned to fight when someone is picking on me. I suppose it was not "lady-like" to be yelling at him on the bus in English in front of a lot of people who may not have understood what I was saying, but I needed to defend myself from such unnecessary and foolish attacks.

I begin to imagine as I write to you now, mother, how we lived in Brazil when I was just a baby. You told me that I was beginning to pick up Portuguese when we were leaving the country. I am studying Portuguese by book and tape and, some day, I hope to speak and write in this language. Even though there is such a major difference in our ages, I still wonder if the conflict we have experienced over the years was because of this age difference. I feel a need to teach you about myself, but I don't know how much of what I tell you will be accepted.

In Brazil many of the women of my age were still living with their parents, and although they had boyfriends, visits were made by the boyfriends to the women's parents' homes. It was assumed that these women would eventually marry and settle down. I did meet a few women who were liberated. These women said: "We are over eighteen, inoculated, and free." Therefore, these women could do what they chose, were free to come and go as they pleased.

It was very difficult seeing the women who still lived with their parents (as I had been up until I was twenty-three) and who had boyfriends. I had not come out as a lesbian to any of these people.

Keeping my lesbian identity hidden from some people was difficult and very uncomfortable, especially when I was asked by someone if I had a boyfriend. I told Afra, a woman divorced and with children, about a lover I had met while visiting in London, England. It was a risk, and very chancy, but she accepted me and we became friends.

I wanted to tell you, mother, that I became so confused over the messages that I received about having to stay far away from boys because my interest in them would disturb my studies. I was not allowed to maintain contact by letters with a boy in another country when I was thirteen because I was told that he would think he owned me. He was a friend, but it was thought that our friendship might get too serious, whatever that meant. Now this friendship and my friendship with my girlfriend Anne were sharply contrasted for me because while you wouldn't even let me write to my pen friend, it seemed safe to you that I had a girlfriend.

In high school I continued to be friends with some of the same girlfriends I had from elementary school, but they now had boyfriends. And I was told to wait because my studies were more important. To me it's quite a joke, but what if I decided to flip this regulation around, say that I am a lesbian and don't want a boyfriend. I know you would not find it the least bit funny.

Later on, your decisions became totally warped in my view because you began to hint that it was time for me to have a boyfriend, and this was verbalized by you when there was pressure from our relatives, and when I came out to you as a lesbian.

I know that when I eventually did come out to you, I chose a time which you may have found difficult. It was the year I graduated from university and moved back into your home. I think I made a big mistake, but at the same time I was glad that I told you. It made me feel good to express who I am even though your response was to walk away without saying a word. What was I to make of this? I felt offended and rejected.

I want to try to explain to you how I became interested in girlfriends that I had while growing up.

I had a good friend Anne who was two years older than me and who lived with her family in Niagara Falls. When I went to stay over for the summer at their house, Anne and I would lie in the same bed together and we would talk about everything from our dreams to our friends at school, our favourite subjects, and what we liked and did not like about certain topics. As we shared this information, we became closer to each other as friends.

I find that it is friendships like Anne's and mine which are viewed as safe, okay, up until a certain age, and encouraged in order to prevent girls from getting sexually involved with boys. When two girls are growing and they begin to explore their sexuality, they are viewed as sick or abnormal.

I have come out as a lesbian openly a few times to you, mother, once by telling you and another time by writing a very brief letter giving you the information about how to contact a parents of lesbians group. Every time your response caused me feelings of sadness, hurt, self-denial, and rejection. Mother, you walked away from me when I told you face to face that I am a lesbian, and, when I wrote you the letter, you wrote back that you thought that it was all in my mind that I was a lesbian. You wrote that I would eventually see it was all nonsense. You cautioned me not to tell anyone else that I am a lesbian or they would not like me.

Hearing what I speak and what I write, you still hope very hard that I will "come to my senses and get married". Since the two experiences of bravely and courageously opening up to you, there really has been no mention whatsoever about my sexual orientation. The topic has been swept under the carpet, so to speak.

Just like the issue around my lesbian identity, you reacted in a similar way when I disclosed to you that my father sexually abused me. It was very difficult for me to tell you, but at times when I communicated to you in letter that my memories are showing me the blocked past, you were very determined and ready to tell me that my father would never do what I had said he had done. I cried so much and felt like I was zipped back into the very same time when the pain and the violation of my body was being made.

According to our family system, the secrets and denial must be maintained. The denial of who I am and what I know I have experienced must be enclosed in a container to be put on a shelf, closeted and hidden. Shh! Don't show or tell.

Anyway, now that I have moved away from your home, mother, and live independently, I have been able to take some control over my life and attend to my needed healing. I know that it is important for me to be truly me and a lot healthier also.

I hope some day you will read my letter and realize that I have made such a courageous attempt to communicate my feelings to you about various experiences in my life.

Sincerely

Asein (pseudonym)

ASEIN (this name means small metal altars upon high poles before which the deified ancestors are worshipped with offerings)

I received a B.A. Honours degree in dance from a major Canadian university. Currently, I am making masks and have made just over forty masks representing various identities I've been exploring. I write poems and someday would like to invoke a choreopoem that could be danced, read, and sung. In addition to my love for drawing and painting, gradually I have been designing and constructing costumes which are used together with a specific mask in exploring that identity. Most recently, I have been sewing and dyeing clothing. I am very interested in the expressive arts as an aid to healing. "I want to continue to unearth the vast richness of my cultural heritage, allowing the ancestors to speak through me."

Marcia Crosby

Speak Sm'algyax Grandma, Speak Haida Grandpa

Dear Gram:

I am writing you too long after you are gone. But never so gone that I do not weep your absence and miss your voice. I was wondering if you were wondering how I was doing? Do you know that I went to university and got a degree? and now I am getting another one — a Master of Arts they call it. They say it's important to have this piece of paper because it will give me the way, the passage, the ticket, the language to tell my story. But grandma, I wonder if you really want me to tell my story. You see I learned about why and where the night and pain and all of the things that you would not let us speak about came from. I learned about what happens to people, like grandpa, when they're sent to residential school. In university, there's nothing in the textbooks that say anything about who we are. I mean gram, we go to school to learn about them and when they think we can think like them and speak like them, then we get a degree. But even though I know how to speak and act like them, I am like you. I am not sure if I can speak and I don't know if it's okay to speak, to tell the story of our pain, to talk about the abuse of our people and why grandpa abused me.

Did you know gram? Did you know that the pancakes he cooked us in the morning were part of the nightly ritual of visiting me in bed in secret in the dark? Did you know that the good smells were a lie? Did you know that my morning baths couldn't make me feel clean? The water, rocking the boat, the boat where he abused me, where he led me to the galley and into the engine room. Did you know that after I walked down the wharf onto the boat and entered that voyage of self-hatred cloaked in family smells and nurturing sounds that I knew you knew? It makes me feel dead inside oh so so tired yes nights, nights and rocking. Rocking alone downstairs by myself. No hands to cradle me, no soft palms to wipe away my fear, no tears, just me rocking, empty and alone with my fear that I was a pregnant eight years old. So so alone, so alone that I remained there remained there, too alone to name my fear and speak the act. Semen sliding down my leg in the middle of the night too afraid to move lying still waiting and waiting waiting to slide down the wall waiting to disappear into the darkness. jesus christ. how long do I have to be alone? When is it alright to tell my family, my community? I was raped over and over, over and over.

Say fondled. No ... abused. No ... touched. No. Not raped. Don't say the word, he made you pancakes in the morning. He made you pancakes and he was so quiet when he touched me. Not a word, not a threat, not a sound just heavy breathing and grunting and touching. And silence. I am so quiet in this world. I will not be silenced. I write now using a huge Webster's dictionary like the one he used to use for crossword puzzles. grandpa was so smart. he always used that great big dictionary. he learned a lot at the residential school.

When I wake up in the morning I sometimes think this is the day to die. Death, inevitable when I think I am all alone in this world with my pain and I wish somebody could fix it because I don't know how. Maybe that wish is like when I was a little girl and I used to dream about saving all the poor dirty kids standing outside the bar waiting for their parents. I wanted to take them home and bath them in the tub that you used to bath us in. I think about being clean and being loved and I wish I could clean up the whole world with that same gesture of love that we experienced in the morning in our tub. Did you think you were washing away the night of abuse? Did you think it would wash away the secret and your silence? I don't know grandma but my faith in the need and the ability to truly clean the world up with a bath is an act of love that ignores life's ugly realities. This is not something I want to do. I want to love the way you did but not in pretended ignorance. I want to love but not in silence. I want to speak the night and speak your gesture of love. I want to speak, to scream, to wail, and to cry out, yet, I need to dance to heal myself. I want to expose the night so we can have our day.

When I write, I dance my words on the page. I speak sadness with the joy, of self-realization, of agency and self-identity. I am whole even in my fractured life of so many worlds: the village, the city, my colleagues, my children, and my family. oh god I just want to dance. I just want the world to flow out of me. I just want my joy to be true. But it's so rare so far away. Let my joy be true. let it last a little longer next time. At times when I think life is pretty good for me as an Indian woman like right now this moment as I speak to you, I take the words, and dance them on the page. But then my Indian woman/child surfaces and is angry and frightened and tired and sad. I work hard to put the punctuation where it belongs (belongs?) to make her dance to make music for her but the form will not produce the

Marcy of childhood, of my young womanhood. I can only dance her with the language that I have now. I hardly remember the joy of childhood. And the times when I experience the satisfaction of being able to write/dance, I must always speak of the abuse of power. When will I dance truly joyfully? I want to write about me dancing for you, scarf whirling around spinning you laughing, remember? I want to write about the possibility of empowerment, agency, happiness and potential for Native women while she dances. I think that if I keep writing the world that it might happen. But how? Where do I find the strength to continue?   It's there in your love, grandma. The bath, laugh behind the soft palm, the gentle proddings.

Go ahead and dance, no one will laugh at you except with delight that you are Marcy, our girl who we have nurtured to speak our silence we cannot speak we cannot tell the secret. Speak for us Marcia. Dance, we will watch and encourage you with our hearts, forgive us for not speaking we could only teach you. We could only give you partial joy and let you realize the rest your self. We are so sorry we could not say the words to make the night go away. We could only love you in the daylight it is up to you now to speak the night. We will love you even if other people don't want to hear your words. We will love you because we brought you up to speak to dance the rest of the story.

Grandma, I want to dance for you again. I want the joy, the self-confidence of dancing for an audience of love. A self with the promise of a future. To become that same child who emerged from time to time despite the pain. I want to tell of the joy I feel when I speak words that come from all the nuances of your love and murmurings, *ah shah, don't cry dear*. I want those soft palms that dried my eyes and gentle rocking to mix with this language I've learned in school. I want the caring you had for our family, our community to meld with my text. I want to tell them our story, the one you gave me with songs and stories of the porcupine and the beaver. Remember when you washed us in the tub every morning grandma and then gently combed our hair? I can only speak of abuse. I want to tell the story of love.

Oh Marcie, forgive me for not speaking. I could not let my self realize the pain.

I can hardly speak your words because I think you might not forgive me for telling the story you wanted kept a secret. Yes, some of our leaders, some of our old people and others in our communities want us to be quiet about life on our social and geographical reserves. They want us to be silent and if we are not then we are not family. But your silence deadened me, gram. This is about love and anger. This is about sadness and joy. About strength and the total collapse of the spirit.

It is up to you to speak the night. It is up to you to tell the story of your and our abuse.

It's up to me to speak, to speak the night. I must speak the night of a colonial history that overlaps with the reality of my own night that continues into day. To tell the Grimm's fairy tale of colonialism. Will I ever speak it so that people will be compelled to listen to a storyteller? I speak the night with pain and with reluctance but if I don't, I will die.

Why did the porcupine leave the beaver up in the tree? *Tit for tat, that's what you get.* No big mystery about an old Indian story that sounds more like an Aesop's fairy tale.

I think about what you taught us. How to be white with Indian stories, drinking tea from a cup and saucer and not a mug. Oh gram this is such confusion such pain. I wish you could have said to me you are Tsimshian our clan is Gisbutwaada, KillerWhale and our people come from a strong matriarchal society. I am teaching you the way of all of your grandmothers. I want you to grow up big and strong like all the great matriarchs in our family. But gram you didn't say it. You couldn't say it. Instead you were silent while your husband abused me. You could only pass on the love of nurturing me in a bath tub. Did the missionaries teach our people we could wash away the dirt of being Indian? Where on earth was all of the knowledge of our grandmothers? I want it. I don't want to have to decipher this cryptic code of love and self-loathing in search of some kind of Indian self identity. It would have been so easy if you could have spoken the world in Sm'algyax. I am crying for us because someone took the language of our grandmothers and replaced it with English, tea in a cup and saucer and such good manners that we could not speak the sickness that happened in our night. Such good English manners that we did not cry rape rape RAPE. STOP.

We are nations of women and men who love our children. We are nations with chiefs because our families eat together at our feasts. What if we gave a feast and nobody came? Help me tell them gram. Turn your face first towards your children. Speak Sm'algyax. Speak Haida. Gently. To us your families and then we will speak as nations. Big chiefs. Big names. Big words for white people don't comfort children at home. Oh gram. How could you be silent? To hell with their manners. To hell with their world. Speak Sm'algyax, speak Sm'algyax.

Speak Haida grandpa. Speak the language they told you not to speak in residential school. Speak the language of family you could not learn in a school without mothers and fathers and aunties to tell you how to behave. Where they tried to teach you to be like them before you could learn how to love your unborn grandchildren. If you speak Haida grandpa will

112

the silence of abuse be over? If you speak our own language will you remember who you are? Speak Haida grandpa, speak Sm'algyax grandma. So we can be a family, be a community, be strong nations of people. Speak to one another first. Sing our own songs and dance our rights and privileges with honour and love. I want to dance with my own people. It's time to dance with you grandma and grandpa. Time to dance with my daughters, and my son.

So I have to go now. I will miss you as I always do because I love you and I need you to know that. I wish those early morning breakfasts were really so sweet smelling and warm, steaming bathtub beside the kitchen stove. I have to go grandma, to let go of my fear of your rejection and my fear that some of our family and community may reject me, deny my truth. I don't think this is such a great way to say good-bye but I guess it's not really good-bye because it's not over.

Love you,

Marcia

MARCIA CROSBY

After graduating with an undergraduate degree in studio arts and literature, I am completing an M.A. in social art history at the University of British Columbia. My thesis is concerned with the relationship between Aboriginal material culture that has been defined as "Indian Art", and the function of those same objects as legal documents within First Nations' territories. During the past six years as a student, I have had the privilege of working as project manager for the Native Youth Project at the Museum of Anthropology, as coordinator for the Cultural Centre in Massett (the village where I live), teaching English as a sessional instructor for Simon Fraser's First Nations' Language Teacher Program in Prince Rupert, publishing an article in *Vancouver Anthology: The Institutional Politics of Art*, co-editing a special women's issue of the *Capilano Review*, preparing a brief (on Aboriginal heritage) for the Minister Responsible for Culture, as well as speaking at various institutions across Canada on issues pertaining to First Nations peoples and representation.

Editor's note: Marcia Crosby would like to acknowledge Angela Hryniuk, writer/poet/editor, who edited the letter.

113

COME FROM AWAY

Sharda Vaidyanath
Rajani E. Alexander
Heather Crichlow
Pham thi Quê
Chanthala Phomtavong
Naïma Bendris
Aruna Isaac Papp

Sharda Vaidyanath

Pioneer Days

Dear Rahul and Chantal:

Perhaps it's a bit unusual that I should be writing you a letter when I could just talk to you any day about any thing I want to say. The fact is, I'm aware that, as children born and educated in Canada, and today, as young adults involved in a multitude of activities, your family history is relegated to school projects. In fact, so far, you've only collected names to fill a big enough family tree, and, occasionally, you've plucked your baby pictures off albums to secure your past on those charts. But there are missing pieces of family history that school projects may never recover! For instance, why did your parents come to Canada? What were those pioneer days like? Did your father and I have similar experiences? While it may not be possible or necessary to recapture every detail of that story, this letter is my collection of "vignettes" of twenty years in Canada.

I know what a huge sense of relief you must've felt with the completion of my Master's thesis in Canadian studies in 1990. Perhaps you don't realize, it is a definitive statement of my intellectual and personal growth in Canada. It is also evidence of successful survival and partial fulfilment of my goals despite many real challenges along the way.

On a hot summer's day on July 22, 1970, I joined your father in Montreal as a landed immigrant. Even at the airport, I nervously remembered, he was described by a source prior to the arranging of our marriage, as unsuitable. Your father's persistence for an entire year had finally forced my father to agree to the marriage, despite his objections. The issues were: your father earned about $6,000 a year, was a part-time student, lived in low-income housing, and had a huge family in India to support.

I had met him for the first time barely two days before our wedding, on May 8, in Madras, India, and was later sponsored as his dependant in Canada. I feel awfully embarrassed today to confess that until then, I thought Canada was a province of the United States! And when your father announced he had bought a "star" for me, imagine my disappointment at seeing a newspaper, *The Montreal Star*, land on my lap! Indeed, I was a typical Hindu bride-to-be, uninformed and unprepared to begin my life in Canada. In retrospect, my naiveté and sense of adventure were definitely an asset!

I became acutely conscious of a new world when your father left for work. I hid in the closet of our single-room basement apartment in a rooming house. The thought that I was really alone in a foreign country made my imagination run wild with ideas of impending calamities. I shuddered each time I heard strange sounds that seemed to come from huge ceiling pipes. It was more than a week before I had the courage to crawl out periodically to go to the washroom (whew! your father came home for lunch), help myself to food, and consider social invitations.

So, there I was, wide-eyed and eager at my first dinner invitation. Then, minutes later, I stared helplessly at what looked like two dead rats (the hostess explained they were exotic East European sausages meant for special occasions) on my plate. As a vegetarian, I was petrified. I went to the washroom to do some deep breathing and trembling in privacy. As I opened the bathroom door, there stood the host, seductive, waiting to make the first move. I dodged him down the hallway to grab my chair at the table. Who said acting was easy? It was one of many traumatic "introductory invitations" from which I returned a famished, psychological wreck.

Ah! and how could I forget that crimson face at the flower shop? I thought I would surprise your father on his first birthday after our marriage. A particularly lovely arrangement caught my eye. When I explained the purpose of my choice, the clerk at the counter lowered his head in apparent embarrassment. Some clumsy seconds later he said: "Madam, this is a funeral arrangement."

And then followed my very first Christmas celebration with a family which included newlywed members. I learned to carry on a conversation in full view of the couple's wild kissing and necking on the couch. I had never seen such a scene, even in the Indian movies! Even more than two years later, after Rahul's birth, I still got a lot of unsolicited attention. This time, they were lingering stares that made me very uncomfortable. Finally, a neighbour politely informed me, "Boys don't wear pink around here." What a relief, all the staring and teasing smiles now made sense. I had innocently indulged in my favourite pink infant clothes for Rahul, before I knew the sexes were colour coded! But there were other challenges to routine life.

The move to a first-floor apartment on Lincoln Avenue highlighted our miseries in Montreal downtown living. The crunch came Christmas Eve 1971. The apartment was flooded with water from leaking heating pipes, a culmination of total neglect of maintenance despite high rents. In a fit of insanity, I prepared a placard protesting the treatment of our landlord and stuck it to our window. The message read: "We are suffering, no repairs done to this apartment." Perched on the window sill, your father and I watched the crowd gathered outside. The administration office ordered me to remove the notice. I refused! The mysterious giant-like landlord confronted my puny frame at the door. I screamed my complaints before he could utter a single sentence! He shrunk into submission. In two days, all repairs to the apartment were done, but I wasn't satisfied. I continued my fight for the rights of tenants before the rental board. I recovered two months' rent and had my lease revoked. It was my first major victory in Canada.

Perhaps the most disturbing memories in these past twenty years were my continuous encounters with the proud displays of Playboy posters of nude women in the basement bars of many a French-Canadian home we considered for purchase. I can vividly recall every detail, particularly the demeanour and comments of "the lady of the house" during those visits, as if it happened yesterday. In one instance, when I may have unwittingly betrayed my discomfort, the lady of the house commented, "But he's a man, he needs it." To me, the issue was not nudity *per se,* but the acceptance of "women as sex-objects" by some French-Canadian housewives. I wondered then, how could any woman who allowed such a use of her home also be respected by her husband and children? It was also during our search for a house that I became increasingly, painfully, aware of tensions between English- and French-Canadians. When a French-Canadian acquaintance who accompanied us on these rounds told us, "These are French-Canadian areas, you wouldn't want to live here", I was speechless.

Then, there was another incident that left in me a permanent wound. It was the sight of a most beloved elderly neighbour named Mrs. Maffrey being carted away from her apartment, like carcass on a hand cart, her head barely inches from the ground. What indignity! She had taught me knitting just the night before. We had become good friends; she had given me an intimate understanding of the life of the elderly and sick in Canada. I prayed to be spared such loneliness and abandonment.

Then, after our move to Gloucester, Ontario, during the summer of 1976, I was faced with a challenge that demanded every skill, intelligence, and sensitivity I had. There were writings on our walkway, "Go home from where you came." There were eggs on our windows. Your father and I felt tense, self-conscious, even frightened for your safety. We pretended to be totally unaffected. But one day, Rahul, who was then barely four years of age, stood in our family room in the basement with an entire can of talcum powder smeared on his body from head to toe. He looked half afraid, yet half serious and with his eyes sparkling through patchy white said, "Mom, you should do it too; it will make your hair golden!" Rahul had suddenly become conscious that **he** and **his mother** and **his family** looked very different from his neighbours. We had black hair and brown skin but all the neighbours around didn't. He had an instant cure for this, talcum powder! I fought my urge to have a good laugh, knowing the issue was a serious one for a child like Rahul (besides, Rahul might have felt ridiculed).

I couldn't scold Rahul for the incredible mess in the basement, knowing this was done in all innocence. I gently conveyed to him I loved my black hair and his black hair and didn't want to exchange it for any other colour. I explained people have different skin colour, hair, eyes, and come in different sizes from different parts of the world. That day, Rahul learned a little about racial genetics and understood that physical differences were not meant to be a statement about "right" and "wrong" looks. It was the beginning of a process of knowing and accepting being "different". I had survived my first "test"! I felt more confident dealing with other such issues as the years passed. You grew up poised and well adjusted with the knowledge that physical attributes were irrelevant for full participation in society.

It was, however, in the early '70s that experiences of pregnancies, child-birth, and a miscarriage brought my loneliness, struggle, and isolation to sharp focus. Besides, I was still dependent on your father for a great deal beyond financial support. I knew my confidence as wife, mother, and human being needed to be consciously nurtured every day to contend with even routine life. I explored a multitude of avenues to become self-reliant and to find my niche in the world outside our home. The nagging fact was, we were now living in Ste-Dorothée, a semi-farming community where the nearest bus stop was at least a mile away. I did not have a driver's licence. The responsibility for children under three years of age meant limited choices. I felt trapped.

My salvation, however, were the "phone-in" shows on some Montreal radio stations. Every morning, after your father left for work I would organize my routine around these shows. As soon as the topic for discussion was announced, listeners were required to dial a certain number with comments. If I was interested in the prize — especially newly published books (we couldn't afford a baby-sitter for the "dinner for two" prize, hence I didn't care to respond) — I'd race to phone to be the first one to reach the station. These were frantic, tense moments because I also had to keep track of the two of you. I knew you could go off like time bombs. Your screams and crying could interfere with the taping of my comments! It was such a thrill each time when my comments were not merely aired but were also considered prizeworthy. I could actually afford for your father a superb birthday gift without spending the house money. But my lack of mobility was debilitating and it is impossible to forget how even obtaining my driver's licence in Gloucester, Ontario, seemed like climbing Mount Everest! There was no escape. A driver's licence meant a promise of freedom from what seemed like endless cleaning, cooking, and caring for children.

I had already failed three road tests. Can you imagine the guilt I felt each time your father had to take time off work to take me to a Transportation office for yet another test? Besides, each new registration meant spending more money we really couldn't afford. Though your father was patient, I couldn't get over the fear of an accident and leaving two young children motherless. The extraordinary stress caused hair loss and weight loss. I felt dizzy as your father accompanied me for my fourth road test. For the first time, a female examiner appeared. What a break! She didn't bark orders; I returned to the lot a winner at last! Indeed, driving alone on the Queensway was a major achievement! Yet, the feeling of insecurity gnawed at my daily life.

A turning point in my life came when someone suggested I just wasn't worthy of any job except sales. It startled me. I had been employed as a teacher in India for two years and had an impressive record of achievements beyond academics. The comment was humiliating. I was compelled to consider university education in my search for an identity.

I can vividly recall that face that looked up at me and with a brush of a hand told me: "You can't get into the school (of journalism) that easily. I have to consult the office." Unaware that I had already received a letter from the school accepting me for registration (in the university's journalism program), the man at the registration desk seemed decided I did not look "right" for the school. His flushed face and impersonal tone betrayed his attitude to a visible minority woman seeking admission into an overwhelmingly white-dominated school. I did not know in 1979 that this incident would be only the beginning of a series of psychological challenges I would have to overcome as a mature, visible minority woman claiming her right to re-train and seek a job. I was "brave" and worthy of admiration to some. To others, I had robbed a promising, young candidate of a seat in the school. The "value" of training someone like me was debated by some students and professors. And when an instructor declared in the presence of an entire class, "You will never make it in the media; you have to run home to feed your kids", I was fired with a determination to obtain my journalism degree. Nevertheless, I was beginning to believe I was the world's favourite victim! As I approached graduate studies in Canadian studies, my academic problems were compounded by personal tragedies.

The benchmark in this saga was my mother's untimely death, in April of 1988, by cancer, in Montreal. The death occurred within five months of her arrival in Canada. To me, the episode crystallized unresolved and complex family problems that I could no longer ignore. My personal life and academic work became inseparable. The Master's thesis on "marriage" was inspired by my mother's tragic life. The insights about "the Hindu way of life" gained through family discussions before and after her death demanded I consider my academic options uncompromisingly. It was the toughest undertaking in my entire life. My life had truly come full circle with its completion. For now, it will suffice to say, I was confronted with revelations of oppressions within ethnic/racial groups. It forced me to abandon simplistic ways of explaining racial discrimination or prejudice. Indeed, graduate work was a privileged opportunity to grow in every way. I hoped this would instigate your interest in my thesis.

In retrospect, despite a million fears that plagued me, I am grateful for these past twenty years. They include the reward of memories that always provoke laughter and pride in accomplishment. How can I forget that first day of class in basic music theory? I had the distinction of being the only student who did not know A, B, and C were also notes of music! Now, five Royal Conservatory piano performance exams later, my love of music includes an informed appreciation of Western classical music. Then, there was my ignorance of sports which provided you with endless opportunities for teasing. Indeed, from having your father write my first journalism sports assignment, the football game between Carleton and Queen's universities in 1980 (while we munched popcorn and listened to students' obscene language), I've advanced to sometimes sharing and appreciating your commitment to sports. In fact, you inspired my interest in fitness and horseback riding.

But that day, when I sat nervously behind the wheel while your father cuddled a roly-poly dachshund male pup on the back seat of the car, is the story I love to tell. Despite my mortal fear of animals, your loneliness had forced me to consider a house pet in 1984. The thought that somehow that little creature could crawl to the front seat and attack me made me lose my direction on our way home from the breeder. It was quite a drive before we reached home. The fear was mutual. The pup and I played hide-and-seek all weekend. On Monday morning we were alone. We reached a pact across all kinds of barriers — chairs, boxes, tables, and what not. Once I established eye contact, we struck a deal: I stay in the kitchen, and you stay in that box. You stay cute and silent and I'll talk to you. It was the beginning of a loving friendship between me and animals. Today, I am tickled pink to think that I have actually served as a member of the Board of Directors for the Ottawa Kennel Club!

In 1970 I strongly believed that I had an obligation to learn to truly belong to Canadian society. The opportunity I've had to learn and grow is a privilege I truly cherish. But have I done right? Only time will tell. I am only sure that I cannot be easily ignored or dispensed with. I've learnt to survive outside the closet!

Your loving mother,

Sharda Vaidyanath

SHARDA VAIDYANATH

I was born on July 29, 1946 in Tattamangalam, Western Village, Palghat District, Kerala, South India and immigrated to Canada after my marriage. My son Rahul attends university and my daughter Chantal is in high school. I received my two undergraduate degrees (B.J. and B.A.) and a Master of Arts degree from a Canadian university. My immediate goal is to persuade Canadian universities to include feminist courses in Eastern religions. On June 12, 1991, at the Canadian Psychological Association's Section on Women and Psychology Institute in Calgary, I presented a paper titled: "The Hindu Marriage: Ideological Barriers to the Hindu Women's Achievement of Egalitarianism". I presented my M.A. thesis: "The Intersection of Concepts of Marriage in Canada" at CRIAW's Global Vision/Local Action Conference in Edmonton in November 1991. My article, "Setting the Record Straight: Hindu Concepts of Marriage in the Canadian Context", in *Women and Social Location: Our Lives, Our Research*, ed. Marilyn Assheton-Smith and Barbara Spronk (Charlottetown, P.E.I.: Gynergy Books) is in print and scheduled for release in November 1993. I am currently Convenor for the Status of Women of the Ottawa/Carleton regional chapter of the National Council of Women.

Rajani E. Alexander

Is Canada Racist?

Dear Rahel:

   I want to tell you of your country, my country, our country. I do not know how things will be when you are older but I think incessantly of your future, and so let me put down some thoughts.

I came here five years ago, two before you were born. I remember it was very warm and sunny then and very still. The air seemed so clear and the streets so open that I wondered if I could get used to this postcard freshness. I walked by the waterside and drew my breath in deeply as I looked at the mountains. I was unemployed then and there was delight in being about and outside during hours when I had been accustomed to being at a desk. But a part of me was also fearful that I would never belong, or work again, in this too-pretty place that was now "home".

That first year we received a lot of presents from friends and family back home in India, sent with good wishes for our marriage and our new life in faraway Canada. It became a joke with your father and me that we almost dreaded another parcel because, often, the customs duty exceeded the cost of the gifts! We did not have a car then, and I would walk down to the Customs office to pick these up.

After one such trip I was waiting for the "Walk" sign at a light, while juggling the two large cardboard boxes that had arrived for us. My face must have been hidden by my load; it actually was hard for me to see too much in front of me, I remember. That was probably why the two persons crossing with me did not bother to speak softer when one said: "Look at those niggers sitting in the sun with nothing to do." As we reached the other side of the road, I saw three elderly people, two men and a woman, two Indians and one Black, sitting under a tree by the inner harbour. Tears were welling up in my eyes, and the heat spreading over my face long before the speakers moved out of sight in another direction.

Sometimes that incident seems very far away, and at others, sharp and clear in my mind. It did not occur to me but I felt it was **about** me. I felt pain and confusion — and anger. I regretted that I had not followed those two men and challenged them, and also wondered if I would have dared.

An Arab friend told me her particular tale. After dinner one evening in a Vancouver restaurant, she started walking the few blocks to the bus stop. A group of youths appeared, surrounding and taunting her. She hurried her steps, but they gathered around, each grabbing a handful of her hair, her long, beautiful, waist-length black hair, running wildly about in a crazy maypole parody — "You ugly East Indian bitch". She escaped when the brighter lights of the block they had reached scattered the group. She cut her hair very short after that and has never grown it again.

I have heard many such accounts from men and women, "visible minorities", stories of expressions of racism, some subtle and implied in a gesture or look, others open, raw, ugly, and loud. One of the most incomprehensible things for me is when someone says, "that wouldn't happen to you", especially after recounting a personal experience of racial hostility. Why not? Because I work at the university, they mean, because I speak English well, seem confident, and do not dress differently from the perpetrators. But I am diminished as a person each time it happens, whether I read about it in the paper or hear about it in a friend's anguished voice. And it could happen to me, every day and any day. It just has not happened yet.

As your mother, Rahel, endless questions run through my mind about your life stretching ahead from this vantage point of three years. What will you become, discover, enjoy — many of the questions I know mothers besides myself have. But there are layers of other questions that relate directly to who I am and who you are. As a half-white girl (although you are so beautiful and golden, not a patchwork as that phrase suggests), will some of your experiences be bitter, difficult, cruel, in a playground or school hallway when I cannot be at your side? Or, what about boys, men, dates? I did not grow up with these options. I am not comfortable thinking about them for you. When I travel to India on holiday and mention such concerns to relatives, they look at me in horror, on the verge of telling me to pack my bags and return to where, they think, the choices are not so "different". I want to laugh then, because a part of me still believes the process of your growing up, here in Canada, can be a discovery, an adventure, one learning for you **and** me.

And I recognize that part of that process is looking at the question that is so personal although it seems large: Is Canada racist? I am aware of some of the early history of non-white immigrants to this country, as well as the genocide and cultural rootlessness of the native Indian communities postcontact. I have seen photographs in the archives of Japanese, Chinese, Black, and "East Indian" labourers, living in their separate enclaves in this British colony. I know of Komagata Maru and that people of Indian origin could not vote here until India became independent in 1947. I will tell you of these and you may later draw a thread linking these experiences to fears some now have that Asians will overrun Canada and this province and change it for the worse.

Yes, Canada is racist. There is a history, even a tradition of racism. Yet we must know that the links in this chain are not unbreakable. Many people in many different places, places we have been to and places we will go, are also resisting change and "difference". Canada is not unique in this, nor particularly strident. This is a very personal fight. You and I are in it. And because parents must avoid absolute statements, I will also tell you the other side of this story. There is hope here, and that is why we will stay and why we belong.

I have come a long way in five years. I now have friends here, resources, and, as I said, hope. I know I am not the average female immigrant from India. I have the benefits of education, facility with English, and recognized work experience. I have, however, met many women here who reaffirm what I have in common with them as a **person,** not what is different. My hope is that this can be true for other immigrant women as well, regardless of background.

As women, you and I will be doubly armed. What I mean is there is a fight on at least two fronts — racism and sexism! And some of it, of necessity, will be with our sisters. This is when you and I must respond gently yet firmly to observations from other women that "it must be awful to have grown up Indian and seen women suffer so". Our search for cultural sensitivity in others, though, must not be morally self-righteous. I, too, have my own prejudices and assumptions. I hope to learn through you, because of you, to bite my tongue.

Life is many-layered and complex, my little Indian and Canadian woman. Let us fight the good fight!

Your ever loving Mummu

R Alexest

126

RAJANI E. ALEXANDER

Born and raised in India, I earned a doctorate in history from the University of Notre Dame in Indiana, U.S.A. I have worked as a researcher, consultant, and academic in both India and Canada. My most recent position involved the planning and management of the Co-operative Education Program in Humanities and Arts areas for the University of Victoria. Currently Ottawa-based, I am enjoying working at home after the birth of Maya, my second daughter. Maya's arrival has made my letter in this anthology even more personally significant. I enjoy writing, travelling, and cooking.

HEATHER CRICHLOW

There is Racism Here

My dear sister:

Canada is not really paved with gold as we thought it was. Jennie, do you remember how we dreamt about what it would be like? Do you remember pictures on the calendars and postcards Uncle John sent us, and thinking that it would be a wonderful place to live? We saw only the big cities, the beautiful scenery, but, never the people. I have been here for over nine years and, in that time, I've noticed there is something wrong here.

Now, don't get me wrong; there is so much to see and do in Canada if you have the money with which to do it. One can travel to the Rockies in the west and the Maritimes in the east. I have been to the Rockies; and the mountains are breathtaking. It's better than on those calendars. I've been out east too. I attended a conference of the Congress of Black Women that was held in Halifax, Nova Scotia. It was great to get together with so many Black women in one place. The Congress works towards helping Black women and their families overcome problems encountered in Canadian society.

However, I am going to tell you about one negative aspect I've found in this beautiful country. THERE IS RACISM HERE. We never thought about that when we were daydreaming of Canada. Racism is directed against Blacks, or people of colour, or visible minority persons. How do you like that "visible minority person"? I am in that category. I am a visible minority person: I'd rather be called a "woman of colour" but, anyway.

You know I work for a private company. I got that position because of a referral. I was laid off when they "downsized" the other company I worked for. The manager there liked my work so he referred me to the company I work for now.

I was the only Black person working there. I guess that my co-workers were okay; but they used to tease me about my accent. There was one fellow there, Gordon, who always asked me about Black men and their private parts; and why if the white girls had a Black boyfriend they never go back to white men. I told him he should not believe such myths. I can see now why they think Black men are so well endowed. White men seem to be classic examples of the replicas of Greek statues with their tiny penises that caused such an uproar in Barbados.

Well, my dear sister, I never intended to come to Canada to be a mere clerk. So, at work I did all the in-branch training manuals and courses, and I applied for most of the jobs that were posted in the company. But, I was never offered a different position. There were people I trained to do my job, and when they applied for the same positions I did, they got the jobs. I knew there was something wrong. So I asked the manager if there was something else I could do to get promoted. He said "No", I was doing just fine but that the others were more experienced than I.

This continued for another year, but suddenly we got a new manager, Mr. Peters. He was more liberal than Mr. Andris. I asked to sit in with one of the lending clerks to learn her job. I did credit checks, started the lending in-branch course, and sat in on interviews in the evenings after I had done my work.

I approached Mr. Peters and told him what I was doing and that I would like to help Judy with her work. This is what he said: "I don't think that would be a good department for you to work in because I don't think the clients would feel comfortable talking to you about their financial problems."

Soon, I saw another girl helping Judy. She was white.

I guess I could have reported him to Human Rights, but I didn't. But, I knew I had to do something.

Occasionally a personnel officer visits from Toronto. They talk with the staff about any problems they may be having. We were invited to speak to the personnel officer in groups of two.

After some trivial exchanges about policy and procedure — they do like that phrase "policy and procedure" — I decided I better take the bull by the horns.

"Well", I said to this lady, "does this company have a policy on employment equity?"

"What do you mean?", she asked.

"Affirmative action", I said.

"No! Not really. Why?"

I proceeded to tell her of my efforts to get promoted, that my annual appraisals were great, and I had done all the courses, but I never seemed to be getting anywhere.

Well, my dear, the next position I applied for that I had the qualifications for, I got. It was so good to get out of one rut and into another.

The position I applied for was downgraded. The job wasn't any different, but the name was changed to a lower grade, and so was the salary. I was assured that if I performed well for the mandatory six-month probation, the job would be changed back to what it formerly was, and I would also get a raise. This did not happen with any of the positions I wasn't awarded.

Eventually, I was upgraded and did get the raise. However, I had to work on Saturdays as a supervisor without the name and the pay, or revert back to my original position.

We are not supposed to be treated any differently because of the colour of our skins. As long as we have the qualifications, we should be given an even chance. There is a proclamation of Human Rights that states this.

Jennie, there is not much overt racism; if there was, I would come back home. Sometimes they say things at work like "I bet your son is going to be a great athlete", and "you people dance so well". It is assumed that anyone coming from the Caribbean is leaving abject poverty.

I noticed, too, that when there were personnel officers visiting the office, the supervisor started telling offensive Black jokes. I told him I did not like it and would appreciate it if he would stop telling them. He did.

Jennie, when they are angry, they smile. I still don't understand that. They are so polite about their anger. I know enough now not to trust those smiles.

I know I am painting a shattering picture. But, this is the reality.

There is something else I have to tell you about. It's about schools, not the education system *per se*, but about the teachers.

When my precious little Robert came here, everyone was amazed with his knowledge and intelligence. You know how bright he is. He was placed in grade three with his age group. He had no problems with anything. He excelled that first year because he had all the basics he learned in the Caribbean. The grammar and multiplication tables, he never had to discover them; he knew them. All he had to do was integrate and learn about Canada.

In grade four he continued to excel. He was so good with essays, the headmistress promised that she would have them printed and illustrated to be placed in their school library. It never happened though.

Robert started having problems — not educational, but social. He was always fighting on the playground and soon he did not want to go to school. He said to me: "They don't like me anymore, mom, the teacher neither."

That really broke my heart.

I made an appointment to see his teacher and asked Uncle John to go with me to the school. We first talked to Robert. He hated being called nigger, having his foot stamped on, and being punched. So, he retaliated the only way he knew how, by punching them back, which usually led to a fight.

Well, we saw Mr. Jones. All he saw was Robert punching those kids. We relayed what Robert said. We told him he should be more sensitive to all his pupils and listen to them. We told him what he usually saw was Robert's response. He was not always the instigator.

Mr. Jones was surprised that Robert did not want to return to school, but he promised to watch and listen, and to let him answer some questions in class. He stated Robert knew the answers, and he wanted to give the other children a chance to answer. But, this was having a negative effect on my child.

Well, would you believe it, Robert came home the next day wearing a Happy Face button given to him by Mr. Jones, for being a good boy.

Things certainly improved. There were still fights, but not as many. Although being called names still bothers him, he does not try to beat them up. We told him that only stupid, ignorant kids call people names because of their colour; that he was a great kid, intelligent and good-looking, and that he should try to ignore those children.

At the end of that school year when Robert had to be transferred to another school, the headmistress called. She wanted to see me.

The headmistress told me she was sending Robert's records to the new school along with a recommendation that he be allowed to enter the accelerated science enrichment program. He would probably attend two afternoons a week. She said: "I know he can do it; don't let him miss this opportunity."

I was so pleased. The kid was not getting as dull as ditch water. There are so many horror stories about bright Black children from the Caribbean being steered from academic to technical classes.

Well, Robert went to this other school, and the first semester (term), we did not get a call from the teacher about the accelerated learning program. We waited until the parent-teacher meeting in the second semester to chat with the teacher, Mr. Ewen. He told us Robert was such a bright kid, that he was ahead of the other students with his questions and answers. We raised the question of the science enrichment program with Mr. Ewen who claimed Robert was not ready for it. The contradictions in his remarks were very apparent.

We wrote a letter to the headmaster with a copy to Mr. Ewen stating our dissatisfaction with the interview, and that it seemed that Mr. Ewen did not want Robert to be enrolled in the program even though he would benefit from it. We also stated that from the interview we had concluded that Mr. Ewen had lower expectations of Black and native students than he did of the white students.

The very next day we were informed that Robert would be placed in the science enrichment program.

It makes me wonder what would happen if we did not complain once again.

Robert now goes to a school which has a large native enrolment. Most of our Black acquaintances were alarmed that we were sending him to a school like that. I think this is the best thing we could ever do for him. The children are not teased about their clothing. Their cultures are recognized by the school. They have special days where parents come to the school for cultural days. The teachers there seem to be attuned to the students, even though there are no native teachers yet.

Robert is doing very well. My fifteen-year-old son is planning to go to university. He has it so nicely planned. He is going to get a scholarship, he says. His teachers say he can do it. I pray everything will work out as he would like it.

As you know, when I left home I always wanted to go to university; and after years I am taking one class in the evening. English 100 — Literature and Composition. The course requires analyzing short stories, plays, and poems. What was surprising is that most of the literature has the word "nigger" as opposed to Negro, coloured, or Black. The professor is very sensitive. He told the class that at the time these people were writing, that is what they called Black people. He said, too, that he hoped that no one was offended. Probably he meant me, as I am the only Black person in the class.

It is a good experience to be back in school. I have a goal to get a degree in business administration. I hope it will lead to a more rewarding job.

Even though this letter sounds negative, I feel there is much we can do to make our lives more rewarding in Canada. Previous generations of Black folks in Canada have contributed much to Canadian society and have made our way easier. I feel confident we can do the same for future generations of Blacks and other visible minorities and, in so doing, help all of Canadian society advance.

All the best

Love

HEATHER CRICHLOW

The oldest of six children, I emigrated in 1982 from Barbados to Canada; in 1986, my son and I became Canadian citizens. I am an active member of the Congress of Black Women of Canada and am particularly concerned about the fate of Black youth in Canada. In 1989, I started writing short stories for children. My contribution to *Sharing Our Experience* is my first published piece. My family and I live in Regina, Saskatchewan.

Pham Thi Quê

In a Jewellery Factory

Dear D.L.:

I was happy to hear your news. The important thing is that you are well. You complained that you could not find work in Oslo. But at least you were able to receive unemployment assistance not long after you arrived in Norway. There, as in France, people are considered to have a past, and since in your past you worked in your country, you have the right to register for unemployment assistance until you find a job in your new country.

Here in the New World, you break with your past and start all over. There is no unemployment assistance for anyone who has not worked in Canada. The offers of employment in the newspapers require work experience in Canada. Other offers in employment centres are reserved for those eligible for unemployment assistance. It is a vicious circle: if you are not given the opportunity to begin working without experience, how can you meet the requirements of offers of employment? And if you have not worked, how can you be eligible for unemployment assistance? If you are not eligible for assistance, how can you have access to the jobs listed in the unemployment centres? Let me tell you a little about my tribulations in Montreal.

There is a jewellery factory in Montreal, where immigrants of all kinds — two Chinese, one of whom is a man, three Filipino girls, a Laotian woman, a Polish lady, and many Vietnamese of all ages and both sexes — have ended up. Why did they come to be there? For various reasons, but mainly to work to earn a living. The language of work, that spoken by the bosses, is English. But everyone speaks their native tongue if talking to others of the same nationality, or, if they are alone, like the Polish lady or the young Laotian girl, they communicate in French. If they all spoke, you would think it was the Tower of Babel.

However, that doesn't happen often, as we are supposed to work like machines, without a break and in silence, to produce as much as possible. At the end of the day, everyone completes their report on the work they have done: how many pearl necklaces have been made? how many pairs of earrings have been mounted? Only the highly skilled worker does not have to complete a report. She creates the most complicated models, the designer's cleverest compositions. She executes the most difficult orders and performs the most delicate repairs. She is treated with a great deal of respect, as is her husband, the foreman. After all, did they not begin when the factory was just a modest enterprise with a total staff of only three?

The work day begins at 8:30 a.m. and ends at 6 p.m. We are allowed a break in mid-morning for a small snack — a cup of coffee or glass of milk hastily consumed — or a trip to the washroom and to wash our hands. The real break is at 1 p.m., when we are allowed half an hour (unpaid) to eat. Everyone brings their lunch so as not to have to spend their hard-earned modest salary at a fast food restaurant just below on the street corner. Lunch may consist of a sandwich, fruit, rice with meat prepared at home, or Chinese soup made right there by pouring boiling water, available to everyone, over the dry mixture. There is no time to dawdle, so the meal must be simple. On fine summer days, we take our lunch to the square to watch the pigeons hopping about.

The only diversion for the young people is eating out together on Friday in the winter, when the factory closes at 1p.m. (in the summer, the work day ends at 6 p.m. every day of the week). But they (the young people) hurry afterwards to "moonlight" on other jobs to recover the money spent eating out on the weekend. The weekend is not exactly restful either: as long as there is still work to be done, we work. It's like two or three days in one, working at the factory during the day and moonlighting at night until the wee hours of the morning, be it in ready-to-wear, furs, or jewellery.

The first thing I did upon arriving in Montreal was to go to an employment centre. I eventually ended up at a centre reserved for executives, those who hold degrees. But you cannot have any of the jobs that suit you because of a certain section 38 under which anyone who is not eligible for unemployment assistance is not entitled to those jobs. Since I have never had the opportunity to work in Canada, even though I worked for more than twenty years in my country and five in France, I was not eligible for unemployment assistance and, therefore, for the jobs posted in the centre. The jobs most accessible to everyone are in material handling or manufacturing. You barely earn enough to live on. This is why the whole family — father, mother, and children — works. Only those under eighteen go to school. The salary is even lower than the minimum wage in France, and raises are so slight that the difference between the authorized minimum wage and that of a worker with one year of seniority is approximately thirty cents an hour. And yet these girls find a way to dress elegantly on a small budget, thanks to the sales.

When you are hired, you learn on the job and perform the disagreeable tasks that professionals despise. You must not learn the trade too quickly. You are taught how to string as quickly as possible, the correct way to fasten a necklace, and how to transfer the pearls. The important thing is to know how to handle the needle quickly and deftly, with the fewest possible errors, because errors do not pay. As long as orders are pouring in, you work non-stop up to the last minute. Eight hours of concentration and mental stress spent tied to the work table are enough to put you on edge. And when the orders are slow, you are plagued with thoughts of being laid off or unemployed.

The atmosphere is not healthy or comforting either. While co-workers band together to defend their interest (regarding wages or overtime) to the bosses, there is a great deal of petty rivalry and unspoken jealousy among supervisors and workers. Should you do something outstanding, the news spreads throughout the workshop and your neighbour's resentment is expressed in a bitter if not mean word. At times the nervous tension is so bad that what starts as gibes back and forth explodes into a free-for-all. On the best of days (the prosperous ones), there is constant chatter until the foreman manages to calm everyone down. Now and then, it takes the manager to restore peace and quiet. But solid friendships form between people in similar situations, students working there temporarily and people who discover that their tastes or personalities are the same.

It is not a very wholesome atmosphere, owing to the lack of job stability. Ten weeks after I was hired, I was laid off for lack of work; I thus lost my first job but still was not eligible for unemployment assistance.

I do not regret having started so low. I had the opportunity to be in contact with a level of society that until then I had not known. What I regret is having wasted precious time struggling inside a vicious circle and allowing my health to deteriorate while fighting for a promotion to a level lower than the one I started at in my country.

While continuing to hope for a position in which I might be able to use my full potential, skills, and experience, I nevertheless regret the enormous waste of my grey matter. This experience robbed me a little of my health, enthusiasm, generosity, and confidence in human wisdom and goodness.

Let this be a consolation to you, my dear D.L., in your disappointments in Oslo. Best regards, until the next time.

Sincerely,

Phtquê

PHAM THI QUÊ

Born in Cholon, South Vietnam, I carried out research on the feminist movement in Vietnam in the first half of the 20th century as revealed in the literature and media of the period. I then decided to study the status of women in general and, in particular, their status in late 19th and early 20th century French literature. Established in Montreal, I became involved in the activities of the Vietnamese women's association and wrote a series of articles on such topics as sexual equality, ethics and women, and employment equity, published in Vietnamese in the association's journal. In addition to teaching French to immigrants, I work with others in various university research projects dealing with Quebec residents of Vietnamese origin and their interaction with the host community.

(Letter translated from French)

Chanthala Phomtavong

From Laos to Canada

Dear Friend:

Since I left my home or my country thirteen years ago, I have been living in Canada. I feel very homesick some times. I still think about my life when I was small. My mom passed away when I was one year old and I stayed with my dad. After that my dad passed away when I was eight years old. I stayed with my two sisters and one brother. Four of us had a very hard time. We had no place to stay. We were like trees without roots.

I had to work hard to get money to spend for education. We grew vegetables in the land that our father left for us, and then sold them in the market. In my country, you need a lot of money to finish your higher education. My brother and sister tried very hard to have me finish my post-secondary education and my teacher training.

In 1978, communists took over my country. Life in my country was getting worse, so I decided to escape to Thailand with my husband.

We escaped at night by going by boat across the Mekong River. My husband jumped under the small boat in the water and pulled the boat away about three metres from the river bank. After that he used a paddle to cross the river. It was very scary for us, for if the communists saw us, they would have shot at the boat. It took us about one and a half hours to get to Thailand.

When we got there, the Thai police put us in jail, and treated us very badly. For example, we had money and gold, and they took it all. To get out of the jail, we had to pay them about twelve hundred dollars in gold for the two of us.

Then they sent us to a refugee camp. I stayed there for one and a half years with my three-month-old son. At that time my husband had to go back to Laos to fight against the communists with a group of Lao people called the "Lao Kao".

When my husband was gone, I didn't have enough food to eat, because they just gave us food twice a week. No one was allowed to go out anywhere. We had to stay in the refugee camp. I had no country to immigrate to because I didn't have a sponsor. I volunteered to teach young children Lao and French languages. I wrote forms in the French language to the Department of Immigration in Canada to sponsor us. I know French because a long time ago our country was a colony of France.

A few months later we got sponsored to come to Canada. In 1979 I was living in Walheim, sixty kilometers from Saskatoon. The Grace Church sponsored us. We were the only family in town who spoke Lao. When my sponsor wanted to tell us something or give us something, we didn't understand them and didn't know how to communicate with them. I felt like I wanted to go back home by that time. One day they brought someone who knew how to speak French. Her name was Diane Moffit. She came from Montreal and she spoke French and translated into English for my sponsor to know and understand what we needed, what we wanted. It was very hard for us, too, because we didn't know how to communicate with them. They sent me to learn English two days a week. By that time I was very worried as to how I might learn to speak English within such a short time.

After a month my sponsor took my husband to find the job at Flexi-coil. At first the company didn't want him because he didn't speak English and he didn't have experience in Canada. But this company is very good. They tried him first for a couple of weeks. Finally, he got the job because he can do the work like anybody else. This company trains and helps a lot of immigrant people.

Dear friend, for me it is very difficult to find a job. I'm not a teacher any more. If I want to be a teacher in Canada, I have to have my certificate. I have to go back to school, finish my grade twelve, then go to university for four years. I spent a lot of time studying to get my degree. I spent a lot of money for education, but they never evaluated me. I got no credit at all.

I can't afford to go back to university because, in my family, only my husband got a permanent job. Plus, I have three children, and I have one child who has hearing loss. I spent a lot of money to pay for a good quality hearing aid. No one helped us with even one penny.

I applied to an E.S.L. program because for this school I don't need to pay. But they only give us twenty-five weeks' instruction for English as a second language. It is not enough time for me to learn to use English for applying for jobs, to write application forms, to use English in the work area. I hope this program (E.S.L.) will give me more time than just twenty-five weeks, and will continue. It is very needed and helps us a lot.

I am very worried about my kids' future too. My second boy is very intelligent. He likes computers and wants to learn about computers. I can't afford to buy a computer for my boy to practice at home. If I have a permanent and secure job, I think I might afford to get him one.

Dear friend, you can't believe, right now, even for a housekeeping job I have to train first. I had to train for ten weeks in the nursing home in the housekeeping area. I "learned" about mopping the floors of all the residents' rooms. I never got hired because of my speed. They want my speed the same as the people who have ten years' experience of working in the nursing home.

I try very hard, so I can make a living. Dear friend, I work as a sewing machine operator. I had never done it in my life. I work very hard even to make minimum wages. If I work the same time my husband works, in the day shift, I can't afford to pay for babysitting. I make only five dollars an hour and my babysitter costs two dollars an hour for one child and I have three children. That is why I have no choice. I have to work the night shift from 4:30 p.m. to 1 a.m. in the morning. In the day time I babysit.

I have applied to so many places, for so many jobs. They always ask if I have experience in Canada, at the least two or four years, and if I finished my grade twelve in Canada. They never try us; how do they know we can do the work or not. Maybe it is racism, maybe it is lack of Canadian education. That is why they do not hire us.

I never give up. My dream is to have a good job, with good pay, in the day time. I will go to school at night to reach my goal, to learn new things, to have more education to reach my new career. I also pray to God to help my family have a healthy life, and I hope that all my dreams will come true in the good future.

Your friend,

L. Phomdavong

CHANTHALA PHOMTAVONG

My name is Chanthala Phomtavong. I have three children. I'm from Laos.
I was a teacher in my country but right now I work as a caretaker in Canada. It
is very difficult to get a similar job or have my education or degree recognized
here, because of the language barrier. Government support of E.S.L. programs is
needed so people like me can continue learning English. The program helps us
immigrant women. Also needed is evaluation of degrees from other countries.
I hope my idea will come true.

Naïma Bendris

Confronting Endemic Stereotypes

Dear Touria,

I was very interested to read your last letter in which you told me about a meeting you had with a group of Canadian field workers who arrived in Morocco a few months ago and were extremely surprised to discover from day to day a different situation in Moroccan society from the one they had imagined before visiting our country. They were even more astonished about the situation of women since their picture of them was totally fictitious.

You mentioned that you were appalled by the western world's reductionist perception of women in the Arab world.

When I came to Canada, I myself was shocked to note the extent to which many Canadians are misinformed about us.

The impression the public has of women in the Arab world is merely a reflection of stereotyped images projected by western media and literature in order to fuel the collective imagination. With a monopoly on information, the western media are attuned to every collective fantasy. They provide the western world with a picture of Arab societies that corresponds to the fantasies of readers and viewers who register these images and retain them in the form of prejudice.

Women in the Arab world have never received as much media coverage as they have since we witnessed the rise of Islamic fundamentalism, and the media are content to convey a false, frozen picture of them. Women in this part of the world are depicted in a degrading situation in which they are seen as submissive, secluded, unobstrusive, passive, and veiled. The fantasy continues to the point of imagining them as princesses, concubines, or slaves confined in harems under the domination of one man, their master. These images of them are devoid of any concept of assertiveness, creativity, potentiality, or militancy. The western media completely shroud the other situations of women in the Arab world, such as women at all levels of education and in various areas of the labour market, women who are assertive, who act, who are innovative, who fight for recognition of their civil and legal rights. These are determined women who help build their society. The changing status of women in these societies has not been accompanied by a corresponding change in their image. The general impression others have of the Arabs has not really altered and has even worsened with the Gulf War. The imaginary Orient remains an exotic, sensuous, and colourful dream world for some, and a world of barbaric, fanatic Allah worshippers to be feared and defeated, for others.

This is why some Arab immigrant women in Canada have organized, rallied together, and attempted to change public opinion about themselves by arranging many activities related to women from this part of the world.

With other women, both from these societies and from Canada, I also set up a committee whose goal is to eliminate prejudice and present a truer image of women in the Arab world. Our aim is to help challenge certain preconceived ideas and "unveil" the taboos and stereotypes. We also wish to remove any obstacles to the integration of women from these communities into Canadian society, obstacles which could result from the common perception of the women of this ethnic group.

Our committee organizes training workshops, conferences, and meetings to explain to people that there is not just one but rather many conditions or situations of women in the Arab world; that their status is by no means homogeneous, uniform, or static but rather diversified and changing; that the Arab world is composed of many societies with similarities but also differences; that there is an entire mosaic of local cultures, traditions and values, customs and standards peculiar to each society. In sum, we would like to present a multi-faceted picture.

I was recently invited to give a training session to women teaching at the centre d'éducation du Québec (CEQ). I began my talk by asking participants, "What immediately comes to mind when women in the Arab world are mentioned?"

The usual stock phrases emerged, such as veiled, illiterate, submissive women or women from another era. Almost all of them had read the book by Betty Mahmoody, *Not Without my Daughter,* which has further reinforced their prejudices about women in the Arab world, even though the story took place in Iran. Another popular misconception is that all Arabs are Muslims and all Muslims are Arabs. Many people think that since the Islamic religion originated in the Arab world, it is a criterion for being an Arab, and they are unaware that the majority of Muslims are outside the Arab world, while some Arabs are Christian or Jewish.

To get back to my training session at the CEQ, I made a presentation in which I attempted to offer a more realistic portrait of the various situations of women in the Arab world, and we then viewed a film by the Algerian producer Merzak Allouache, entitled "Femmes en mouvement" (women in movement) in which we listened to a number of militant feminist members of different women's associations in Algeria and women working in the public sector. The film showed participants another aspect of the social dynamics of women in Algeria, and it was clear that their perception was totally different at the end of the session. They told us, "We really thought that women from that part of the world led a dismal, nightmarish life, but we now see that, just like us, they present their problems and claim their rights; they act and fight for their cause."

I am very satisfied with these events, and my goal is to reproduce these kinds of activities across Quebec and develop in people a new way of looking at us. I would like to break the vicious circle of these endemic stereotypes in order to create more harmonious relations, and I think that knowledge and respect are prerequisites for a peaceful, fruitful relationship. This is my wish and that of all women in Arab communities, and indeed of women of all ethnic communities living in Canada. The social integration of women from Arab communities is also dependent on interpretation by the Canadian media. This integration must be conveyed through films, radio and television broadcasts, texts, articles, and talks which totally integrate women from the Arab world without focusing on their difference or turning this difference into folkloric exploitation.

In closing, I promise to keep you informed of future activities undertaken by my committee which, I neglected to tell you, is affiliated with the Centre d'Études Arabes pour le Développement, a non-profit NGO (non-governmental organization). The centre was founded in 1984, and it consists of people who wish to develop ties of solidarity and exchanges between the Arab world and Quebec on the one hand, and communities of Arab origin and the Quebec community on the other hand. To do this, it organizes conferences and workshops, prepares files, conducts research, and talks to the media on various themes and topics of current interest related to the Arab world and inter-ethnic relations.

As always,

144

NAÏMA BENDRIS

I was born in Morocco, in Rabat. My letter is addressed to Touria, my young aunt on my mother's side who lives in Fez, Morocco. I spent part of my childhood and teen years with her, until I left for three years of language studies in a French university. I have been living in Canada for nearly twelve years now, and have studied sociology at the Université Laval, in Quebec City. Currently, I am working as a social sciences research officer at the Université du Québec à Montréal. I am a member of the Women's Committee of the Centre d'études arabes pour le développement (CEAD). The Women's Committee is concerned with focusing attention on the various situations of women in the Arab world, and on the situation of women who were originally from these countries but now live in Canada. The Women's Committee also works to establish links between women living in Canada and those in the Arab world. I am a member of the Comité québécois Femmes et Développement, and participate as a resource person in a study on ethno-cultural communities and AIDS, carried out by a research team of the Community Health Department at Montreal's General Hospital.

(Letter translated from French)

ARUNA ISAAC PAPP

Sujata's Death

Dear friend:

I am writing to inform you of Sujata's death. She passed away on November 13, 1989. The family says that she had chest pain and was complaining about a headache. She was taken to the hospital but within moments of arriving, she died.

I am sure you remember her from our support group. She had become disabled during her third pregnancy ten years ago. Her daughters and son are in their teens. You, like all the other women in the support group, kept asking her why she had joined a group for battered women when she maintained that her husband was a god, a very kind and gentle man. I know that some of the women in the group wanted her to leave the group but Sujata kept returning.

I first met Sujata the day Sgt. Harris called me to say that he had received a letter from a man indicating that his sister was being abused by her husband, and the brother was afraid that she might be killed. The Sergeant asked me if I would go with him to the victim's house because she did not speak English and he needed someone to do the interpretation. I agreed.

We were met at the door by her husband, and Sgt. Harris explained to him the reason for our visit. Her husband was very angry and asked if he had to allow us to enter. Sgt. Harris replied that we could always come back with a warrant. After thinking about it for a while, her husband opened the door and allowed us to enter. He had been informed by the police that we would be coming so it was not a surprise visit, especially since he had received a copy of the letter. Sgt. Harris asked her husband to call his wife so that we could speak with her.

Her husband went to the stairs and yelled up to his wife in his native tongue, saying, "Your coffin bearers are here, you better come down." Her husband knew that I spoke his language and understood what he was saying, but he looked at me with such hate and challenge that it caused me to shudder. Sgt. Harris looked at me and asked: "What was that about?" I told him that we had been introduced as "her coffin bearers". Her husband, with a smirk on his face, said to the Sergeant: "Since the day we have been married her relatives have been making trouble for us. They will not allow us to live our life. My wife and I have no problems, except the relatives interfering." Sgt. Harris said: "I am sure that is true, but we need to talk with your wife about this letter and ask her what is happening."

Just then Sujata came down the stairs. When she was told that the police had come to speak with her she began to cry. She refused to talk to the police officer and said in perfect English: "I have no problems, my relatives have made up this story, my husband has never beaten me, I have no complaints, I want you to leave." The more she talked the louder she began to cry, and within a few minutes she was trembling. I made her sit down and told her that if she did not want to speak to the police at this time, that was fine. I offered to make her a cup of tea and find her a blanket. Sujata agreed to this and calmed down a little.

Sgt. Harris came over to Sujata and said: "I received a letter from your relative and this letter makes me very worried. I know that your husband is a good man and he does not hurt you. I believe you, but I have this letter and it is my job to talk with you and your husband so that I can go back to the police station and write a report saying that you are okay. Do you understand that?" "Yes, yes", said Sujata, "I understand. I am physically disabled but I am not stupid. I know my relatives are trying to make trouble again. You must have spoken to them and now you are here to bother us." Again the Sergeant explained to Sujata the reason for our visit. Finally she agreed to allow her husband to go with Sgt. Harris to another room and I remained with her.

I was sitting in the living room with Sujata who was having tea. I asked her about her youngsters, how they were doing in school. She said that they were all doing very well and were very good youngsters. The father dropped them off in the morning and picked them up after school. They stayed home after school and were not allowed to go out without their father. Sujata said that her husband was a very good father. He did not allow the youngsters to receive friends or phone calls. He was very careful they did not mix with bad kids, and followed the religious teaching. The father even checked the families within their own community to make sure that they were not a bad influence on his children. Last year her husband was late in picking up the kids and when he arrived he saw their older son talking with a white girl and a boy. Her husband was furious and demanded to know what they were talking about. The other kids got frightened and ran away. But being the good father that he is, he made arrangements to take their son to India and got him engaged to a fourteen-year-old girl who is from a very nice family. Sujata said: "My son knows that he has to be loyal to her. If he deceives this girl and finds another woman, it will be a great sin and God will never forgive him. Nor will the father. As soon as the girl in India is of age they will be married."

I asked Sujata what she had done before she came to Canada. She said that she had been living in Glasgow, Scotland, and worked as an assistant in a small firm importing goods from India. Her familiarity with the suppliers enabled her to establish herself and this allowed her husband to go back to school. But after her third pregnancy she became disabled. Her husband was finding it difficult to find a job in Scotland, so they decided to move to Canada. When she became disabled, she was sent back to her relatives, because her husband refused to support a disabled wife. She learned to live with her disability and to cook, clean, and look after the family without the full use of all her faculties. Sujata had become a very good cook. After two years of separation and learning to do things for herself, she came back to Canada to look after her husband and their home.

Every time I tried to ask her about the abuse, she would refuse to talk about it, saying that every married couple has fights; they were no different. Sujata insisted that her husband was very kind because he allowed her to remain in the home. He had many offers of marriage from parents of younger, beautiful, and very rich girls but he had put them off. She had so much for which she was grateful.

I asked her what happened to her during the holidays that had caused a fight and the police had been called. She said that she had fallen down the stairs which she said is expected to happen to a disabled lady. I agreed. Then I asked about what had happened last week, what had started the fight. She said it was nothing. She had been saying her evening prayers and did not hear her husband come in with the groceries. He had bought a lot of food and needed help with it, but since she was in the middle of her prayer, she did not hear him arrive. He came into the room and, while she was bent over with her head down, he had put his feet under her and lifted her up, banging her head on the ground. She was very surprised, and being beaten, she began to scream. Because she was screaming, her husband got very angry and began to kick her around the room. He said that she prayed too much and that he was her god and she should pray to him. He was the one providing for her and taking care of her. He was angry that she had not interrupted her prayer to assist him.

There were tears running down Sujata's face as she continued to defend her husband and make excuses for him. And I asked her: "Do you still think he is a god?" "Yes", she said, "He is a god, no one else will give me the status of a wife. If I am not a mother nor a wife, what am I? You know he can leave me anytime he wants to, but he has been kind and I have food and shelter. Is there any place in this world I can go to and feel safer, happier, and be respected? I live with my children, and I rejoice in their well-being and their progress, I cook for them and they tell me my food is good. What more can a mother ask for?" I had nothing to say to Sujata. She was right, she had no place she could go to. Her relatives who were concerned about her were not willing to offer her shelter. The government shelter and safe houses are not a permanent solution for South Asian women.

Sgt. Harris had been questioning her husband for nearly two hours. He confessed that on several occasions he had beaten his wife. During a fight she was trying to get away from him and had fallen down the stairs and broken her ribs. Another time she had broken her arm. He had hit her on the head with a chair once which had required eighteen stitches. He told the Sergeant how difficult it had been for him to look after the children and his wife. For ten years he had been alone in this hell.

Her husband said that due to immigration problems, unemployment, no support from the wife, etc., he had become a man with a very short fuse. He took out his frustration on his wife because he blamed her for all his troubles. He had prayed about it and he was talking to someone in the community about his troubles, and he thought that this was making a difference in their lives.

Sgt. Harris came into the living room and sat down near Sujata and said: "Your husband has confessed to me that a lot of abuse is going on in your marriage, and he tells me that you are the victim. I would like you to press charges against your husband so that this kind of thing will never happen again. You need to protect yourself and we are here to help you." Upon hearing this, Sujata began to cry again. She had feared that this would happen and she began to curse Sgt. Harris. "You have frightened my husband into making this confession. He has never hurt me, I am not a victim. I am only a victim of my fate. God has been unkind to me. Please go away; leave, leave us alone." We had no choice but to leave. The police did not charge her husband. He was advised to go for counselling.

Today Sujata is dead. Her family did not have an investigation done because they feel that when she was alive she protected her husband. In death they want to carry out her wishes.

My friend, I am writing to you because I hear echoes of your words in this letter. Can you hear them? You always get beaten up, you have had broken ribs and a broken nose. You are frightened of being alone in your home with your husband, yet you try so hard to protect him and his actions. You take all the blame for what he is doing to you. You always say: "If I had not done this, if I had kept my mouth shut, if I had cooked a different meal, if I had not spoken so harshly about his mother, he would not have beaten me." You are fooling yourself. He will never stop beating you. He has become used to beating you. He knows you will protect him.

Last year several South Asian women were killed by their husbands. I knew three of these women. I am so tired of attending funerals of women I know. Every night when I lie down to sleep I wonder which one of us will get killed next. I don't want to have to attend your funeral. Please get out while you have time. You can have a safe life. I will help you. I care about you, so do your children. Take care, God bless.

Your friend

Aruna

ARUNA ISAAC PAPP

I came to Canada in 1972. During the past fourteen years, I have worked as a counsellor for victims of wife abuse, and have founded three organizations which assist women living in violent family situations. Currently, I am a self-employed consultant doing cross-cultural training for mainstream agencies, dealing with cultural, religious, and systemic barriers faced by immigrants when they come to Canada. I serve on several boards, including the Board of Governors Centennial College, Centenary Hospital, and METRAC. In 1991, I was honoured by the YWCA of Metro Toronto with the "Women of Distinction" award. I have three daughters and a son.

TAKING A STANCE

Dolores Gabriel
Beryl Tsang
Rosemary Eng
Sunera Thobani
Jaya Chauhan
Mayann Francis
Minnie Aodla Freeman

DOLORES GABRIEL

Anger

Dear Black Baby:

What has life been like to ME, a Black Woman born in Nova Scotia?

This is not a difficult question to answer but one that brings back so much. I have so much I could tell and so much I've wanted to say for so long. Finally a chance to use my voice in a way that might change, or at least cause others to think about some of the things they say and do.

Life for ME, a Black woman in Nova Scotia, has been a life filled with hardships, struggles, pain, rejection, and most importantly, ANGER. So much to be angry at, and always the knowledge that there was so little that I could do about it. The fact that this society has placed ME, a Black woman, at the bottom of the ladder has not only served to limit my political, social, and economic power but also tried, and I repeat, tried to take away all the good that is inside of ME. I am Strong, I am Proud, I am Black, I am Beautiful, and I LOVE ME, even if nobody else does. I love my thick lips and my beautiful dark skin. I love our tight hair and our wide hips: I LOVE ME.

Oftentimes I encounter a face, a situation, or a word, and it stirs up so much anger in me. I get angry at lots of things and when I do, I stop, say a prayer, and ask God to give me strength to face this cold, cruel world. I get angry at a lot of things and always, without failure, God gives me the push and inspiration that I need to carry on.

I GET ANGRY! I GET ANGRY! I GET ANGRY! I GET ANGRY! I GET ANGRY!

Angry at the cruel and mean things that other kids would do and say to ME. The very same things they now say to my son. Things they say because they have been taught that it's okay to do and say those things to people with black skin.

Angry at the idea that there are still Black youth who have to see "nigger" scrawled on desks and bathroom walls every day they go to high school. It makes me think the more things change the more they stay the same.

Angry at never being able to go through a day without fighting for the very rights that I am supposed to be guaranteed under the Charter. Rights that I'm supposed to have as a Canadian citizen, but rights that are violated whenever others warrant they should be.

Angry at being overlooked when I go to the cashier with purchases at the grocery store or department store. The policy is supposed to be first-come, first-served, but the rules always seem to change when a white customer ends up behind me in the line.

Angry at employers who merely look at my skin before they immediately reply: Oh, we're very sorry to bring you all this way for an interview, but the position was filled this morning.

Angry at the question, Well, what was he doing in that part of town at that time of night? Why must we respond to such a stupid question? We have just as much right as anybody else to go where we want to go regardless of the hour.

Angry at statements which hint at the greater sexual potency of Black men and women. As a Black woman, I am not a sexual savage nor am I eager to be sexually exploited. The word NO means the same things for Black women as it means when uttered by a white woman.

Angry when young innocent Black boys/girls are harassed by the police officer because, "we all look alike". Just as there are white people with different skin tones, various eye and hair colours, we, too, have unique features/qualities that make us different from other Blacks. It is time to dispel the myth that we all look alike.

Angry when materials such as *Huckleberry Finn* remain a part of the required readings for courses at the university level. How can a young boy teach an old man about everyday experiences that the older man has already experienced? God gave Black people brains too; and they are very healthy: Don't demean us by casting us in roles which indicate otherwise.

Angry at the fact that I refused to eat one of my favourite fruits, watermelon, for years because of racial overtones associated with Blacks eating watermelon. I know that I have never seen anyone — black, green, purple, red, and even white — with lips the size of a watermelon. I've decided I will never again let someone else's ignorance dictate what I can and cannot eat.

Angry at the thought that everything black is bad. Words such as black magic, black sheep of the family, blackmail, etc. Or inferring that it's okay to tell a white lie. A lie is a lie, is a lie. I don't ever recall reading any part of the Bible which indicates that it's okay to lie any time.

Yes, I get angry, but I don't give up hope. The hope that one day people will just see Me for the person that I am on the inside. I refuse to apologize to anyone for my BLACK SKIN. I love it and it's never going to disappear; so deal with it. I have so much to give, and better things to do with my time and energy than just be angry. Give me a chance to be all that I can be, let me show you all the good that I have inside of me. Please! Black Baby, you too have much to give and do. Do not become discouraged. Keep on doing and being the best you can be. Remember I believe in YOU!

Dolores Gabriel

The following poem is dedicated to my great-grandmother, Granny. She is currently living in Halifax, Nova Scotia, and is now approximately one hundred and four years old. We have been fortunate enough to have her with us for a long time, and I'm sure she'll be around for many years to come. I have often gone to her to talk when I needed guidance, and I have also sat and listened to her talk many times. She has not always been so willing to remember the past as it brings back painful memories.

On one occasion, when I was sitting and listening to her, she made several remarks about things she wished she could have done and said.

"You are so lucky to be able to read and write. I can't do those things and my desire to learn to do them is dwindling. But God has been so good to me. I have lived long enough to be a great-great-grandmother; not many people do. But times are changing. When I was younger, we didn't have much but we made out okay and things will be better for your son. Although I am grateful to the man above for all the things he has done for me, I can't help feel as though we, as a people were cheated. Oh well, the main thing is that I am here today. We did what we had to do to survive, yes sir, we did what we had to do to survive."

155

I've Survived

Frustration, Anger, Rejection, and Hate
Burn deep within my 96 year old soul
Like acid eating away at me

Wrinkle upon wrinkle from worry and fight,
Reading, writing, and arithmetic — I've never been taught.
I was not in control of my destiny; white man controlled it for me

NIGGER, SCUM, WENCH, — were learned too well.
Life has been nothing but a battle to conquer;
A fight:　To overcome feelings of hate.
　　　　　To hold back from saying NO to a white man when he touched
　　　　　my dark breast
　　　　　To remember to tell my children to love the little white child that
　　　　　spit in his face.

Yes, my children, my beautiful children;
They've not forgotten but memories are fading.
I've taught them well,
Taught them to be strong, to fight back, to overcome.

I've not overcome, but I've survived
I've not lived, but I've survived
I've not succumbed, but I've survived
I've survived, I've survived!

Dolores Gabriel

156

DOLORES GABRIEL

I am currently employed with the Halifax District School Board, as an elementary school teacher. As well, I am doing part-time studies at Mount Saint Vincent University towards my Master's in Education. I have always loved working with children and am the proud mother of one, my son Obadiah. The experiences that I have chosen to write about reflect my feelings about life for Black women in Canada, specifically in Nova Scotia. They also reflect my love and admiration for women all over the world, who have to struggle every day to ensure the survival of their families and loved ones. My hope is that my writing will give women the strength and courage they need to go on fighting, yet one more day.

BERYL TSANG

Celebrating Chinese New Year for the First Time

Dear Mother:

It is Chinese New Year and for the first time since leaving home, I am celebrating this holiday. For once I am happy that I spent all those Saturdays shopping in Chinatown learning the traditions that went into preparing for special occasions like today. I have cleaned my home meticulously, careful not to sweep near doors so that I would not "sweep my luck out the door". Red paper bunting hangs from my door and window frames. Incense and offerings to the Gods sit on my mantle and in my kitchen is a ten-course vegetarian meal which I will share with my friends.

As I sit here waiting for them to arrive, I cannot help but feel your presence all around me, gently haunting me, making sure I carry out all the proper rituals the right way. I wish so much that you were here. I have so much to say to you. Since I have no other way of speaking to you, all I can do is write down my thoughts and feelings. I hope that you will forgive that the letter is in English. When I "sweep" your grave in the spring during Ching Ming, I will pray the smoke which contains its essence will travel to the world where you now live and let you know in Chinese that I have not forgotten you or all that you have taught me about being Chinese.

Just before you passed away you told me a story about a woman and a rice bowl. She lived in China and was unable to keep her bowl filled with rice so she took it across the ocean, over one thousand li away, to a place called Gold Mountain. There, she hoped to fill her bowl not only with rice but also with gold she hoped to find. When the woman reached Salt Water City, on the edge of Gold Mountain, she found that the stress of her journey had caused her bowl to break. Since it was the only one that she had, she painstakingly tried to put it back together. The elements, however, conspired against her and caused the pieces to warp before she could reassemble them. She reconstructed the bowl but it was not the same. It was still the same shape. It would still hold rice but it would not hold the small pieces of gold she worked so hard to save. When she tried to put them there, the bowl would crack. It was as if its essence as a receptacle was gone, replaced by something new which she could not comprehend.

After you finished the story I remember exclaiming in English, "What a stupid story. It doesn't mean anything." You explained in Chinese that the story had a deeper meaning and if I had only listened to it with my heart, and not just with my ears, I would have been able to make sense of the woman and her rice bowl. The rice, you said softly, embodied that which kept our physical beings alive. The gold, on the other hand, represented those things which made our lives meaningful. The woman, you told me, did not merely see her rice bowl as a something which held her daily meals but as a vessel which held promises for the future. "Some day, little Pui-yee", you whispered, "you will better understand this story."

I realize now that the story you told me was not actually about a woman and her rice bowl but about a mother and her daughter. In her daughter the mother saw all the wonderful things that could be. The daughter, living in a new place with new rules, started separating herself from her mother and her mother's values. The mother tried to make her daughter Chinese. The daughter, though, resisted, remaining Chinese only on the outside. The more her mother tried to instil in her the Chinese rituals and practices that she felt were important, the more the daughter pulled away. While the daughter accepted her mother's home and food, she disassociated herself from her mother's ideas and beliefs. Her identity was Canadian; her mother, though, did not know what this was.

Was this story meant to be about you and me? I cannot help but think that it was. I remember sitting on your lap when I was three or four and having you tell me that no matter what I did, I must always understand my roots. I must remember that I came from people who laboured with their hands, who endured poverty and hunger and who, through study and perseverance, became officials to the Ch'ing government. As a girl living in a male society, you explained, I would have to endure many trials. As a Chinese in a white world, I would constantly be questioned. People would always say I was not good enough; so I would have to try harder than everyone else. Participating in Ching Ming, where I swept the grave of dead family members, going to Chinatown on Saturday where I met other Chinese children, and celebrating Chinese New Year where I gave thanks, you patiently explained to me, would give me my identity. And identity, you believed, would give me my strength.

Of course I did not listen to you. What did you know? You could not even speak English very well! You had no idea how the society outside of Vancouver's Chinese community functioned. You could not, I thought, teach me how to live in this new world because you had no understanding of it yourself.

So I grew up apart from you, denying that I was Chinese, having only "white friends", speaking only English, trying hard to adhere to the white, Anglo-Saxon, Protestant values of our upper Westside neighbourhood. When others called me a Chink, I honestly did not believe that they did so because I had yellow skin and slanted eyes but because I did not somehow "behave" in a Canadian manner. To be even more Canadian, I made a point of laughing at the broken English of the Chinese grocer whose store I bought candy from at recess; I sang the "Maple Leaf Forever" a little louder in class; and I started watching "Hockey Night In Canada" every Saturday at 5 o'clock. How angry you used to get at me when I insisted we leave Chinatown and all of your friends so that I could go home and watch hockey!

In spite of my efforts, I always found myself being confronted with negative images of Chinese people. Do you remember when I came home crying in grade three because my teacher had been mean to me? You reprimanded me. You said that teachers were never mean and that if they were it was because the student deserved it. You thought that teachers should be respected. I never told you why I was upset, but I was upset because she read us *The Five Chinese Brothers* and all the children laughed at how stupid they were. The story hurt me and when I told her so, she ridiculed me.

Without even realizing it, I spent the rest of my childhood and teenage years rejecting all of those negative images of Chinese people. I didn't want to be associated with Chop Suey Houses, the dirt and squalor of Chinatown, or the loud banging of mah-jong tiles. At the same time I did not want to be like the "middle class" Chinese kids I knew in high school. The kind who did what they were told, valued education above all else, got honours at school, and became M.D.s, C.A.s, or L.L.B.s. Although you never said so, I know that this was the kind of person you wanted me to be. Professional. Respectable.

You died before I went to high school. If you had been alive, I think you would have been disappointed with me. There I fell in love with abstract art, Canadian history, English literature, and Victorian theatre. My grades suffered as I pursued these interests. I had no idea what I wanted to do with my life when I went to university and I really did not care. It was there, however, that I found out who I was and realized what I wanted to be. This process began on my very first day of classes. A Chinese man, about my age, looking rather "nerdy", and wearing shabby clothes, asked me if I would like to join the Chinese Canadian Students' Association. Its goal was to promote recognition of the academic, community, and professional achievements of Chinese-Canadians on campus. I was insulted. The very idea that a group like this should be allowed to exist was offensive to me. It merely served, I rationalized, to further segregate Canadian society which, I thought, already had a tenuous sense of self.

I dismissed the whole episode but, as my education progressed, I became more and more aware that I was being treated differently and that there was no reason why I should have been. Fellow students told racist jokes that did not seem like jokes at all but real beliefs. Campus theatre groups would not let me audition for roles in their plays, stating that it was too unbelievable to have a Chinese in a Shakespearean or any other "Western" production. Professors often disregarded my opinions. When this happened, I assumed that it was because my points were invalid, irrelevant. Yet I noticed that when other students raised the same questions, they were listened to.

These things remained lost inside me until one day in my last year when I discovered I was a victim of discrimination, in particular racism, maybe even sexism. Then I was enraged. The force of that realization was so strong that my next reaction was denial; discrimination could not exist in Canada! If it did, Black people, like Lincoln Alexander, could not become Lieutenant Governors of provinces; Japanese people, like Dr. David Suzuki, could not become television personalities; Native Canadians, like Bill Reid, could not have whole galleries and exhibitions devoted to their art!

At the same time that I came to this revelation, I was taking a course on Canadian history. Part of the course involved looking at the history of ethnic groups and racial discrimination in Canada. This course showed me that Canada, the country I was so proud of being a citizen of, was inherently racist. Did you know that the Chinese were prohibited from practising law, medicine, dentistry, and pharmacy until 1947? Segregated schools existed until the late 1960s and even now people educated outside of Canada cannot practise their professions here.

If you were here when I made these discoveries, what would you have done? Would you have told me to suppress it; rise above it; not make "waves"; ignore it and focus on my own achievements; fight? I wish I knew. Maybe then it would not have been so overwhelming for me. Looking back on the incident and at our relationship, it all seems so ironic. I spent so many years closing my ears to what you had to say. Then when I needed your words of wisdom, it was too late.

You would be proud of me if you were still alive. I got an education (Bachelor of Arts Honours with a specialization in History, Master of Arts in progress). It may not have been the kind of education you had in mind, but I acquired the knowledge necessary for living life with love and compassion. I am a professional. I am not the Doctor, or Accountant, or Lawyer you wanted me to be. Instead, I am an anti-racist educator. I teach people of different races that they can live together without conflict and they respect me for it. I am an active member of the Chinese community. It may not be the community of Chinese shops, restaurants, and mah-jong clubs that you were a part of, but it is a community of men and women committed to finding a place for the Chinese in Canada. Most of all I remember the past. It may not be our family's past. It is the Chinese-Canadian past — the past of railway workers, laundrymen, and Chinatowns — but it gives me an identity and that identity gives me strength.

My guests are arriving, and it is time to serve dinner. Please know, Mother, that I am glad that you brought me to Canada. While I would not take the gold that you worked so hard to save for me, I found my own gold.

I love you,
Your daughter
Pui Yee Tsang

BERYL TSANG

I was born in Hong Kong but grew up in Vancouver. I hold a Master's degree in Modern East Asian History and work as a community organizer, race relations consultant, and writer in Toronto. When not working, I am active on the boards of several equity-seeking groups including the Chinese Canadian National Council. My current work in progress is my son Kirir Alexander Tsang with whom I explore the "meaning of life".

162

ROSEMARY ENG

To Future Young Journalists of Colour in Canada

Dear Future Young Journalists of Colour:

You are on the brink of entering one of the most fashionable professions today. From television newsroom shows like *Murphy Brown* and the celebrity status gained by Woodward and Bernstein when they exposed Watergate, journalism has become regarded as a glamorous line of work. I hope you won't get sidetracked by that. As journalists of colour you have different responsibilities. Though Canadians don't like to think of themselves as such, they are far more steeped in colonial tradition than their neighbours in the United States, where I am from. Mainstream journalists here may choose to be concerned about issues regarding people of colour, but my perception is that people belonging to communities of colour rarely get the chance to interpret their own issues as part of the mainstream journalism process. Your road is going to be different from your white counterparts who are reporting about their culture for people of their own culture. You will be working with people who may know nothing of your heritage and who may not care, either. I hope you realize you will have to set your standards differently. Your successes will have to be in a different context. When your reporting of events from your perspective as an Asian, African, Hispanic, Aboriginal person can be accepted as a legitimate "Canadian" view, you'll have accomplished much.

As one of the first Chinese-American women in journalism, I see the road ahead of you as far tougher than mine was. Back in the '40s, I was inspired to go into journalism by Brenda Starr, a glitzy redhead metropolitan daily reporter, whose life was reported in brilliant colour in the *Chicago Tribune* Sunday comics. I was enthralled with the idea that a woman could have such an exciting job. In junior high school, in a "news writing" class in Cincinnati, Ohio, I was assigned a book report on Marguerite Higgins, one of the first U.S. women to become an overseas correspondent. Her

real life was as exciting as Brenda Starr's paper one, and I was hooked.
I applied to Syracuse University (in New York state) which has a school
of journalism more than fifty years old and was accepted. My parents'
friends would ask what I was studying to become. When I said,
"newspaper reporter", they would all reply, "I never heard of a Chinese
going into that."

It was easier back then to become a journalist because the job wasn't so
hung up on image. People I worked with in newsrooms in Massachusetts,
New York State, and California were gutsy, unpretentious, low-paid,
and oftentimes without university degrees. But they shared a sense of
decency and made their contributions to open information, honest
government, open-mindedness, and equality. When I won awards,
including one for a series in California on how controversial proposed
legislation to establish no-fault divorce could be more humane in part
because children would no longer have to testify against their own parents
in the old process of establishing fault, the old-timers in the newsroom
were nothing but congratulatory. We shared the same idealism. Starting
work for newspapers in the early-to-mid '60s, being Chinese was neither
a positive nor a negative factor in being hired. I must admit, that being a
woman was a problem when tough assignments were more routinely
handed out to men.

I think you will have a much harder time than I had because I have found
white Canadians tolerate differences much more poorly than Americans.
My experience is that many white Canadians still think this country's
strongest cultural link is European. When I came to Canada more than
fourteen years ago (a conciliatory gesture to a white-Commonwealth-
citizen husband who was raised with monarchy, tea, and "civilized
people"), the experience was a shock. Doughty old women in clipped
accents complained loudly about how Canada was letting in the wrong
kind of people after I stepped aboard the bus.

At a pre-school multicultural foods event, teachers rushed to apologize
before my son could tell me about one child who made a scene screaming:
"I hate Chinese food and I hate Chinese people." (No wonder her mother
wasn't very friendly.) Wives of friends of my husband, who is now my ex-
husband, hoped that their spouses could be transferred to Asia or Africa
so they could have cheap servants. At a mom-and-tots afternoon in a
church near the Squamish Indian Band reserve in North Vancouver, one
mother was outraged that native children dared to trick-or-treat in the
neighbourhood. Last year at a junior secondary school parents' meeting,
I commented that a video portraying ruthless Vancouver-based Asian
gangs would do more harm than good in a school where there were few
minorities and little general knowledge about minority people. I told how
my son had to tolerate being called "chinky chinaman" and "Chinese pig"

through various grades of elementary school. One mother's reply was: "You immigrants have to expect to be called names." No one in the room disagreed. If this has happened to me after my family has been in North America for more than three generations, you've got a **long** way to go here.

One event that made a major difference in my life was covering a national meeting of the Congress of Black Women of Canada held in Vancouver. I was working as a correspondent for a Toronto newspaper. The women were angry. They were sick of bottom-level jobs. They were fed up with how they were represented in the media. They had had it with taking the emotional brunt of the frustration felt by their men in this society. Native women and Asian women there also identified with what was said. I realized then that what I thought was happening to me was happening to "us". It turned out the Toronto paper never ran my story and the event was not covered by any Vancouver print media either.

I know so many factors — space, time, other important events — can bump stories from running. But because these women so wanted their issues to be understood, I felt a special regret the story did not run and put their concerns before the public. I phoned Congress member and former MLA Rosemary Brown to apologize that the story didn't run. Her reply was simply, "quit blaming yourself". To me, the thought was revolutionary. When the old women complained on the bus, when the pre-schooler hated Chinese, when shopkeepers made it clear I should buy quickly or get out, I was sure I must have contributed to making those things happen. I was blaming myself for Canada's racism. I realized, in sitting through the Congress sessions, that many issues of those women were mine as well. When issues of people of colour are kept silent, what is heard is white-dominated media which continually touts Canadian tolerance. I hope for you that some Canadian publication someday might run something like Rose Del Castillo Guilbault's excellent weekly column, "Hispanic, USA", in the *San Francisco Chronicle* in which she writes about everyday Hispanic life as an integral part of American life. I'd love to read a column with similar insights about the Indo-Canadian, Asian-Canadian, or Caribbean-Canadian communities.

If you want your people to have first-hand and fair media representation — not white interpretation — you must take every route that's open to you to make a statement. The opportunities won't come very often and you'll have to take the initiative. I proposed to the *San Diego Tribune* years ago a series on the history of the Chinese in San Diego. They went for it, a four-part series complete with photos showing that the Chinese had one of the first coastal California fishing fleets (which they were forced to cease operating). If your people have been overlooked, try bringing them into media coverage.

In a piece I wrote for the *Toronto Star* on Canada's first Chinese woman labour organizer, I and a union worker were able to pose as seamstress applicants in Vancouver and get a first-hand look at the abysmal conditions immigrant women have worked and still work in. Take advantage of your ethnicity.

In Vancouver, there's an ambivalent attitude toward minority participation in the media which tends to be managed by white, first-generation male immigrants from the British Commonwealth, many with the colonialist outlook intact. I don't understand why they are less regarded as immigrants than we are. In the latter part of the 1980s, I had been told my "stringer" position was being terminated at the *Vancouver Sun.* The paper wanted the hours absorbed by a new staffer downtown. What was insulting was that this happened at the same time a *Sun* article appeared saying too few trained minority reporters were available for hire. I pointed out the juxtaposition of these events in a letter to then-*Sun* editor Nick Hills, and sent clippings of stories I had written about minority issues for the *Globe and Mail* and *Toronto Star*. "It's to the credit of these newspapers that they have taken interest in the Vancouver Chinese and did so before the Asian immigrant influx became so controversial...", I wrote.

Whites at the time were getting panicky about the numbers of new Asian immigrants in Vancouver. Several *Sun* articles on the subject heightened anti-Asian feelings and so angered members of the local Chinese community that they were threatening to cancel their subscriptions. Newspaper management seemed puzzled about the bad relations.

I mentioned to Hill: "I recall once phoning in my North Shore coverage schedule and asking to speak to your Chinese staffer, Wyng Chow, who was working the city desk at the time." My letter continued: "Someone called out his name using a mocking sing-song intonation. It was extremely offensive. If you want to bridge the gap between your newsroom and the Chinese community, I'd suggest a big first step is stop making fun of minorities in your newsroom...."

After ten years working for the *Sun* covering the three suburban municipalities on Vancouver's "North Shore", hundreds of news calls to the city desk, hours on the phone transmitting stories to copy takers, and piles of stories I had written for that paper, with no incidents or errors, I received a reply from Mr. Hills saying: "I have talked to then-managing editor, Gordon Fisher, and he says he has no knowledge of your presenting yourself as a reporter schooled in the Chinese community."

How many reporters covering minority issues **are** "schooled" about the issues? This is what you're up against. Don't get sidetracked by the glamour of yuppie journalistic stardom. You must keep fighting for us.

ROSEMARY ENG

I was born in Chicago, Illinois, where my paternal grandfather ran a Chinese goods store in Chicago's original Chinatown. My maternal grandfather operated a laundry in Staten Island, New York. A graduate of Syracuse University in New York, I have lived in Canada for seventeen years. I am now a staff writer for *Business in Vancouver*, a weekly newspaper. I am concerned about society providing part-time, flex-time work for primary caretakers of children and about the voices of minority people being heard through mainstream media, the two issues being intertwined for women of colour.

SUNERA THOBANI

Fighting Sex Selection Technology

Dear Sister:

I am writing to tell you of some disturbing events occurring here in Vancouver. A doctor based in California has started advertising sex selection technology in the South Asian community in British Columbia. He is promoting the use of ultrasound to determine the sex of the foetus as early as twelve weeks into the pregnancy, and quite shamelessly acknowledges that the results of this test are used to abort female foetuses. I am sure, dear sister, you will understand the shock and outrage some of us felt at seeing this kind of practice being promoted through our community media. As we have often spoken of the complexity of the issues of sexism and racism in the past, I felt I must write and tell you how I feel in light of this particular experience.

Needless to say, my first feeling was one of anger. How dare this kind of thing be advertised! This was instantly followed by the feeling of betrayal in the knowledge that the community media had agreed to run this advertisement. For those of us living so far away from our lands of origin, the sense of community has come to acquire even more significance than perhaps it did when we were growing up in the lands of our birth. As you also know, in the West the community has often been a source of strength and support. In a hostile environment where racism is on the rise again, we are feeling the need for the unified forces of the community to act together in facing and challenging this racism. And the community media have had a central role in providing a means of communication, in providing information and promoting the services that are available for us within our own community.

This is a place where we will not instantly become labelled as "alien". It has amazed me how many community-owned businesses and organizations exist, these being the ones that many of us go to. Even at the basic level of shopping, it is wonderful to see familiar faces. It is so different from going shopping at the local Safeway; the counter clerks are always so rude and make one feel insignificant all the time. They look down upon us. Going there to shop always ruins my day. It takes me hours to ease that tight knot of anger that forms in my gut. It is also convenient to be able to shop for all the things that we need, whether clothes or groceries, in one vicinity. The market on Main Street has become second home, a place where we don't stand out as "aliens", a place where we are not shunned and humiliated on the basis of our colour. The community newspapers have played an important role in advertising these businesses, in creating this sense of belonging. So you understand why the shock was greater and the sense of betrayal so deep when these communication vehicles are used for the furthering of the devaluation of women.

Of course, I know that the community media are also a means of social control of the community. We have argued about that often enough in the past. Whoever controls the media determines what goes in for publication and so sets the agenda. I have forgotten the number of times this paper has been approached in the past to carry news and announcements of such important issues as Bill C-43[*] and other issues relevant to women, but to no avail. I need not point out to you that the community newspapers are male dominated, as is the general political life within the community. Anyway, although I knew the limitations of what we can expect from the community media, the sense of betrayal was there, nonetheless. But that did not stop me. Of course, a letter was immediately written to the editor of that particular paper, protesting the advertisement.

For a long time afterwards, I could not get over my gut reaction, that of anger. In fact, I still have not got over it. Most studies of the subject show that in the overwhelming number of cases, it is the female foetus that is aborted. In reality, it is male selection that we are talking about, not sex selection, which implies that both sexes are selected. The use of this technology is sexist and results in the perpetuation of male supremacy. This use of male selection carries to the extreme the devaluation of women in our world today, with this devaluation acquiring scientific and medical legitimation. We women are deemed to be so worthless as to not even merit being allowed to be given birth to.

In deciding to raise my voice against this practice, I have had to deal with various issues. The first of these is the issue of racism. Many hours have I spent arguing with people, both from within and outside the community, as to how this is racist. The general reaction I get is that yes, there is no

---

[*] At the time of writing, Bill C-43 was the proposed abortion law that would restrict abortion in Canada to cases where a woman's health was endangered by the pregnancy. In other instances, abortion would be criminalized; both the women undergoing the abortion, and the doctor performing the procedure, would be open to prosecution.

question that this is sexist. But it is not racist. The argument that is offered is that given the experience in India, where female foetuses are aborted at horrendous rates after determination of sex, this doctor only acted upon that information and so targeted the Indo-Canadian population. It is a fact, they state again and again, that this practice occurs in alarming numbers in India. Painful as the knowledge is, of course we know of the use of this practice in India. But what this doctor has claimed, and the way the whole matter is being presented in the media, is that this practice is rooted in our culture, that this preference for males is an inherent part of our culture. I can almost see the sign of exasperation you must be making at this point. We have been through this one before!

As you know, every ill that befalls us has been blamed on our "culture" in one way or another. As women of colour living in the West, we have been told that our society is a backward, traditional society and that is the main reason why women in our communities are oppressed. Since colonial times, we have been told that patriarchal attitudes and oppressions are inherent in our culture, and that machismo is very much a Third World phenomenon. Of course, I would not deny that our culture is patriarchal, but this singling out of cultures of people of colour as inherently backward and oppressive is what is racist. Culture is a changing, dynamic process. If women are devalued in our culture, then we also have a strong tradition of resistance to this devaluation of women in our communities. Why are the most reactionary and oppressive elements being promoted and legitimated in the name of culture? Why not the revolutionary and progressive elements? And what is more, our community is not a monolith with every one of us having the same attitudes and practices. If there are people who support this kind of practice, then there are many others who are opposed to it.

What this doctor has done is to re-create that racist stereotype of our community, the legacy we have inherited from our colonizers. In many Third World countries this practice is used as a form of population control. It has been argued by many that the world's poverty is to be blamed upon over-population, and that the Third World peoples breed excessively, thereby increasing the pressures on the limited resources of our planet. After all, scarce resources and endless wants are a fact of life, it is explained to us. These kinds of myths have been around for so long that even many of us have internalized them.

There is much lip service being given to the "preservation of our culture", even as the most reactionary practices are being enforced onto us in the very name of this "culture". What there is little of is the exposure of the designs of the imperialist masters who benefit, and their racist myths that population explosion in the Third World is to be blamed for the growing poverty and injustice in the world. Why is it not being exposed that it is their control over the world's resources and the distribution of these resources that are at the core of the growing poverty, not population growth? We should be asking who is benefiting from these reproductive technologies, who is making the money. And who is defining what is "culture".

But let us go back to the doctor. Once the story hit the mainstream media, the Indo-Canadian population became the focus of much attention. Inside the community, there was a general reluctance to talk about this issue. And I must admit, I felt some of this reluctance too. I have already mentioned the rising tide of racism in this country. Although Canada prides itself in being a multi-racial and multi-cultural society, people of colour know only too well the hostility and racism we have to live with every day. The events of Oka in the summer must still be alive in your mind. After this summer, there was no doubt in the minds of First Nations peoples and people of colour that things were going to get much worse before they got any better.

The looming recession will serve to compound this rising tide of racism. In light of that, there was much concern about what kind of use will be made of this event, particularly as it has been portrayed, i.e., that sex selection is inherent to the Indian culture. Will this become yet another stick to beat the whole community with? Of course almost everybody I spoke to agreed with the need for an honest dialogue within the community about this, but to have it out in the mainstream media might prove to be detrimental to the whole community. It would work to increase hostility from the mainstream society with the racist myth of our cultural backwardness being given yet another shot of life by this event. However, with the mainstream media carrying the story, this debate was taken out of our hands.

The most disturbing element of this whole affair has been how the issue continues to be portrayed as one of relevance only for Indo-Canadian women. Sex selection continues to be viewed as an isolated phenomenon. Needless to tell you, this event has forced me to do my homework on reproductive technologies, sex selection is just one such technology. It is only within the context of the totality of reproductive technologies that we can fully understand the impact of sex selection. Reproductive technologies target all women, and we know that one of the cornerstones of patriarchal power lies in the control of women's sexuality and reproductive abilities. So while all women are targeted by this technology, we see that specific kinds of technologies are being earmarked for specific groups of women. White, middle-class women are being targeted with technologies such as in vitro fertilization and surrogacy, even as Indo-Canadian women are being targeted with sex selection technology. The Anna Johnson case in California has shown how women of colour can now be hired by affluent couples as "surrogate mothers" to carry embryos that are not genetically linked to them. Women of colour can now be used as breeders for infertile white women.

Reproductive technologies thus reflect, and also re-create, the divisions of race and class that exist within our world today, and which also, of course, exist among women. We see that more money is being put into research and technologies that benefit a small number of affluent women, i.e., those who can afford such technologies as in vitro fertilization, while the basic health needs of poor women are being ignored and remain unfunded. And as women of colour are disproportionately represented among the poor, the potential for our exploitation by the use of these technologies is immense. Here in the West we see that the priority of these technologies is to increase the reproductive abilities of white women, while Third World women face forced sterilization measures and myths of population explosion. Such is the world we live in today and we are expected to believe that all this is the result of our "cultural attitudes".

Lest I leave you with the impression that only the Indo-Canadian community has a preference for males, consider the following:

- The Vanier Institute of the Family based in Ottawa stated that Caucasians in North America prefer that their first-born child be a male child.*

- In a study carried out in 1954 of American college students, the results showed that 66% of the women and 92% of the men wanted an only child to be a male child, with 4% of the men and 6% of the women wanting a female child. When the study was carried out again twenty years later, the results were found to be similar.**

- The State of Pennsylvania has outlawed the use of abortion for sex selection in a Bill which went into effect in January 1990.***

- In Denmark, a woman demanded an abortion upon finding out that the foetus she was carrying was a female one. As abortion is available on demand for eighteen weeks, doctors cannot disclose the sex of the foetus until after eighteen weeks.****

---

* Editorial, *Vancouver Sun*, September 20, 1990.

** Gena Corea, *The Mother Machine: Reproductive Technologies from Artificial Insemination to Artificial Wombs* (New York: Harper & Row, 1985), pp. 190-191.

*** Ellen Goodman, "Sex Selection by Abortion Repugnant", *Vancouver Sun,* January 5, 1990.

**** Quebec, Conseil du statut de la femme, *Dilemmas: When Technology Transforms Motherhood* (Quebec: 1987), p. 5.

- When the first "made to order" male child was born in England, a doctor claimed in a newspaper that his clinic had been "swamped" with similar demands.[*]

Of course, the fact that women are more than 50% of the world's population and work two-third's of the world's work hours while earning only one-fifth of the world's income and owning only 1% of the world's property,[**] illustrates better than anything else could the "preference" for males in our world today. While I do not want to make light of the fact that our community is patriarchal, that is also true of all communities in Canadian society. I recognize the exploitation of women by the men in our communities, and the violence that is done to our humanity by them. But we need to understand that exploitation and struggle against it within the context of the totality of patriarchal relations in the world, and also recognize how this patriarchy is re-created in our everyday lives. The capitalist state is a patriarchal and racist state, and we are learning that both racism and patriarchy are an integral part of this system of relations. It is only within this context that we will recognize the manipulation of our "culture" and be able to re-claim it in the struggle to end our exploitation.

In closing, I will address the issue of "choice" and "preference" that often tends to dominate any discussion on this matter. Surely women should have the right to "choose", we are told, and surely all sex selection does is reflect the "preference" that prospective parents have?

Sex selection results in the aborting of female foetuses in the overwhelming number of cases that have been studied. Therefore, it is not a "preference" that we are talking about here, but the systematic elimination of the beginnings of female life on the basis of gender. How can this be anything but a reflection of the devaluation of women in our world today? As women, we are defined as worthless creatures throughout our lives, incapable of being rational or objective. The only purpose for our existence is to become sexual objects for the gratification of men and to become sacrificing mothers to "their" children. Sex selection is racist and patriarchal medical science revealing to us the extent of our devaluation. So once and for all, let us dispense with this notion of "preference".

As for "choice", women are relatively powerless in our world today. Women of colour are even more powerless as a group. So what does "choice" mean for us when our "choices" are limited so monstrously by

---

[*] *Ibid.*, p. 5.

[**] Margot I. Duley and Mary I. Edwards, eds., *The Cross-cultural Study of Women: A Comprehensive Guide* (New York: The Feminist Press, 1986), p. 48.

our exploitation? Are we going to call the little space for manoeuvre that we create in our lives through bitter struggle "choice", accepting for it all the connotations that that word has of the real freedom to choose?

My dearest sister, for me the most painful aspect of all of this has been to face the extent of the internalization of our devaluation as women by ourselves, by the women who have asked for the telephone number of this doctor, the women who claim to be "choosing". What kind of "choice" can it be to abort the foetus they carry on the basis of the sex of that foetus being the same sex as themselves, the female sex? Can anything reveal more than this the extent to which we as women have internalized our own devaluation? I think not.

As a single mother raising my daughter, I know only too well the pressures that we face within our own communities. Do we have any choice but to fight back?

Yours

Sunera

SUNERA THOBANI

I am a researcher/activist whose area of interest is the interaction of race, class, and gender within capitalism. In June 1993, I became the President of the National Action Committee on the Status of Women (NAC). I am also a poet and a single mother.

JAYA CHAUHAN

Involvement as Credential

To: the Coordinator of Women's Studies Program

Re: Contractual Appointment in Women's Studies

I am in receipt of your letter inquiring about my involvement with the women's movement in the United Kingdom, as my curriculum vitae does not reflect a commitment to feminism, a prerequisite for the position. I have been a member of a grassroots group — Black Unity and Freedom Party — since the early '80s. The major aim of this group is to form unity amongst Black people to advance the struggle for the liberation of the oppressed. The group undoubtedly recognizes that the perversity and exploitative nature of male behaviour needs to be confronted and dealt with. Nonetheless, the capitalist state is the real cause of the perversion of humanity, pitting one group against another: women and men, black and white, rich and poor. In the '90s the situation is even more complex since capital is freed of labour, and thus, the creation of communities of resistance is vital. For obvious reasons I do not state my involvement with this group on my curriculum vitae.

My politicization is rooted in my oppressive upbringing. However, I am wary of the feminist concept of the personal as political, especially as regards race and the fight against racism. The "personal is political" personalizes the enemy and reduces the fight against racism to a fight against prejudice, and a fight against institutions and practices to a fight against individuals and attitudes. I am very much in agreement with Sivanandan, Director of the Institute of Race Relations (London), who said that the "personal is political" is concerned with altering the goal posts, whereas the "political is personal" is concerned with the field of play; the "personal is the political" may produce radical individualism whereas the "political is personal" produces a radical society; the "personal is political" entraps one in the self-achieving, self-aggrandizing lifestyle of the rich; the "political is personal" finds value in the communal lifestyle of the poor. Western governments, multi-national corporations, and their agents, the IMF and the World Bank, are responsible for the exploitation of the Third World and its people, the looting of its resources, and ecological devastation. The causes of famine and hunger in the world are made opaque by the agents of the state.

Although my experience in the particular field of Women's Studies is limited, I believe my qualifications to be appropriate for working in this area. I have the additional "advantage" of unavoidably having experienced the racism which runs across the gender-line: too many women scientists (this being my field of expertise for which I am qualified to speak) have lost touch with their oppression on gender grounds because they are "respectable". My awareness of gender oppression is inextricably tied into my experience of oppression as a non-white woman. The link between violence and sexuality is something you live rather than something you theorize about because both are triggered by gender and racial fascism. Canada will not be a new country for me because I undertook my post-doctoral training in Edmonton, and in the final analysis the struggle of the oppressed and exploited has no boundaries since we share a common enemy.

A brief personal history is justified to explain my position. I was born in Kenya in 1955, my parents having emigrated to Kenya from India in the mid-'40s in the heyday of British colonialism. My father often talked of the great benefits British colonialism brought to countries like India and Africa: the railways and the roads. However, the reality is that means of communication were constructed not to facilitate internal trade in local commodities but to make business possible for the timber companies, trading companies, and agricultural firms for the white settlers. Britain was desperately in need of labour as a result of the loss of men in the war.

Initially, my father had come on his own, leaving behind my mother and three sisters. My eldest sister was married in India and she has always lived there. My father returned to India and brought back my mother and two sisters to Kenya. These two sisters of mine were married in Kenya. My older sister and I were born in Kenya. My father was a shoemaker. My mother was a homemaker, and she also undertook sewing for other people to supplement my father's meagre earnings. My oldest sister was married to a motor mechanic and she experienced some complex marital problems with her in-laws. Hence, in 1965, her family left Kenya for England to start a new life for themselves, lured by the relatively better prospects of work and education in England. Once in England, my sister suggested to my parents that they should send my sister (two years my senior) and myself to England to take advantage of the free British education system. In Kenya, my parents could barely afford the school fees and my sister was aware of their financial hardships.

Thus, in July 1967, at the tender age of fourteen and twelve respectively, my sister and I left Kenya to join our older sister and her family in Luton, England. It was the very first time we were separated from our parents and leaving them behind was difficult. We cried all the way on board the plane and, to further exacerbate the situation, we were sick as dogs, only to arrive in England and find no one there to meet us at the airport. There was an error in the flight information my parents had sent, and therefore, we were not expected until the following day. The airport staff very kindly looked after us and several hours elapsed before we were met by my brother-in-law. Since my sister's family did not have a telephone, the airport personnel had to inform Luton police who in turn informed my sister. Luton is some seventy miles from London's Heathrow Airport, and with all the confusion at the airport, my first day in England is somewhat blurred in my mind.

As it turned out, in actual fact, we were separated from our parents for six months only, before they joined us in England. My parents were in the precarious position of being homeless should the Kenyan government decide to prohibit those with British passports to live and work in Kenya. In 1967–68, Idi Amin's regime had barbarically expelled Ugandan Asians who held British passports from Uganda, and in Kenya, Asians felt similarly threatened and insecure. This led to a mass exodus of Asians from Kenya as well as Uganda.

My parents had made tentative plans to travel to India before joining us in England, but that was a big chance to take, as the political situation was very unstable. Britain did not need cheap labour in the late '60s and was afraid of being swamped by the very people whose sweat and toil was responsible for creation of the affluence of the country. My parents had not seen their families in India for some thirty years. The unfortunate course of events that followed was that my grandmother died before my mother was ever able to travel to India. This has always been a deep regret, for our mother talked so fondly of her mother and all the hardships she endured in raising her family. My grandfather died when my mother was very small, and my grandmother raised her children single-handedly. My grandmother has been a great mentor of mine, and despite never having met her, I feel as though I know her. She placed a great value on education and there were times when they had to go hungry, but she ensured that her children went to school.

In the hierarchical caste system, we are fairly low down, and therefore one could wash dishes and sew clothes for those who could afford such services. My mother was taught sewing when she was young. Sexism in education was pervasive at the time, and my uncle was put through school to become a barrister-at-law. My mother did learn to read and write Gujarati, and to this day, at the age of seventy-nine, she is an avid reader.

My father, who only recently died, has to be commended for all the hardships he must have had to endure in leaving India to settle in Kenya and, later, England. In England, he worked as a porter at the airport until his retirement at the age of sixty-five years. When he first went to Kenya, there was poll tax paid according to age and therefore his passport reduced his chronological age by some five to six years. He died at the age of eighty to eighty-one years, but was officially declared seventy-four years. There is no birth certificate to prove his age, but he certainly paid an adequate price for the reduced poll tax paid in Kenya. I would have liked my father to come to Canada to visit me so that he could have experienced another new country, but, sadly, this was not to be. The bittersweet memories of my relationship with my father linger and I miss him sorely. This small piece is written as a tribute to him on behalf of all his five daughters in whose hearts and minds he continues to live.

Returning to myself, at the age of twelve I was put in an alien culture, and had little choice but to utilize available resources as best as possible. Due to British imperialism, English was the main language of my school in Kenya, and this had its obvious advantages when I came over to England. I was hard-working at school and well-liked by the teachers, so that I did not let the ignorant form of racism from my peers hinder my progress. I went on to college armed with ten "0" levels to pursue three "A" levels in the sciences.

The next stage of university was not a natural progression from college which was the case for my peers. In England going to university usually means living away from home. My parents were of the firm belief that a young female, more so than her male counterpart, should be reared under the protective paternal eye. For the female, the parental home is her rightful home and only after her marriage should she leave, when the husband would take on his paternal role. It was an arduous battle to convince my parents that I should take advantage of a university education and that I would not be led astray by the "western" way of living. This was a constant worry to them as their peers judged their parenting abilities on that basis, and in the event that a youth does not abide by the laws of the community, the family faces ostracization. My socialization, therefore, involved the concept of arranged marriages within a caste system, and I knew there was no immunity from this tradition, an integral part of the culture.

I was fortunate at university to have the ardent support of another Indian classmate who had to cope with similar family circumstances. It was during those early years at university when I began to ask questions about my life that I realized there were no easy answers. My consciousness was raised regarding the power relations of dominance and submission which are rendered complex by the interaction of gender and

178

race. I also became aware of my privileged position, and that I owed it not only to myself but to all those other sisters to fight the system, if personal freedom and liberation were to be achieved. I have also been very fortunate in my friends, who have been a great source of inspiration in my struggle to come to terms with my oppressive socialization. The extended family system which is alien to those in the "first world" has much to offer to the individual, and whilst I cannot deny the merits, there is a heavy price to pay for personal freedom. I use "first world" critically, as such terms implicitly reinforce existing economic, cultural, and ideological hierarchies.

I have always made the point of seeking out women's groups in my environment, but unfortunately race and class issues have been a barrier to my active involvement. I initiated a Black women's group when I was in Reading, but sadly, there was no continuity in the group and it disintegrated. Over the last year, I have been a volunteer for Karuna Trust/Aid for India, a charity organization akin to Oxfam, which specifically gives aid to the untouchables in India. In the name of religion, this sector of the Indian population is grossly marginalized. The women's movement can play an important role in ensuring that development agencies from the west do not collude with the Indian state, but offer a genuine alternative for self-determination to these people. We are all subordinate to the same forces of wealth and power which scan the globe in search of profits to be made out of the most basic human needs. The striving for sufficiency and security is the same for people all over the world, and the liberation of all is part of an indivisible process. It is, thus, imperative to unite across the boundaries of race, gender, and geography, if we are to alleviate our common subjection to global economic forces which render us powerless.

I am most impressed that you will be including the Women and Science course in Women's Studies. Scientific objectivity incorporates the dichotomies of "intellect versus emotions" and "self versus other". White, upper/middle class, heterosexual Christian men are largely the creditors of western science with the result that these characteristics are identified with "the self", hence valuable and "normal". All that is not "self" is alien and different, therefore in need of explanation. Women are equated to nature, and both are oppressed. A broad dynamic that labels all that is different from the scientist's "self" as inferior is responsible for the oppression. There are conflicting evaluations of the resources the women's movement can bring to the growth of scientific knowledge. Although science will not be transformed by more women in science, it will create a supportive environment for anti-sexist and anti-racist approaches to science. We are inevitably forced to remake science, but not in conditions of our own choosing.

I trust that you will find the above useful in your assessment of my capabilities to teach the Women and Science course.

The struggle must continue.
In sisterhood,

J. Chauhan

JAYA CHAUHAN

I was a practising Sensory Scientist (working on taste and smell of foods) until 1990 when I began teaching in the Women's Studies program at Memorial University of Newfoundland. In the 1991 school year, I taught full-time at St. Francis Xavier University in the Department of Sociology and Anthropology. These two years of teaching outside of my Ph.D. work marked a major career shift and an important turning point in my life. I have been able to critically reflect on my status in academia and in society. Currently, I am enjoying living with my partner in Edmonton where I hope to find paid work which will reflect my commitment to social change and justice.

MAYANN FRANCIS

Letter to the Virgin Mary

Hail Mary full of grace, the Lord is with thee. Blessed art thou amongst women and blessed is the fruit of thy womb, Jesus. Holy Mary, Mother of God, pray for us sinners now and at the hour of our death.

Now I lay me down to sleep, I pray the Lord my soul to keep. If I should die before I wake, I pray the Lord my soul to take. God Bless my family and friends. Bring peace and love into the world. Thank you. Amen.

Dear Mary:

I pray to you every night and every morning. Tonight, however, I decided to write you a letter. I am tired. My shoulders are heavy. There are times I want to put my head on your bosom and cry myself to sleep. You see Mary, being a woman and Black is not easy. Day after day, I must prove that I am a somebody. I must prove to everyone that I know how to think. When I walk into a store (it could be any store), I need to prove to the sales clerk that I am not there to steal. Never mind that I have an American Express Gold card and an American Express Corporate card. Why would a Black woman enter an expensive store except to steal? Oh Mary, it is difficult. Because there are so many negative experiences in my life, I often wonder why God created me. And why Black!

Last night I had a dream. I dreamt that I died. I found myself in a place which was peaceful and beautiful. The streets were lanes of flowers: red, white, yellow, and black. Could these flowers represent the races of people on earth? Along the lanes were trees blowing in the wind. The sun was a bright orange. I could not see the ocean, but I could hear the waves in the distance. Suddenly, I heard voices, familiar voices. Voices of women and men. Excitement gripped me, for I recognized those voices. Where are you? Please do not hide from me. I missed you. One by one they appeared. There was my Father, Martin Luther King, Harriet Tubman, and Sojourner Truth. With tears streaming down my face, I ran to my father and held him tightly. He asked me how everything was on earth; was there any change? They left a world where there was slavery, racism, sexism, violence against women, and oppression. I told them there was very little change. Slavery no longer exists in the way known to Sojourner and Harriet. Systemic discrimination and institutionalized racism inherent in our social systems replaced slavery of the 1700s.

"Father", I said, "why is life so difficult for me? You really did not prepare me for a world that would hate me because of my sex and my skin colour."

"Daughter, this was not something I would have been able to foresee. Nonetheless, your mother and I did our best to help you realize that you are an important person. We told you to get an education and to be proud of who you are."

"In school, I did not study about Black people. I remember very well the story about Betty and Tom, Flip, Pony, mom, and dad. None of them looked like me. I only remember little Black Sambo. I did not know that Black people were scientists and inventors. I remember little white girls not wanting to hold my hand because they thought my colour was dirty and would rub off on them. Some of them called me 'nigger'. When I was in grade six, I remember a little boy told me that he did not like my girlfriend because she had a black face. I was confused because my face was also black. I ran quickly home thinking that maybe I had turned white. I asked God about this, but I did not get an answer."

"How come you did not tell your mother and me about this?"

"I was afraid. I did not want to talk about it because ... well, it was painful. I thought there was something wrong with me."

Dr. King looked at me and said: "I had a dream that my children would be judged by the content of their character, and not by the colour of their skin. I taught them to be strong men and women. I fought for my people. I hope it was not all in vain."

"Dr. King", I said, "the struggle still goes on. I am very proud of you and what you did for Black people and all humankind. You made a difference in our lives. The Black woman's plight in society is still one of oppression. Even though we have made great strides, we still remain at the bottom of the hierarchical order in white society. First is the white male; second is the white female; third is the Black man and other racial men; and fourth is the Black woman and other women of colour. Society has seen to it that the Black woman is placed on the bottom. This low ranking has not stopped us. The history which was hidden from us tells us that our backs are strong and we will overcome. Harriet, I remember reading what you said a long time ago:

> 'I had reasoned dis out in my mind ... there was one or two things I had a *right* to, liberty, or death; if I could not have one, I would have the other; for no man should take me alive; I should fight for my liberty as long as my strength lasted, and when de time come for me to go, de Lord would let dem take me.'[*]

When the government and companies started to talk about affirmative action for women, I do not think they meant women of colour. We were an afterthought. Initially, the feminist movement did not take me or other women of colour into consideration. Do you think if white women achieve power, they will then treat the women of colour with respect? Do you think they will want to work for us? I often wonder about this because society through institutionalized racism and sexism has discriminated against visible minorities and women. Now that some of these barriers to equal access are breaking down, white women are slowly being allowed into the ranks of white brotherhood. I worry because they (white women) are all part of the same socialization process which gave them privilege, and maybe racist tendencies might be buried in their subconscious. I hope I am wrong."

My father turned to me and took me in his arms. "We must say good-bye", he said. "You are not meant to stay here. Your time has not yet come. I called you here because of your pain. You must return. You cannot give up. Please believe that justice and equality will prevail. Be strong and dry your tears. There will come a time when all of this hatred will be gone. There will come a time when race, colour, and gender will not matter, because love will conquer all. I want you to always remember the teachings of St. Paul.

> Love is patient and kind; love is not jealous, or conceited, or proud; love is not ill-mannered, or selfish, or irritable; love does not keep a record of wrongs; love is not happy with evil, but is happy with the truth. Love never gives up: its faith, hope and patience never fail. (I Cor. 13:4–7.)

---

[*] Quoted in Lerone Bennett, Jr., *Before the Mayflower: A History of the Negro in America 1619-1964*, revised edition (Chicago: Johnson Publishing Company, 1962, Penguin edition 1970), p. 146.

"But father, I do not want to leave, it is so beautiful here … but wait … there is something different … I feel free … I do not feel pain … there is love … why do I feel this way?"

"Do you remember what I just said? There will be a time when race and gender will not matter and love will conquer."

"But father, you did not answer my question."

He smiled at me and said: "Yes, I did."

When I opened my eyes, I felt as though a weight was lifted from my shoulders. My father gave me the strength to face tomorrow. If I do not have the courage to move ahead, then nothing will be accomplished. Tonight I will go to sleep with a smile, for tomorrow I will have renewed strength. Thanks Mary, for always listening.

Love,

Ann

P.S.

*Hail Mary full of grace, the Lord is with **me**, blessed art thou amongst women and blessed is the fruit of thy womb, Jesus. Holy Mary, Mother of God, pray for us sinners now and at the hour of our death. Amen*

MAYANN FRANCIS

I am currently employed as the Employment Equity Officer at Dalhousie University, Halifax, Nova Scotia. Born in Sydney, Nova Scotia, to Caribbean parents who immigrated to the United States but subsequently settled in Canada, I received my early education in Sydney. I then lived in the United States for sixteen years before returning to Halifax in 1990. After having experienced racism and discrimination in both the United States and Canada, I believe racism in Canada is subtle, pervasive, and therefore a greater threat to one's personal dignity and self-worth. Both countries, however, leave a lot to be desired when it comes to women and people of colour. While living in the United States, I obtained my Masters in Public Administration from New York University, with concentration in labour and personnel administration. I also hold certificates in Paralegal Studies and in Equal Employment Opportunity Studies. Prior to my return to Halifax, I worked as Administrative Manager in the Human Resource Department of the Brooklyn District Attorney's Office. While in New York I also worked as a corporate paralegal both on Wall Street and in the Rockefeller Centre area.

Minnie Aodla Freeman

Dear Leaders of the World

Dear Leaders of the World:

First, let me tell you a little about myself. My name is
Mini, which means gentle rain in my language.[1] I was born
in James Bay, Northwest Territories on an island called Cape
Hope. I was born in a log house that my grandparents built
in the late 1800s at our winter and summer place. Because
my mother died at the very early age of twenty-one, during
a German measles epidemic, my grandparents brought me
up. I grew up with very traditional Inuit values and was
taught what is right and wrong very harshly, which I do not
regret today. It tells me that my grandparents loved me a lot.

I began to grow with all the traditional equipment of my
grandparents. Those equipments, whether physical, mental,
or psychological, are still with me today. I use them a
great deal in dealing with my daily life. Then one day our
Canadian government decided to put all the Canadian
native children into residential schools. It was their way of
planning to turn us into another type of people, which they
failed because no one can ever be what they are not. Yes,
they can adapt to each other but not become one and the
same. In those residential schools I learned to write, read,
and multiply, and live by the clock.

Then the government decided that I would make a good
nurse, so again they decided to kidnap me, and send me
away. This time to further south where I had to live in a
residential nursing school. It took three years. In those three
years I learned more about human suffering than how to
apply gauze to a wound. At that time no one ever sat down
with me seriously and asked me what I would like to do.
I was made to fumble along in the qallunaat[2] world.

---

1 Editor's note: The RCMP anglicized Ms. Freeman's first name.
   Minnie is her legal name.
2 Editor's note: qallunaat means "white people".

I was very young. I would take all the suffering that I was going through. In fact I took it all as a learning process and I learned about people. I love people; I love watching people and, especially, talking with young people. People fascinate me a great deal. What are they saying? What are they doing? What makes them tick or even tock?

Then I fell in love. Fell? That was the funniest thing I have ever done in the qallunaat world. I came from a society that pre-arranges marriages even before the birth of the child. I was one of those. But I fell. The biggest fall I have ever had. I have no regrets either way as my grandmother dissolved the pre-arranged marriage, believing that I would starve to death because he was not a very good hunter. It seems my grandmother unknowingly put me from one frying pan to another. I ended up marrying a very poor scientist. I still have no regrets. I have three beautiful children, two boys and one girl. I have two loveable grandchildren and another one on the way.

Twenty years ago I finally found what I would really like to do. This was after I brought up my three children. First, I founded Inuit Broadcasting Corporation and I made sure it serves seven communities in the Northwest Territories. There are thirty-five small communities throughout the NWT and I made sure all eventually should be serviced with broadcasting. I am also a writer; I have written a book and a play,[3] lots of children's stories, and poems. I travel both nationally and internationally to be an advisor on Inuit culture. My fumblings in the qallunaat world taught me a great deal. It proved that one culture can survive in another. I will always value my culture. It makes me know who I am and it is my very foundation as a human being.

I have asked a few people if it would make any difference to write to the world leaders concerning peace in the world. All the people I asked are those whom I respect and consider their knowledge very valuable. But I was very discouraged by their answers. Some were cynical, some not trusting, and others believe that any leaders of any country are there for their own personal gain. Maybe it does happen to some leaders, at least to the weak ones, or to the ones that do not really care for their own country. Believing that not all leaders are alike, I decided to write. After all, I came from grandparents who were leaders of our community for over sixty years. They taught me that you have to care, no matter how rich the people or how poor the people, and care about all your surroundings, whether it be the environment or the many animals on the land. On the land,

---

3 Editor's note: Minnie Aodla Freeman is the author of *Life Among the Qallunaat.* (Edmonton: Hurtig Publishers, 1978), and a play, *Survival in the South,* published in *Paper Stays Put: A Collection of Inuit Writing*, ed. Robin Gedalof (Edmonton: Hurtig Publishers, 1980).

everything is inter-connected. As you all know, we the people live in one world, one globe. We also know that we have come a long way to survive in it beautifully. As people, we have achieved victory over the deadly diseases by hard work of research and careful testings. Each time when a new deadly illness comes along we grow up further and educate ourselves more to find a cure for it. Today we are walking on the moon and we will walk any distance to find the answer to whatever we want to know.

But we have only one world and it badly needs good care from everybody. We cannot undo all the uneducated harms that we have done to our world. We should learn something out of each wrong that we have done to the world and especially to each other. We should no longer pollute the grounds or waters. We should start thinking that our grandmother, mother, or whoever puts our food on the table may be the real providers. I know a lot of cultures think that the breadwinners, the ones that go to work, pay for the food; forget the dollars and cents for now. In the end the earth and the waters are our main bread.

Education from our past mistakes has shown us that nature takes its own time. If forced, it will do something else. The world is no longer huge like we used to think. It began getting smaller when we first started flying, and even smaller when we invented the television. It got still smaller when we orbited the Anik 1 and 2. Any native of his own country will tell you that all the rivers, streams, and lakes are inter-connected to the seas. If you pollute in Spain or England, you pollute in Canada or in Ecuador. Not only do we discriminate against our own environment and treat it very badly, we also discriminate against each other very badly. We do not sit with each other long enough to understand each other. We do not educate each other enough to understand each other's cultures. We care for only what matters to us. We do not want to care what grows in Mexico, yet we eat it in Canada and vice versa, all over the world.

At the present time, we need peace in the world very badly. We have enough natural wars that we have to fight every day in our daily lives. We do not need wars with weapons, hand grenades, explosives, or missiles. These cause world-wide exterminations or executions of human beings. They are similar to what happened to Jewish people during the second world war. We have enough wars on our hands to deal with. We fight every day with diseases. We fight every day with car accidents. We fight every day with abuse within families. We fight every day with new illnesses, and we fight every day for the safety of the world environment. The wars bring all the above-mentioned illnesses. If we could just look at the most recent war in the Gulf. The land became torn, the environment became polluted, the people died, the women got abused, and the people engaged in the war discriminated against each other. It is all illness and we need to fight it.

Again, at the present time, we need world peace. You, the leaders of the world, are given that opportunity by us, the people, to lead us into a peaceful world. We have sat long enough and watched other people getting killed in wars, wars that are absolutely unnecessary if two people or different cultures could only meet half way and discuss whatever problems that need to be solved. I know that it sounds a very simplistic dream and I make it sound very easy to solve. I know two brothers who hated each other with all their might, yet they forgave each other and began to share all the family joys that they missed out on over fifty years. They accepted their differences and began respecting each other's choices.

In our own uneducated ways we have tried to divide up the world. We have tried to put boundaries, lines, and fences in our surroundings. We may feel better by doing it. But the environment has no divisions. What grows at the next door neighbour's may look to be growing there, but the roots of whatever is growing next door may be in your own side of the yard. We cannot control the thinking or behaviour of the environment. But we can control the deadly illnesses of the world. All of us have to start caring for what happens in the Gulf, whether we sit in Canada or England or any other country. My grandmother used to say: "if you care at home, you care everywhere." So we have to begin at home to fight our illnesses.

Thank you if you took time to read my letter. I read of your leadership every day.

> Minnie Aodla Freeman, an Inuit first, very Canadian, and most of all a woman who cares about what's happening in the world.

MINNIE AODLA FREEMAN

My short stories and poems have been published in various books and literary magazines since 1975. My play, *Survival in the South,* published in *Paper Stays Put: A Collection of Inuit Writing,* ed. Robin Gedalof (Hurtig Publishers, 1980), has been translated into German and Greenlandic, and adapted as a play performed during the Dominion Drama Festival in Newfoundland and at the National Arts Centre in Ottawa. *Life Among the Qallunaat,* published in 1978 by Hurtig Publishers, has been translated into German, French, and Greenlandic; as well, it has been filmed by the National Film Board and is now a school textbook. I have served as Vice-President of two chapters of the Canadian Writers Association (Newfoundland and Hamilton, Ontario), participated in National Book Week reading tours (western Canada and eastern Arctic), and currently serve on the National Committee of the En'owkin International School of Writing (Penticton, British Columbia) and as advisor to the National Museum of Civilization (Hull, Quebec) in connection with a major exhibition on women artists.

FOR THE RECORD

Irshad Manji
Mila
Ann Haney
Minnie Peters
Alice Masak French
Lee Maracle
Evelyn Hamdon
Carole Anne Soong (née Wong)

IRSHAD MANJI

Dear Mum, I am Sorry

Dear Mum:

I am ashamed. I am an immigrant woman, like you. But because one of us is "more immigrant" than the other, one of us is more oppressed than the other. Thanks to me.

Since childhood, mum, I have oppressed you. I have ridiculed your accent, told you not to cook curry, demanded that you speak English in public, called you "cute" when you made people chuckle, and thought you "stupid" when you made them uncomfortable.

Do you remember, mum, the lunch my university held to honour its scholarship winners? I sat next to an eighty-year-old woman and you next to the university president. We were discussing languages; after pointing out that the smallest accents can cause the biggest misunderstandings, you explained how most people interpret your pronunciation of "beach" as "bitch". Do you remember that when the b-word shot out of your mouth, our entire table fell silent? The president cleared his throat and my shocked eighty-year-old neighbour whispered, "Oh my!" In retrospect, your story was funny. I should have laughed with you. Instead, I felt like crawling under the table and shouting, "Forgive her — she knows not what she does. She is an immigrant!" Worse yet, mum, one horribly racist and patronizing thought kept popping into my mind: "How many times have I warned my immigrant mother not to embarrass me like this?"

That, mum, was one in a string of racist and patronizing thoughts about you. I can recall, as a ten-year-old at a sleepover with the Brownies, sharing Rice Krispies treats that you — "my mum", I proudly said — had made for "the gang". But when the all-white gang examined the treats with scrunched-up noses, then spat out what they had just bitten into, my heart sank. Rather than defending you, I ridiculed you. "My mum has got to be the yuckiest cook in the world", I giggled to break the tension. "She probably put curry in these!", someone screamed above our laughter. That's right, **our** laughter. Mine included. I decided not to explain that the treats looked and tasted a bit different because you had made them with coloured and not plain marshmallows. It was easier simply to laugh at your "dumb" and "gross" immigrant ways. It was easier to let my "friends" oppress me. It was easier to let them let me oppress you.

And, mum, if this behaviour is okay for a ten-year-old, it is not okay for a twenty-two-year-old. I realize that. So why, just last week, did I talk to you like an overworked immigration officer would? Why, when you asked me to clarify a point in the Canada Pension Plan, did I automatically assume that you knew nothing about it? Above all, why did I lecture you on the need to get your facts straight? Why did I react this way to a Muslim woman whose guts and brains allowed her to divorce an abusive husband, stand up to manipulative lawyers, fill out her own tax forms, and gather enough money to have a house built while dealing with contractors' delays? I reacted this way because, lurking within me is the memory of you as an Avon lady; baby in one arm, make-up bag in the other, able to sputter only a few English words, and missing home profoundly. Mine is a memory of the "immigrant image" that my friends and **their** friends consider shameful. To suppress that "shameful" memory, I shamelessly oppress you.

Occasionally at least, mum, I have taken pride in watching you flaunt our immigrant past. When you appeared at parent-teacher nights in a sari, or brought samosas to my school parties, I didn't run for cover. How could I run when I saw people gasping at your beauty in that sequined sari? How could I run when I saw them praising your samosas? How could I oppress you when I sensed approval, not oppression, from others? (Remember how hard I encouraged you to wear a sari at my scholarship lunch? I now wonder if my motive was pride, or the feeling that I needed something — your dress, maybe — as an excuse for any embarrassing moments: "Look at her. She's wrapped in a sari. What does she know?")

Actually, mum, you know a lot. Most immigrant women do. That's why I wish I could stand atop a mountain and yell to all immigrant mothers below: "Learn to separate your children's **constructive** advice from your children's **destructive** criticism. Take their advice. Don't take their criticism!"

Of course, mum, you sometimes fought back. I still dread the lines you would throw at me year after year: "You think I can't teach you anything just because you get straight A's ... just because you're high school president ... just because you'll be going to university ... just because you're at university ... just because you graduated from university." I constantly denied that any of this led to my arrogance. I still deny it.

194

Instead, mum, my racism comes from a lifetime of being urged — by teachers, by friends, by t.v., books, and magazines — to hate my real self. My distinct self. My brown self. My immigrant self. In the classroom, on the playground, at the mall, and under the spell of popular people, I responded to the suffocating lifestyle of the white man (and I do mean "man") by becoming a white woman. That way, I could escape total suffocation. And even though I would remain oppressed as a woman, as a "white" woman I could oppress somebody else. That somebody was you.

Mum, please recognize — help all immigrant mothers to recognize — that raised-in-Canada kids can be as oppressive as we can be oppressed. We will swallow the intimidation of others, then regurgitate it on those whom we believe, because others believe, least represent Canada; those who are most vulnerable, yet most forgiving: our mothers. Mum, be forgiving no more. Beware. Then be determined to be unapologetic.

I opened this letter by confessing that I am ashamed. Let me close, mum, by saying that I am sorry.

Love,

Irshad

IRSHAD MANJI

I immigrated to Canada from Uganda in 1972. The difficulties my mother faced in being treated with respect at work as well as at home gave me an early sense of what "double disadvantage" means in Canada. That sense was refined when, as a student, I joined the board of the Vancouver Society on Immigrant Women. I then took the lessons of grassroots activism to Parliament Hill, where I coordinated legislative strategy for the women's spokesperson for the New Democratic Party. I am currently a journalist specializing in equality issues and speechwriter for NDP Leader Audrey McLaughlin. I am also writing a book on feminism for young women. I attribute my activism to my mother, whose courage continues to inspire me. My contribution to this book is that of a letter from a young woman of colour — me — to an "older" woman of colour — my mother. It discusses not only the experiences of a visible minority female growing up in Canadian society, but also how those experiences can lead a daughter to mistreat her first and best friend. This is a letter of both apology and awareness.

MILA

A Struggle for a Career

Dear Nira:

I was excited to receive your letter and to hear about your career as a university professor. Compared to you, my academic life is rather depressing. At present, I am a Research Associate without stipend at a university. I am doing independent research in the area of history and the development of women's education in India, and the educational problems and prospects for South Asian women in Canada. I am glad to be at least a Research Associate, because I have been unsuccessful in establishing an academic career in Canada. In this letter I will tell you about my struggle to attain a higher education and find a job in Montreal during the last twenty-eight years. I feel strongly that my gender, race, and status as an immigrant have been a significant hindrance to my success.

At first, let me give you a brief idea about Montreal's educational system. Montreal is a bilingual city in a province which is French. Therefore, educational institutions are divided into two languages, English and French. School boards control elementary and secondary schools which provide education up to grade eleven. Then, there are two-year colleges (CEGEPs). After college, university education begins which provides undergraduate and graduate degrees. When I first came here, CEGEPs had not been established. High school education was up to grade eleven and followed by four years of undergraduate program in the university. In the 1960s, there were one French and two English universities. One of the English universities already had an international reputation and the other was still trying to establish its reputation. In the 1970s, another French university was established.

In the early 1960s, Canadian immigration policies and practices facilitated the entrance to Canada of educated professional middle-class South Asians in the interest of capitalist economic development. In 1964, my husband had an appointment as a professor at one of the universities.

The chairman of his department told him that he would try to find something at the university for me. On the basis of his oral assurance, we made the decision to move to Canada from the United States. At the time of our arrival, I had two Master's degrees, one in Bengali literature and language from India and another in education (M.Ed.) from a prestigious university in the United States. I also had two years of teaching and administrative experience at a girls' high school in India.

I had previously heard and believed that there were more opportunities for higher education and a professional career in a developed country, such as Canada, than in Third World countries. As I had a keen interest in higher education and the ambition for a professional career, I was delighted to get an opportunity to come to Canada. I arrived in Montreal with great hope for a professional career. Unfortunately, upon arrival, my ideas regarding the opportunities for higher education and career advancement changed, hope turned to disappointment.

In 1964, we came to Montreal for only one year. For this short period, I wanted to work rather than study. After joining the university, my husband was told by the chairman that he could not find anything for me. I was disappointed. I felt cheated because without his oral assurance about me, my husband would not have come. They badly needed professors at that time. I could not believe that a powerful man at the university sincerely tried and could not find anything for me. Maybe I was denied a job because of my gender and race.

Then, I searched for the names of teachers' colleges in the Montreal telephone directory. One day, I went to a teacher's college to meet somebody personally to know whether any teaching positions were available. The conversation regarding the availability of teaching positions was negative. Moreover, I had the impression from that conversation that I was not welcome in Canadian society.

Afterwards, I became aware that there were job placement offices in Montreal. I contacted those offices and informed them of my educational qualifications and experiences. The officers told me that I was too qualified. They could only find jobs for secretaries, typists, etc. I was surprised at the demand for women at the clerical level because it was uncommon in India. I gave up hope of working in Montreal.

Thus, after studying and teaching for so many years, I was forced to stay at home. My hope of career advancement began to look doubtful. In 1965, we left Montreal for India.

In 1968, I came back to Montreal with my husband and a two-year-old daughter, leaving close relatives, friends, and a comfortable lifestyle at home. My husband re-joined his former university. So, I decided to try again for a career in Montreal.

I realized from my earlier job search experiences that if I wanted a professional career, I would need a Ph.D. I believed I could do a Ph.D. in the field of educational administration, since that was my major in the Master's program at the U.S. university. Therefore, I started inquiring about the Ph.D. program in educational administration at all the Montreal universities and found that none of them had a Ph.D. program. Moreover, the education faculty of one university was situated far from the city. So I thought about doing another Masters degree in history and talked to the chairman of the history department of the one of the universities in the city. I was told I had to start from the third year undergraduate level.

I felt humiliated. After doing two Master's degrees, especially one from a prestigious American university, how could somebody possibly start from the undergraduate level? I felt something was wrong in the education system. I had sufficient background in history from studying in India as well as in the United States. I know overseas education is devalued in this country. But what about my U.S. Master's degree? I had doubts about whether there was a firm regulation or whether gender and race played a part in this decision. In any case, I could not accept the idea of registering as an undergraduate student. I decided not to do a Master's degree in history.

I was desperate to keep myself academically active. I started taking French-language courses. At a university, the Ph.D. program in educational administration started in 1969. I applied and was admitted as a full-time Ph.D. student. I was assigned to take six courses. Taking courses in French was a challenge. Instead of being afraid, I was rather proud of myself. Of course, being a university student and taking care of a family with a child without domestic help, except from my husband, was strenuous. The chairman of the department was my advisor. He was an understanding, supportive, and encouraging man. However, two young professors, whose classes I was attending, discouraged me from the first day. I remember one professor wanted to talk to me after class. He said that I would not be able to succeed because courses were offered in French and it was a French university.

I could not understand what would be the barrier to my success as I graduated from the U.S. university with an "A" average. I was taking French-language courses at the same university and was quite comfortable following the lectures in French. All the books were written in English, and I was permitted to write papers and examinations in English.

Those professors themselves had graduated from the United States in English which was a foreign language to them. What was the difference between my situation and theirs? It seems to me that as soon as they saw me — a short woman of different skin colour — in their class, instead of waiting to see my ability, they assumed that I was not capable of higher education.

I discontinued my studies after a month. Discouragement was one of the reasons; the other was the responsibility of raising a child. But I could not stay home without any intellectual stimulation. I took several French-language courses up to advanced level in the same university. After three years, when I had confidence about my French-language ability, I made an appointment with the new chairman of the education department, who was from Quebec, with a view to continuing my studies for the Ph.D. Our conversation was in French. Still, he expressed his doubt about my success at a French university. Then I learnt that my "dossier est fermé", which meant re-arranging all the required documents and re-applying. I was disappointed and lost the desire for studying at that university forever. Again, this situation raised the question in my mind whether it was my language ability or my gender and race that were mitigating against my educational opportunity.

Then, I was confined at home for three years because my son was born. But my educational and career aspirations did not die. I always wanted to pursue higher education at a prestigious university. Since I was now over forty and had been out of the university atmosphere for several years, I decided to enrol for a single course before applying to do my Ph.D. I received the highest mark in the class (for conducting empirical research). As a result, I was inspired to go on.

I struggled for eight years without success. I will tell you the story. In 1976, I met a professor (Professor A), the chairman of the department of educational administration and policy studies, and conveyed to him my desire for a higher degree. He told me that they had only an *ad hoc* Ph.D. program, and that the Ph.D. candidate had to be a full-time student. At that time, I was unable to be a full-time student because I had two young children to raise. He suggested that I enrol as a special student and take the compulsory courses which would later be transferred toward a Ph.D. program. I agreed and was admitted as a special student and began by taking the compulsory course which he taught. He was an excellent teacher. In the term papers, I got remarks such as "excellent" and earned mostly A's. But, my final mark in that course was a B. I was disappointed. I met the professor to ask about the inconsistency between the marks on my term papers and my final mark. He told me I would not be able to succeed. I asked him specifically the reasons for his doubt, saying: "If it is my ability I will try my best to improve, or are there any other reasons, such as my gender, race and physical appearance (short)?" He nodded, "yes". I was surprised to see that attitude in a university professor. Maybe it was the reality which I did not recognize at that time. I had confidence in my ability. I could not think about discontinuing my studies. Then, he suggested that I meet Professor B who worked in a field that interested me.

I met Prof. B, who agreed to be my advisor. From 1977 to 1982, I took courses, worked with her, and prepared a thesis proposal. We developed confidence in each other. While I was in India from 1978 to 1980, I did research on my chosen topic. She encouraged me to work on that topic up to 1981. In one letter, she wrote:

> I am really glad that you have continued to work on your thesis... I have gone over your proposal again. Basically it is very good — shows depth of study and sound thinking.... I am sure this would be acceptable for submission for a Ph.D. application. This is good.

She was only concerned whether I would get the co-operation of the subjects of my research. Her confidence in my research ability is illustrated in the following letter of recommendation which she wrote when I applied for a graduate fellowship:

> I have known Ms.... as a student in my classes, as a thesis advisor, and as a research assistant for three years. She is an extremely capable student, meticulously thorough, and at the same time creative and insightful. I believe that Ms.... will complete, very capably, any project she undertakes and recommend her highly for a Graduate Fellowship.

Also, in an informal conversation regarding the marks I received in a statistics course, she mentioned that my mark was the highest any student ever received in their department. So, I had no doubt about my future success.

In 1981, I arranged the subjects of my research. I was ready to apply for the *ad hoc* Ph.D. program and to submit my thesis proposal. At that point, she told me to change the thesis topic because I might face difficulty working on that problem. I was confused but changed topics twice within six months. Then, in some informal conversations she showed her doubt about the possibility of my finding a job in the administrative field, especially as I was a non-white woman with little teaching experience. She suggested I change the discipline of my study and talk to other professors. Finally, at the end of that year, she told me that she would not be able to guide me any more because she was going on sabbatical and would retire soon. I was shocked and lost after working for so many years in one field and with the same professor.

I changed the discipline because that was the only alternative I had. I started taking courses with Professor C. I began to do research in the area of women and education in India. I formulated a new thesis proposal with Professor C. He was not ready to be my thesis advisor but suggested the name of Professor D who was interested in my area of research. Unfortunately, Prof. D was abroad at that time. I wrote to her requesting she be my thesis advisor and sent her my thesis proposal. She replied: "If you want to wait till I come back before submitting your proposal, then I may be able to be your Ph.D. supervisor." I was hopeful. After she came back, I took a course with her and wrote a final Ph.D. proposal under her supervision. I received an A in her course — as I had in all the courses I had taken with professors B and C.

In early 1984, I applied for admission to the *ad hoc* Ph.D. program and submitted my thesis proposal. All of my hopes for a higher education were shattered by the final decision of the department committee responsible for the admission of *ad hoc* Ph.D. students. The chairman of the department informed me that in exceptional cases they sometimes recommend an *ad hoc* course of study for "candidates who are outstanding, who are capable of independent work, and for whom adequate resources are available." ..."On the basis of my performance over the years" and my "research proposal", they decided that I had not demonstrated "sufficient ability to work independently" and that my "critical judgement and capability for originality" were not at the level they require for a prospective Ph.D. candidate. I was shocked by their decision which devastated my entire career goal and academic life.

The real reasons for the committee's judgement are still a mystery to me. (The only thing I know is that Professor A was on the committee.) I obtained A's in most of the courses. My professors advised me to take courses in different disciplines to qualify as a future *ad hoc* Ph.D. student, which I did. They constantly encouraged me to submit a thesis proposal on the basis of my performance in courses and independent research reports. If the professors with whom I took courses and prepared my Ph.D. thesis proposal were not convinced of my critical faculty and capability for independent work, why did they advise me to take courses during the long eight-year period?

I was so disappointed that I went through a long depression. I lost courage and the desire for higher study in any discipline or in any university forever. I developed an inferiority complex. Eight years of hard work without success affected my physical and mental health severely. During these years, I never slept before 2 a.m. I took several night courses in the harsh winter, and used to come back on public transport (changing three times) with a fearful heart. I lost the possibility of economic independence and a better social position forever.

Still, I could not stop my intellectual curiosity. Since 1985, I have been researching the history of women's education in India. I confined myself to libraries and home. I was isolated from the academic atmosphere. After a while, I found this isolation was a killer. By 1988, I was desperate to find a job or some place where I could meet educated people. I applied for jobs in some private schools and undergraduate colleges. I contacted a number of women's organizations, including the Canadian Advisory Council on the Status of Women, for help. Finally, from a prominent woman I got information about a program in Women's Studies at a Montreal university. I personally met the principal, conveyed my research interest, and applied for Adjunct Fellowship. Since 1989, I have been an Adjunct Fellow and later a Research Associate, without stipend, at the university; my colleagues are very supportive. I am enjoying research facilities and an academic atmosphere. In my mid-fifties, I have found a new life. But research requires money. Since I do not have any income, I will not be able to fulfil my research interest without financial assistance.

My struggles for an academic career led me to conclude that I am quadruply disadvantaged in this country. Firstly, in Montreal, the educational institutions are white-male dominated. It is hard for the professors to believe that a short woman of South Asian origin has the ability to achieve an academic career, especially in the administrative area where even white women have little access. Secondly, my overseas education and teaching experiences are devalued. Thirdly, my lack of knowledge of the education system and lack of a network in this country because I was brought up and educated overseas both work against me. Unfamiliarity with the education system and resource persons in this country hindered my proper decision for career achievement. Fourthly, family responsibility took precedence over my career achievement. While I was a student, I always wanted to spend more time in the libraries, discussing with friends and finishing my papers. But, I often had to leave behind my unfinished paper to come home to make a nutritious supper and serve dinner at the right time.

I strongly feel that if I had stayed in India, I would not have been so lost. I had my teachers who were familiar with my work and always helpful. I would not have felt so isolated because I had relatives and friends. I would have had domestic help and so could have spent more time on my career.

In the future, I wish educational institutions in Montreal will arrange some capable and understanding resource persons who can advise foreign students so that they can be successful in their lives. I hope that other educated South Asian women will have an easier time than I have had.

With warmest regards,

Mila (pseudonym)

MILA

I am a Research Associate at a Montreal university. Born and educated in India, where I received my B.A. and M.A. degrees, I worked as a teacher and vice-principal at a girl's high school in India. I came to the United States and obtained an M.Ed. degree. In 1964, I immigrated to Canada and since then have been residing in Montreal with my family. I studied and was a research assistant at the Department of Education, in a Montreal university, for a number of years. My research interests include the history of women in education and society, and the life history, experiences, and contributions of professional minority women in Canada. I am currently working on a project about Canadian South Asian professional women in Montreal.

ANN HANEY

who wrote this letter on behalf of Hilda Abas, her mother

On Working Hard

Dear Diane:

The last time we spoke I was trying to explain to you the importance of working hard and never giving up. I want you to understand that if you really want to achieve something, you must expect to work hard for it. I don't expect that you will fully understand this now. But one day you will. You will learn throughout your life that these responsibilities are needed for you to be independent and proud of yourself as I was throughout my life.

In Lebanon, my family was very poor, and the poor were looked down upon. We wanted to get ahead and make more money, but it was impossible. The government allowed the rich to remain rich and the poor to remain poor. When I was on my way to Canada in 1950, I had such dreams of my new life! I thought Canada was the land of milk and honey and I would be rich instantly. I was leaving my family to meet my husband — a man I had never met before. Oh! I was so excited when the plane landed at the Winnipeg airport. My excitement turned to disappointment almost immediately after the plane landed. First of all, I walked out of the plane and into a very cold October weather wearing a light pink Lebanese dress. Then, there was no one to meet me.... I was a very frightened sixteen-year-old in a strange country where no one could understand my language. My husband and his younger sister eventually came and off we went to my new home.

We finally arrived at the place which was to be my home. It was a small farm shared by my husband, his parents, and two brothers. We all lived in the same house. Soon I discovered that I was expected to cook, clean, and work on the family farm.

I was always very busy and never had time for myself. If I wasn't milking cows, I was busy raising my twelve children. My first child was born ten months after arriving in Canada and my twelfth child was born twenty-three years later. I decided that I should learn to read and write English. Unfortunately, raising children and my many other responsibilities were too time-consuming to allow me the opportunity to learn the language. I always felt that I missed out in life because I couldn't read or write. But, I promised myself that all of my children would get a good education.

As time went by, and my twelfth child was three years old, I decided that I would have enough time for a part-time job. I applied for a position at the local hospital. The position involved housekeeping and kitchen duties — jobs that I was very familiar with. Even though I couldn't read or write, I was hired. I worked very hard in the hospital and always tried to do my best to please my supervisor. If I was called to work for only two hours, I would go because I needed the money and I also liked getting out of the house. I worked at the hospital for nine years and never once did I regret working there. A permanent position finally came up in housekeeping. I immediately and excitedly applied for the position. I should get this job — after all I had worked at this job for nine years and always performed excellently! My interview with the hospital board ended with great disappointment for me. The board decided that I was unqualified because I could not read or write. My feelings were hurt and I was humiliated. I actually felt devastated because I had worked there happily for nine years without making a mistake, and now, suddenly, my independence was taken away because I could not read or write.

I finally came to the realization that I simply could not be happy just working at home. I had so much to prove to the public and to myself. I was not going to give up! I wanted something more. It was something that was lurking in the back of my mind for years. I wanted a business — a business of my own. I was known in the area as a great cook, and I love feeding people. My heart was set on a restaurant and bake shop.

The desire for my own business was the beginning of another battle for me. It was a battle between my family and me. My husband and my sons thought I would never survive because there would be too much paperwork, and I couldn't read or write. There were many arguments to discourage me, but my mind was set. Now I had to prove myself to my family, and especially to my husband. I had managed to save money from my hard work on the farm, selling cream and eggs, and working at the hospital.

In 1984, my payoff came. I started my own bakeshop and restaurant in Hodgson, Manitoba, through loans and the money I had saved. My restaurant and bakeshop is nothing fancy but my goal had been realized. I enjoyed people and cooking because, as a housewife, I was always cooking and catering. My family helps me a great deal in managing the paperwork and working with me at the shop. I still have a positive attitude as I work fourteen hours a day, and I still want to keep on going. What I did was put aside the fact that I couldn't read or write and always reminded myself that I could do better. I'm very proud of my business and I feel that it is a success. My husband helps me also, and, at times, I can't get him out of the restaurant. He gives me a lot of support now and that's the greatest feeling to have.

What I'd really like to say to you is that even though you suffer from hardships and frustrations, you can still achieve your goals. Just remember — never give up! Once you've achieved your goals, you will feel pride in yourself. You will be independent. Live free and enjoy life.

Love,

Ann Haney for Hilda Abas

ANN HANEY

After graduating from the University of Winnipeg with a Bachelor of Arts degree and the University of Manitoba with a teacher's certificate in 1974, I decided to teach in northern Manitoba. I taught grade 3 at Moose Lake, for one year and I was a classroom teacher in the elementary grades at The Pas, for thirteen years. In 1975, I married Clarence Haney and we now have three sons: Ryan, born in 1977; Neil, born in 1978; and Chris, born in 1983. Our family moved to Morden, Manitoba in 1989 where I taught for one year. My career then took a new twist as I began teaching literacy to adults in Winkler, Manitoba. I feel very fortunate because I love my job. I owe my success to my parents who encouraged and supported me every step of the way.

HILDA ABAS

Hilda (Hajar) Tasse Abas was born in 1934, and immigrated to Canada from Lebanon in 1950, bringing with her the morals and values of the Moslem religion. She consented to a pre-arranged traditional marriage to Joseph Abas of Hodgson, Manitoba. Together they raised twelve children. Hilda helped on the family farm, and from 1978 to 1984, she did part-time housekeeping and kitchen duties in a hospital. Rejected for a full-time position, she became a restaurant and bakeshop operator and owner, with the help of her family. Currently she enjoys the benefits of running her own business, the successes of her children, as well as the happy moments spent with her twenty-four grandchildren.

MINNIE PETERS

Hard Life

Dear Sir/Madam:

I am sending you this letter in the hope that you'll read my story. I want this story recorded so that everyone who reads it will know of the hard life that Indian women led.

I am Minnie Peters, the sixth oldest of seventeen children. I am a Thompson Indian from British Columbia. I was born in the mountains of the Upper Fraser Valley in August 1921. I was born in the mountains because my mother was collecting berries to prepare for the cold winter, and my father was hunting for fresh meat.

Every year, my parents faithfully gathered berries, caught fish, and hunted for meat. The berries were dried, the fish was dried, smoked, or salted, and the meat was dried or smoked.

Because we were poor, we used everything around us. My mother would skin the animals that my father caught to make moccasins for the family, and she sometimes traded them at the store for food. My mother would go to the mountains to collect cedar roots for making baskets and she would trade the baskets for food or cloth. With this cloth she would make clothing for the children.

When I was five, my father, Johnny Chapman, died of tuberculosis. It was at this time that I was sent to the Kamloops Residential School, run by Sisters of St. Anne and Brothers of the Roman Catholic church. That school changed the lives of three hundred Native boys and girls.

The school day began with one hour of church first thing in the morning, followed by breakfast of plain porridge with skim milk and plain dried bread. Everyone did their chores until dinner time. Dinner was usually stew, made with very little meat, some potatoes, carrots, and flour to thicken. After dinner, everyone went to their classrooms to learn English for two hours. More chores followed classroom time until supper was ready. For supper we had soup, stew or fish, and rice pudding with skim milk. It wasn't until after supper that we were allowed to go outside and play or do crafts and have fun with other children. But this would only last for an hour, and then everyone would get ready for bed.

Every Friday, the boys caught fish for the girls to make soup with and serve for lunch, which was a real treat for everyone. On special occasions such as Easter, Christmas, or inspections, we were given two candies each or one orange. We never had salt, pepper, or butter.

Some children were assigned kitchen duties such as cooking for the whole school and staff, setting tables, and cleaning up for the next meal. The girls made butter that was all sold to the town for extra money. The girls also did a lot of baking but never had the joy of eating it.

Other girls worked in the laundry and others mended and sewed. Some other girls cleaned different rooms, including those of the Priest, Sisters, and Brothers. Every month we had new chores to do. I had a turn doing each one. I liked sewing and ironing more than anything else.

The boys fed the animals, milked the cows, checked for eggs, cut the hay, and gardened. They also picked apples and sold them in town for more money.

The school separated the boys from the girls by having them sleep in separate dormitories and play in separate areas. Although the children were permitted to eat in one big eating room, they were not allowed to speak to each other. If they did they were punished. Even in the church, the centre aisle separated the boys from the girls.

Once a month, we were permitted to leave the Residence to go into town two miles away. Parents were required to write for permission to see their children, or to take them into town. Parents had to wait for a reply for a visiting time. Any other visits were on the grounds of the Residence.

The Priest and Brothers, who were training to become priests, treated the children very mean. I didn't know if they just hated us because of our race or if they just hated their work, but we could sure see the hatred in their eyes.

If we were caught speaking our own language we were punished. Punishment meant being slapped on the hands with a stick or a belt, missing a meal, or being whipped in front of all the other children. If we didn't learn well, we were beaten and sent to the dormitory.

I remember speaking my language in the dormitory while we were getting ready for bed and one of the Sisters overheard me. She made me kneel down outside her bedroom door in my nightgown. I wasn't allowed to move until she said I could. I stayed like that all night. I remember being cold and tired. When she opened her door in the morning she asked me to stand up. But I had such a hard time because my knees were so sore. She then beat me and sent me to bed.

Another time I will never forget was when I was in the classroom. I wasn't doing my work right and the Brother grabbed the back of my shirt. He pulled me up out of my seat, swung me back, and then swung me forward, breaking all the buttons off my shirt. Then he threw me back in my seat. Then I had to try and do my work again.

Most of the children were confused, unhappy, and afraid. Some children couldn't adjust to this new life. They couldn't take any more abuse and missed their homes and families so much that they would try to run away from school and go home. But the Priest always caught up to them and brought them back, only to beat them in front of everyone to see.

Over the years, my mother worked in a railway camp as a cook. It was not long before she met her next husband, Charles Stromquist. They lived at the railway station since my stepfather was a section foreman on the Canadian National Railway.

Finally, after seven terrible years, I was allowed to move back home. By this time my mother had just had her second child with her new husband. I took pride in helping mom with the housework and the kids. I felt part of a happy family again.

When I turned thirteen, I began public school in our community. Only then was I certain that I was treated differently because I was an Indian.

Some school children stoned me, chased me off the grounds, beat me, made fun of me, called me names, and laughed at me. My friends pleaded with the school teacher to end this discrimination at the school. But he didn't feel it was his place to say anything. The teacher wouldn't do anything but give me school work, and since he wouldn't help me with it, I failed. My stepfather complained to the teacher many times, expecting some changes to be made. When I was eighteen and it was clear that nothing would change, he took me out of the school and I stayed home to help my mother.

I would stay with my great-aunt and great-grandmother for weeks at a time. My great-grandmother did not speak English at all, while my great-aunt spoke some. She translated for great-grandmother. My language came back to me very quickly.

Occasionally my mother had to go away and would have a friend watch us until she returned. One day I met the friend's younger brother, Robert Peters, while he picked up a parcel at the railway station. Soon after that we started seeing each other. We were married in 1940, one year after our meeting. When I turned twenty the following year I gave birth to our first son. Two more sons and one daughter were to follow.

Robert made his living as a logger and as a farmer. One day while working on the job he got squeezed in a flip of logs. His hip was shattered and he needed an operation. After three years of healing, he went back to logging until his retirement twenty years later. When he retired, he took up farming and continued to farm until just recently. Once Robert retired, I went back to school to learn how to manage a business. Since all I knew my whole life was how to make my own clothes and my own food in the old way, I turned to that for income.

About twenty years ago I started to teach art classes to school children and prison inmates throughout the Fraser Valley. This was a good source of income for me. As well, I continued to fill private orders.

I became very involved in reviving the old ways, my culture. I have been a director for the British Columbia Native Arts and Crafts Society for many years. I helped set up a local moccasin factory which is still in existence today. I opened up a retail arts and crafts shop in our community, catering to tourists mostly.

Right now I am fashion designing in traditional and contemporary styles. I exhibit in fashion shows, trade shows, and competitions. I now have two sound businesses that I operate today.

Today my granddaughters help me, using the same skills I taught them, that were handed down to me before them. I can rely on them for help with my arts and crafts business, and my fashion designing business. I am confident that they will carry on with my businesses when I retire and will continue to teach the next generation.

I now have seventeen grandchildren and ten great-grandchildren. My fifty-first wedding anniversary has just gone by, and I am now nearly seventy years old. My life has been many things to me. My life has sometimes been miserable, hard, happy, and special.

Yet, after everything I have been through in my lifetime, I have been strong. When I look back at all the years spent at the residential school, it seems the whole purpose of it was to learn English and forget our own language. It was all for nothing, because today I speak my language fluently. I have made damn sure that I taught my children and grandchildren everything I know. This way our people will survive.

Sincerely,

Judy Peters for Minnie Peters
Note: Judy Peters is a granddaughter of Minnie Peters.

Minnie Peters

MINNIE PETERS

My skills in bead and leather work, basketry, and knitting are self-taught. My arts and crafts have been widely exhibited in British Columbia and elsewhere. I work closely with my own people of the Peters Band in Hope, B.C. as well as other British Columbia Indian Bands. In 1985, I ran a training program for a group of young Native Indian women who, under my guidance, made all the clothes for a fashion show of Native Indian garments. I serve on the Board of Directors of the Indian Arts and Crafts Society of B.C. as the representative for the Upper and Lower Fraser Valley.

ALICE MASAK FRENCH

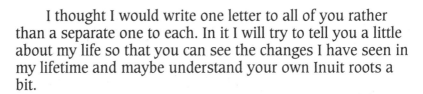

Inuit Roots

My Dear Grandchildren:

I thought I would write one letter to all of you rather than a separate one to each. In it I will try to tell you a little about my life so that you can see the changes I have seen in my lifetime and maybe understand your own Inuit roots a bit.

I was born in the Arctic on the Beaufort Sea on a little island called Baillie Island. I was born at home on the 29th day of June, 1930. My parents, as almost all Inuit in those days, lived on the land and also off it. Our food supply came from the land and the sea. Our meats — like caribou, rabbits, ptarmigan, and ducks — we had to stalk, shoot, and snare, then skin, pluck, and dry or store whole for the winter months. In the summer months we went whaling for belugas so that we and our dog teams could survive the long winter months. We also gill-netted fish to dry and smoke.

Our staples — like flour, sugar, and tea, etc. — we bought from the company stores dotted around the MacKenzie Delta. The main store was the Hudson's Bay Company, but there were a few free traders around. It is not like now when most of our people live in towns where we can go daily, or once a week, to shop, and if we forget something we can go the same day to get it. In those times we didn't forget anything, or, I should say, not anything that was important, like flour, matches, etc. As we could not easily go and replenish them, it was very important to remember what was needed for the next six months to a year, or we had to go without.

Our fathers trapped fur in order to buy the necessities. There were very few jobs, if any, for them to work at. If lucky you could get one, say, as an interpreter for the company stores, R.C.M. Police, or the Mission schools. So you can see there were not that many jobs around then.

In spite of that we lived a good life on the land. It gave us food, shelter, and clothing. Families were much closer then than they are now. Grandparents, parents, aunts, and uncles all lived together or next door to each other so that family ties were close and very important to us. Grandparents were wise because of their experiences and could give sound advice to their children as well as help with the care of the children born to their children to free the parents so that they could go out to hunt and gather.

There were aunts, uncles, and cousins to talk and play with. The home was a lively and busy place. Not much time to become bored. We had no t.v., of course, only a battery-operated radio and sometimes not even that. The battery would run out of juice, and the town was a hundred or so miles away so we would have to wait until we could go into town by boat or dog-team and replace it.

When I was between six and seven years old, I went to boarding school in Aklavik because my Mom had tuberculosis. Dad could not look after me by himself. I cannot tell you how frightening it was. I had never seen such a big house before, nor so many children, Inuit and Indians of all ages. There were a lot of big rooms and white people there. I found out that they were teachers and supervisors for the children. It was very frightening because I had not seen so many people living together in such a big place before.

I am not sure that I would have gone to school if my Mom had not been sick. I may or may not have gone. In hindsight, I am glad I did. My Father had gone to a school in Alaska. The hospital my Mom had gone to was run by the Anglican Mission. There was only one doctor in Aklavik, and he serviced two hospitals; the other was Roman Catholic. I was very young at the time so have no idea what treatment they gave her. She had gone to the hospital during the last stages of her illness. When she died, I went to the hospital to see for myself if what the supervisors had said was true. I ran into her room and saw only an empty bed. I could not really believe that she had died. I felt very, very distressed and lonely. She had been a link outside of the school to my way of life. With her gone, the only other link I had to family life was my Father who was not there and whom I would not see again for three years.

I felt very lonely because my Mom and Dad seemed to disappear from me. My brother, Danny, was left at school, but I did not see him except at meal-times and when we were outside, playing. Even then it was not like home. We were not allowed to speak to each other or speak in our own language at all. He stayed on the boys' side and I on the girls'. It was not like school as you know it. We lived in the same building yet were not allowed to be near each other. Now when you are at school these days, you can go home to Mom and Dad after school. You grow up together, fight, argue, and play and get to know each other as you grow up. Be thankful for that; it was not so for us.

When I was fourteen I went home to be with Dad and was finished with school. He had married again, and I had two sisters by then. Learning to live with family was difficult because I had forgotten how to live like that and in a small family. Even though they were my family, I had become so used to living in an institution. I also had forgotten how to speak in my own language, Inuvialuktun, and my step-mother could not speak in English. Even now I am not fluent in my own language. I can understand it but not speak it very well. I wish I could speak more fluently in Inuveak so that I could teach you better. I think it is a part of your heritage, and you should know how, at least, to speak it.

When I left school, I went back basically ignorant of our Inuit way of life. Fortunately, I had a Grandmother who undertook to teach me my language and the necessary things a woman needs to know, sewing and scraping of furs to make into mukluks [boots], parkas, mitts, etc. Also, how to clean and cook caribou, rabbits, duck, fish, etc. She thought I would be unmarriageable if I did not have those skills.

There is much of our culture I would like to pass on to you. That is why I have written two books, *My Name is Masak* and *The Restless Nomad*. My hope is that you read these well, and understand. But I have lost a lot; there is a lot of richness that you will never know about your people and culture. I hope that as you grow up you will become interested in this part of your heritage.

When your Grandad and I moved out of the north in 1961, we were both very unknowledgeable about the way people in the south lived. I met your Grandfather, who is Irish, in Cambridge Bay in 1958. We fell in love and got married and have been happily married ever since. Your Grandad had lived in Ireland before immigrating to Canada, where he landed at Churchill in 1955. He had lived in Ireland in an old-fashioned house without electricity and was not used to towns and cities. We had to laugh together about the things we did not know, like the first time we bought bananas and put them in the fridge, only to see them go black! We were fascinated just to watch the people rushing about in their cars. Luckily, we have usually lived in very small towns and sometimes in native communities; so we still live off the land and waters to a small extent.

I hope that you, my Grandchildren, will have more schooling and that you will be able to voice your fears for the North. It's part of your heritage and needs all the help it can get. The only way this can happen is for you to be vocal and to know what is happening in the North. You need to be well educated in order to make people understand how fragile the North is. Also to help business and oil companies to understand how easy it is to scar the earth and so expose the permafrost which lies only a few inches below. Once exposed it melts and often becomes a small puddle, then larger and larger. I could hope that the North could remain the same, but I have seen great changes there in my lifetime. This is why I stress education in order to make yourselves heard about the concerns of the North land. The changes are great and sometimes confusing for our people.

May the Good Lord be with you all,

Your loving Grandmother

Alice Masak French

ALICE MASAK FRENCH

I am an Inuit, born on Baillie Island on the Beaufort Sea in the Arctic Circle. After going to a boarding school in Aklavik early in life and remaining there until age fourteen, I returned to my people and learned much about my own culture from my grandmother. Now in turn I tell my grandchildren what life has been like for me. I have written two books: *My Name is Masak* (Peguis Publishers, 1976), and *The Restless Nomad* (Pemmican Publishers, 1992).

LEE MARACLE

Hands

To My Children:

I look up and there you all are bigger than I, except around the girth. I don't mind that, but lately I have been watching you, and caring in a very different way. When you were little, I knew what was best. My mind operated from the safety of long distance forward vision. Now, the screenplay of our lives which rolls around inside me wants to rewind. When you were small, tying up my shoelaces while I pecked optimistically at an old typewriter, I saw young adults in full bloom, ploughing new fields with great vigour. Each time I rose to answer the door with my laces tied together, and ended up flat on my face on floor tiles so worn some of them had no design, I looked into the future: "When they are seventeen, they won't be doing this." I listened to your constant chatter and heard different words. I heard women and men, making sense of the world around them. I saw you cooking, caring, and working. I didn't hear the whine of children wanting me to cook.

Now I look, and I see tiny little girls crying at the store because mommy wouldn't buy them satin shorts. I see little boys wishing for real toys, and not wooden blocks. I see you staring out the window on Saturdays, saying it's boring, now that we aren't middle class and can't take dancing lessons. I watched you go to work in your early teens to pay for the lessons I could have provided had I taken that government job, instead of deciding I wanted to write. I look at your robust young bodies and wonder what they would have been like had they had all the dance lessons, gymnastics training, and swimming lessons you all wanted.

Welfare. Do you remember those days.... I can't forget. I can't forget the basement suite, the old quadruplex in an industrial neighbourhood … our house one of the only two residential houses within four blocks … the eight-block walk to school. I can't forget being pregnant with my youngest son, walking you up that hill. I can't forget, rolling the buggy, then the stroller, up that hill. I can't forget the huge efforts of you, little Tania, your deceptively frail, but strong body, pushing the stroller, while I hauled laundry and groceries by turns the mile or so to our local IGA and laundromat. And Columpa. Always walking on her sore legs behind the stroller, the buggy, crying "Wait for me."

It is 1981, and I am watching your hands pluck fat, red raspberries from bushes under a hot afternoon sun. The young white man on the other side of your row faints from the heat. You too are all a little sick. I didn't bring enough water. I send one of you scurrying for more — I don't even remember which set of hands fetched it. Near to fainting, I call the day off for the smaller boys, but you my girls, had to continue — picking, picking, picking. Several weeks and only a few hundred dollars between us all. We are baked near to black. We are thin and a little sick from the diet of peanut butter sandwiches and raspberries sprayed with who knows what.

I am sick. Sick of not being able to provide. Generation after generation, we have been unable to provide. It is a sickness which began when they came and changed all the rules of survival. Our lineage, your great-grandmother, your grandmother, you and I, worked until our fingers bled and our baked backs could hardly hold us up.

Mine is the first generation entitled to the same education as the rest of Canada. I could have finished college, gone on to university. I tried. I wrestled with academia off and on over the years. I am so close to a degree now, I can taste it, but I am not going back. Not right now, and again I will have to watch you work.

I hear laughter, the mature laughter of you working people hard at the business of planning their lives and realizing those plans. Laughter, full of gracious optimism. Between the laugh lines of my own eyes I can see my regrets and layered over those regrets are years of tenacious, unrelenting struggle by you and me. It is this tenacity, this will, I bequeath to you, and quite by accident. I wanted to create, not a writing mother, though I knew it would take that, but a different world.

Somehow, the world grew, the words rolled out, and the memories piled themselves into untidy little piles inside me. I was young. Invincible, like you are now. No yesterday — just tomorrow. There I am, leaning out the window, dishes still in the sink, you are too small to do them and I am too busy birthing Bertha and all those other people in my stories. They meant more to me than the sum total of dance lessons, satin shorts, or the toys I couldn't buy. At the time, they meant more to me than the shame of being on welfare.

I must know why they were so important, so I can finish growing you up, so I can stop the interminable instant replay button in my brain from punching out your littleness.

You probably don't know how "Bertha"* was born.

There was this little shack nestled between an old unpruned cherry tree and a splendid vine maple grove on the trail to the beach behind my house. Inside, the sound of click, click, click of crab legs against great clay urns could be heard. Every now and then a low whisper and raucous laughter drowned the click, click. A little grass orphan leaned against that shack door waiting for the laughter and imagining, dreaming up the story about it. Through the cracks the little girl could see the hands of the woman who made the others laugh. It is the clearest image I ever had of the woman I called mother for many years.

I got so used to peeping through the cracks of the door to hear the voice and see her hands that at night when she finally came home to gather all of us around the old wood stove to tell a story, I would watch her hands and listen to her voice without looking at her face. My mother's young face, my grandmother's face, even my old great-grandmother's face didn't exist for me when I was small. I was raised by three generations of women whose faces were invisible to me. I grew up thinking I didn't look like my mother. My wrists are slender and my fingers much more delicate. We didn't look alike at all.

As soon as I was big enough to handle an iron and wash clothes, I went to work, gathering laundry from the white ladies in the neighbourhood and "giving them a hand", two actually, for a dime. From seven to eleven I watched my hands collect beer bottles, pop bottles, sweep floors, babysit, pick berries, and, late at night, I watched my hands open my mother's books. My mother's books. An old encyclopedia, a Webster unabridged dictionary, and the children's classics by *Reader's Digest*. The one I loved most was the dictionary. Noah Webster wrote the first one.

I loved it so much I bought my own. This language came alive for me while I struggled to write Bertha, but the story, the memory that prompted her into life was the lonely child peeking through the cracks of the crabshack door trying to see my mother. Bertha would have a face — no hands, just a face. I tried to write her story without ever showing anyone Bertha's hands, but it didn't work — Bertha's fingers became pudgy, like your little hands were.

---

*   Editor's note: "Bertha" is a short story published in Lee Maracle's short story collection, *Sojourner's Truth and Other Stories* (Vancouver: Press Gang Publishers, 1990).

Hands do things and in their doing, they achieve a personality. Sometimes hands do regrettable things — like the hands of the white children who hit me because they somehow felt Custer had failed and they had a sacred duty to finish the job. Hands abused me, large male hands placed themselves on parts of me I didn't know mattered. Hands of teachers pushed, pulled, and strapped me, because I laid my hands on the children who hit me. I wanted to erase hands. Especially the hands that touched my daughters a generation later — large male hands.... I wanted to elevate faces, characters, sounds, bodies, rich with love and affection, but without hands.

I wanted to erase the memory of hands that didn't do things. Hands that didn't pat me on the head at school for a job well done. Hands that didn't clap when I sang solo for my school choir. Hands that disappeared when I sat on a bus seat next to them. Silent hands, infinite in their discomfort about my presence. Hands of men who passed through swinging doors, without holding them for me. Hands that never slipped theirs in mine.

I whisked through my household chores after your father left for the day in search of work. Day in and day out, I struggled to write Bertha into public life without hands. But they kept poking out from behind the curtain covering my memory. I cried. I screamed. I yelled, but those damn hands kept appearing. Little hands, tiny and soft, met my face, caressing little hands and a voice, the gentle even tones of my mother's people whispered in my ears, "Don't worry mommy, it'll be all right. If you keep trying you'll be a writer some day." Those pudgy fingers became Bertha's, and my own skinny fingers her young friend's.

Two years. It took two years to finally finish the story. Two years of fighting those horrible other hands and coming to love yours. You were there under the boards and bricks and foam we called "the couch" to hear the nice white lady feminist tell me "to take the drinking out of the story and we will publish it."

You heard raven rise in my throat, cackle arrogantly at such idiocy. You heard it stop dead in its tracks and with lynx efficiency my voice purred a soft "thank you" while my hands gracefully reclaimed my manuscript. And when she was gone, you watched me pull the drapes, lean on that typewriter and you heard me whisper, "Bertha, Bertha, some day the world will love you as I do." You watched me weep, stare at my hands; then carefully I put Bertha in my box of magic and I began another story.

You were not complacent. One pair of hands fixed coffee from her chair perch, another handed me a cigarette, another a match, while the smallest least competent little hands tormented my head with a hair brush — sure this would do the trick and stop the tears I shed for Bertha. And Tania.

Tania, Tania, Tania. I made such an old woman of you. You kept saying to no one in particular, "the woman is soooostupid, what-does-she-know" in exactly the same voice as my great-grandmother, my grandmother, and my mom. And the click, click of keys against the platter brought back the sound of the women in the crab shack. I wanted to laugh.

"What does she know anyway." It stuck with me my darlings, long after the hands ceased to plague me. You knew, you knew my stories were for me, perfect children, conceived by my memory, my heart, my imagination, my hands. All of me went to work to create this woman who is every Native woman whose hands ever slugged it out in a cannery, in a berry field, until sick to death of work without any pleasure, she put her hands on a bottle.

I left her in that box until just this year — fifteen years. I kept saying, "what do they know". And now we have women who want to see Bertha in a book — Bertha my favorite "child". I worked like hell to get her in print. I had to write all kinds of things, say things, before the world was ready for Bertha. I had to put my life between blank white sheets in 1976. It wasn't the one I wanted to write. Bertha was not in it, nor was Charley or the myriad of other stories and poems I had written, but it was one this country was ready for: my life. There you were, all starched and ready for mama's first interview. Nothing came of it. I sat and glared at the reporter whose questions are now classic statements of colossal ignorance.

I left without speaking. "It is going to take a political movement to jar these fools loose", I mumbled to you without caring whether or not you heard. I threw myself into the arena. Heart and soul, leaflet after leaflet, articles rattled out of the typewriter, until finally, it looked like the day was done when some fool was going to ask me if I "wanted to put white people on reservations".

Native people everywhere had to say things and do things in this country before anyone really wanted to hear from us. Hundreds of us, thousands of us, had to jump up to microphones connected to radios, televisions, and the bullhorns of road blocks, demonstrations, and fish-ins, before anyone wanted to hear from us.

The country has not changed much my children, but some of the people have. There are men and women in this country, poets, writers, social activists of all colours who want to know who we are. My writing helped to do that. Oh, maybe not a lot, but more than a satin shorts' worth.

In 1988, *I am Woman* greeted the Third International Feminist Bookfair in Montreal. She was the best seller at the Fair. My girls, you should have been there. Instead, you were home alone, working and hungry. Hungry for weeks on end because somehow you had acquired the tenacity, the sense of loyalty to your art, to rise above an empty belly and finish your play penniless. You trekked through the heat wave of 1988, not for the white man who promised to pay and didn't, but for your art and your fellow actors. It did not matter to you that those other youngsters had parents at home to feed them, drive them to work, and home again. Finally, I came home in time to take you to the hospital.

You did this because you know that the creative self is sacred. Magnificent and sacred. Fate. The fate of a people who uphold the sacredness of the creative soul in a world that crushes creativity everywhere it finds it. The train stops here. The empty cattle car we have always ridden in stops here. Generations of our women have worked for little or nothing, while those who employed us lived well. I want you to clutch the thread of tenacity and loyalty to your sacred creative self which drove you to walk in the hot sun, work on an empty belly, and walk home again. What I want you to let go of is the notion that for our people, this is enough. I want you to dream, as I did; we have a perfect right to be. I want you to imagine being an eagle in full flight, a raven, cocky and sure, but I want you to imagine being all of those things on a full stomach with a home to call your own. This is not a Canadian dream — before they came it was our reality.

You see, Bertha died because she dared not dream. She dared not envision a home. She dared not conceive these people should treat her better. That was left to me. My second book nearly cost you your lives, but it brought hope to a good many of our people.

In Montreal, I saw hands rise to touch their cheeks, caress and nurture their faces. I saw hands wipe gentle tears of joy, of rage, of sadness from their eyes. I heard and saw hands rise in tumult, clapping for this little brown crab-pounder's daughter. And my dreams became a groundswell in the hearts of those women. I didn't change the world, but I did touch the hearts of some of Canada's finest women and these women will not sit idly and watch us die. And that is something more than satin shorts.

Lee Maracle

LEE MARACLE

I am a writer, a poet, and an orator who speaks internationally on subjects ranging from medicine to social conditions, bringing to all my work a knowledge of contemporary society and my own history. I develop and share my ideas through stories. In *I am Woman* (Write-On Press Publishers, 1988), I describe my personal struggle and the struggle of Native people to "climb the mountain of racism and reach the summit of a new humanity". My other books include the autobiographical *Bobbi Lee: indian Rebel* (Women's Press, 1976, reissued 1990); and *Linked Lives*, a book of poetry published by Trois Editions in 1990. *Sojourner's Truth and Other Stories* (Press Gang Publishers, 1990) focuses on interracial issues and traditional Native cultural values. In the tradition of Native oratory, each of the stories in *Sojourner's Truth and Other Stories* is layered with unresolved human dilemmas. Weaving the essence of Native lives into my storytelling, I write with love and humour about the pain and triumphs, and the spirit of resistance. I co-edited the book *Telling It: Women and Language Across Cultures* (Press Gang Publishers, 1990). My novel *Sun Dogs* was published by Theytus Books in 1992; my most recent book, *Raven's Song,* was published by Press Gang Publishers in 1993.

EVELYN HAMDON

My Continuing Identity Crisis

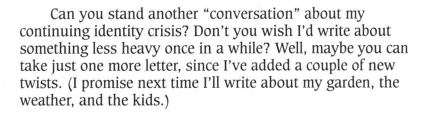

Dear Aunty Lee:

Can you stand another "conversation" about my continuing identity crisis? Don't you wish I'd write about something less heavy once in a while? Well, maybe you can take just one more letter, since I've added a couple of new twists. (I promise next time I'll write about my garden, the weather, and the kids.)

The reason I always write these tomes to you is because I know that for a good portion of your life, you have had to tackle these issues of personal identity as they relate to ethnicity, and because I so admire your self-awareness which is the end product of this struggle. So I find myself turning, once again, to you as an elder, friend, and, I hope, soul mate, with the hope that you will redirect me if I am going astray in my own quest for an integrated identity.

I know it seems as if we spent the better part of a year talking about the Gulf, but it still haunts me. The issues, though not directly related to the war, are a result of the racism directed towards Arabs during that time. So many thoughts, feelings, and fears, which lay dormant were stirred to the surface as that terrible year dragged on. All at once I was seven again; cornered against the school portable by most of my grade two class, while they taunted me with "Look at you, you look like a 'nigger' in the (class) picture." That sea of little white faces hating me, scorning me because of my dark skin, large nose, coarse black hair. How I longed to be pale, have straight, thin, blond hair and, maybe, even a few freckles.

Fortunately, as I grew older, the tolerance of my peers increased, and by the time I reached university, I found that my "ethnicity" was even an advantage in the political groups I became involved with. I suppose it meant that I had suffered first hand, a real plus for an "activist". So, separated from reality by a layer of academia, I found the old issues which I had faced for so many years, issues which had shaped my character, were pushed aside by other concerns.

For many years, my identity skirted my "Arabness" while I focused on my roles as a teacher, mother, feminist, wife, activist, daughter, and on and on. While issues involving race were never out of my consciousness, their personal relevance to me was insignificant. I was part of another "colourful ethnic group" who could boast wonderful food, a generous nature, and fun circle dancing. And having so many well-integrated personalities around (i.e., my proudly Arab relatives) made it easy for me to delude myself into thinking that I was immune to racism. I was outside its jurisdiction. Our family was loved, accepted, respected. The women, such as yourself, successful in business, social services, community work. All was right with my world.

The war changed all of that.

From the time of the U.N. embargo, the word Arab became synonymous with the enemy. Preparation of western civilians for the inevitable war centred around presenting the Iraqi/Arab people as hostile, evil, and barbaric, bent on the destruction of all that we hold dear. Years of negative media stereotyping of Arabs made it easy for people to see us as the bad guys: swarthy, unshaven, bad teeth, amoral. Even the portrayal of Kuwait as a victim and the matter of Arab participation in the so-called coalition forces couldn't change this western view of Arabs. All that remained was for the west, or coalition countries as they became known, to have in their minds that the Iraqis were these same villains they had been seeing in movies for years. After that it was easy for them to embrace the concept of a war with such people. (As a corollary, it also made it easy for them to refer to the tens of thousands of dead Iraqi women and children as "collateral damage".)

While the situation in the Gulf became more tense, so did things here in Edmonton. All of this propaganda had its desired effect on the general population. It was okay to Arab-bash in public. "How long", I asked myself, "had these hostile feelings lived underground?" (Were these people I heard in the media, in malls, in my babysitting co-op, those vicious little seven-year-olds all grown up?) Radio talk shows were swamped with callers venting their anger at "heathen" Arabs willing to take the world to the brink of world war. The few Iraqi sympathizers who spoke their views aloud touched off frenzied cries for internment camps to protect Canadian citizenry from potential Arab-Canadian treachery.

The surfacing of this racism put all of my protective instincts *vis-à-vis* my kids on red alert. It seems all of their lives I have stood vigil, waiting at the ready to defend my children from bigots who would hurt them. Even before Geoffrey was born, I was afraid for his safety because of that horrible nurse I had at a hospital. Remember the one who ranted and raved about Arabs generally but Arab men in particular. And there I was hooked up to the IV, dehydrated, throwing up, barely able to talk, and scared to death I was losing my baby while this woman went on and on about the bestial nature of Arab men and the wretched condition of the ignorant Arab women. Did I rise up, indignant, and put her in her rightful place? Did I deliver a scathing rebuttal? Oh no. Instead I whispered, in tears, that these men she was referring to were my Dad, brothers, uncles, and grandfathers. You see, it was all I could think of to say. I could picture these gentle, jovial, humorous men, and I could not understand how she could hate such men so. And I was afraid that if I spoke up or complained to the hospital administration, she might hurt me, or worse, my baby, when I returned to deliver. I could only think about protecting my child. She must not, at any cost, hurt my baby.

Can you see how the war, coupled with the memory of this and other experiences (including the damaging ones of my own childhood), might lead me to consider drastic measures to "protect" my children? By the middle of January I was on the verge of changing their names to camouflage their Arab heritage. I reasoned that if the parents of the kids Alia was going to school with were saying viciously anti-Arab things, how could I be sure Alia wouldn't be subjected to the parroting of racist epithets? How could I allow her to experience the spirit-killing racism that I had? Knowing how proud you are of our heritage, I am sure this sounds repugnant and cowardly, but I had become consumed with the fear that Alia and Geoffrey would suffer; that they would be haunted for years by bitter memories of racism. I even felt relief (forgive me) that they do not look at all Arab. Obviously, I did not succumb to the fear, and I am glad now that the counsel of the wise teacher, and one or two trusted friends, resulted in my taking pro-active measures. I found myself taking action and taking the kids along. Now was the time for them to learn how to defend themselves and to never be ashamed of who or what they are. The school was wonderful, tackling the issues of stereotyping, racism, and the futility of war in a sensitive and intelligent manner. In the end, we have emerged stronger and I have never regretted not changing their names. But for every day that the war lasted I was afraid for them.

Like you, I felt that I had to counter this dangerous situation with a campaign of cross-cultural awareness. (Remember all of your newspaper clippings flying to Edmonton via Air Mail?) But unlike you, I found that in coming to the "defence" of Arabs, I had to define for myself just what that meant. I realized that my knowledge of Arab culture was inadequate. What was I defending — a "race", a way of life, or what? And in the midst of all of this confusion was my own personal uncertainty. Sure, I am of Lebanese descent, but what does that exactly mean after three generations? When a local broadcaster made a statement about those bloody Arabs, did he know that he was referring to a world that stretches from Yemen to Lebanon to Morocco? To a number of cultures which are as diverse as they are similar? And Arab-Canadians are as diverse as their cousins overseas. Some of us still retain the language and traditions with exactness. Others of us have a "skeletal" version of the culture upon which we hang our Canadian self. Yet others of us have completely forgotten our origins and long ago dropped the hyphenation. I often found myself defending my Arab kin by invoking the evils of racism rather than trying to promote intercultural understanding.

Some of my difficulty lay in that I am acutely aware that Arab culture tends to exclude women. I can hear the protests as I type this ("the Koran elevated women and gave them rights", "look how rapists are treated in Saudi Arabia", etc.), but as you and I know, as in most of the rest of the world, Arab women are second-class citizens. There were days when I found it hard to defend anyone or anything. Here was another patriarchal system which deserved to be overhauled from top to bottom, and I found myself overlooking this, not speaking to this issue because of the lousy war and the racism it had stirred up.

So many of us are aware of this new tradition within the Arab world which is so inward, fearful, sceptical, that it shuns the light of change in spite of what good it might find within it. I am aware that in most Arab circles my brand of feminism would be condemned. The Imams, their pious followers, the priests and theirs, eschew philosophies which call for women to liberate themselves or to discover their own power and use it freely and without apology or shame. I have always wanted to believe that your Mother, my Sitty, was just another in a long line of grand Arab matriarchs who presided with wisdom and dignity over a family and a community. Were we raised in a community and time that was nothing more than a "blip on a screen"? Were we shielded from reality rather than steeped in it? I have always taken my feminine identity from her (as have all of the women in our family), but more and more I think she was a woman who rose above the tyranny of our patriarchal culture and, by force of will and strength of character, kept those traditions at bay. What a rude awakening I have had. Still, I feel inspired by her to continue to find my own way, as an Arab woman, just as she found hers. If she could have the courage then, without benefit of education, English, or even age (imagine being sixteen when she came here as a bride), to redefine the "Arab woman", then who am I to shy away from the challenge? So I made a choice; I chose action rather than victimization — I will not succumb to being triply marginalized (an Arab within Canadian society, a woman within Canadian society, and a woman within the Arab-Canadian society). I will not be quiet and accept all that conspires against my Arab sisters. We are of a magnificent tradition of women who are strong, resourceful, and loving. We can use this to find a new way of being Arab-Canadian women.

There are days when I feel like I am struggling to create something that doesn't exist — a utopian Arab identity full of enlightenment, grace, charity, nobility. Then I ask myself why should the Arab world be so perfect? God knows that the western world certainly hasn't cornered the market on these qualities. As I read article after article about babies beaten by their parents; women beaten and raped by their husbands, lovers, and strangers; thousands upon thousands of women, men, and children homeless, without food or education or proper medical care, in the wealthiest of Canadian or American cities, I think: "So what are these phone-in types talking about, what am I apologizing for: the world is basically a fairly barbaric place — period."

It has gradually dawned on me that what I was experiencing was no different from what a Native Canadian woman would face, or a non-hyphenated Canadian woman, or any other woman anywhere. We are in a position of "defending" ourselves from our culture while at times struggling to be a part, somehow, of the same culture which marginalizes or excludes us. The result: identity confusion.

After all of this self-searching, I have decided that I can best serve the "Arab" cause by opening the windows, letting the fresh air in, asking questions, and forcing any Arab who will listen (male or female), to let those questions penetrate their psyche. In the final analysis, that's what Sitty did — and it worked for her and the community she was a part of.

The struggle for me is to put all of these parts together in some way that can work for me and, maybe, benefit Arab-Canadian women coming after me. I guess it might be a long time in the making. Who knows, maybe my granddaughter will pick up where I leave off. I hope, if she does, that she has a mentor such as I have had in you.

Please write soon and give me your valued thoughts on these matters; I can't wait to hear what you have to say.

With much love,

Evelyn

P.S. I just wanted to add this before mailing: Yesterday Alia came home from school upset because a friend had said, "Oooh, Yuch, I didn't know Arabs had sweaty hands. That's gross!" Guess what Alia's response was. She said — indignantly I might add, "What an ignorant thing to say. Don't you know anything about Arabs?" Then she marched home to tell me and to suggest that we call the friend's mother and tell her to tell her daughter not to be so rude. Hooray! The next generation has entered, stage right, and what a grand entrance it was.

EVELYN HAMDON

I was born in 1954 in Edmonton of Lebanese-Canadian parents. All of my grandparents, both paternal and maternal, came from the Bekaa Valley in Lebanon. I grew up in Edmonton, eventually attending the University of Alberta where I studied philosophy and political science. While attending university I became involved in Fourth World support work, the Free Southern Africa Committee, and the Edmonton Women's Coalition. Later, as a unionized child-care worker I was involved with a group of women who endeavoured to have sexual harassment clauses negotiated into our union's Master Agreement. (This was not considered a priority by our "brothers".) After graduation I travelled overseas and spent six weeks in Lebanon, a very moving experience for me. Currently I am involved in teaching family life education courses for various social services agencies and doing research on a freelance basis. I am married to Kevin O'Brien and have two wonderful children, Alia and Geoffrey.

CAROLE ANNE SOONG
(née Wong)

My Experience
in the Women's Movement

To All Young People:

You need to be aware of our past history so that you do not allow the same problems to be repeated in the future.

I'm writing this letter as a way to share my experience in the women's movement over these past twenty years. Looking back to 1970, I realize how that Report of the three-year-long Royal Commission on the Status of Women in Canada had such an impact on my life. Those 167 recommendations of the Royal Commission were the catalyst which put me on the road to active involvement in the fight against sexism and racism.

There undoubtedly have been some changes for the better that have taken place in regards to women's issues since 1970, but, unfortunately, there are many problems and issues remaining which still keep women, particularly those of immigrant and visible minority backgrounds, at a disadvantage in education, at work, in the home, and in law.

Throughout these two decades I have, on the voluntary or work levels, been putting my energies into changing the status quo and refusing to accept sexist and racist attitudes and behaviour.

My involvement has certainly helped me to develop a sense of personal confidence and empowerment. I really want other women to be aware that this can happen for them as well. When you take those chances and speak out, refuse to accept sexist and/or racist treatment, you will be taking on what may seem to be very tough opponents at times,

229

but as a result you will eventually, no doubt, build up a real sense of empowerment.

Since childhood, as I grew up in the Chinatown area of Vancouver, I was aware of how racism permeated the lives of Chinese-Canadians. Here I was, a fourth-generation Canadian with a maternal grandmother who was the first female of Chinese extraction born in the province and my father, who was born and raised in Victoria. Yet our colour and ethnicity often dictated how we were treated in our country of birth. From my growing-up years I have a number of memories which stand out.

- Memories of teachers who told us that attending "after-school Chinese language classes" was an interference with our "regular school work".

- Memories of the sudden disappearance of my Japanese-Canadian classmates in elementary school and not understanding until years later that my friends, simply because of their ethnicity, had been sent away to the interior of British Columbia and internment camps because Canada was at war with Japan. But they were Canadian by birth, and didn't they have any rights and protection from such treatment?

- Memories of being ushered into specific sections of local movie theatres because we were not white.

- Memories of hearing bitter stories of relatives who could not gain entry into medicine, architecture, and law studies at our local university because they were Chinese.

- Memories of my father telling me that in his childhood days, Chinese-Canadian students were not welcomed in Victoria public schools.

- Memories of how my father and uncles lobbied Ottawa after World War II to give Chinese-Canadians the vote in Canada.

Early on for me, memories such as these served to make me aware of what discrimination did to people.

So in 1970 along came the *Report of the Royal Commission on the Status of Women in Canada,* and it was the impetus for me to work with a group of women to organize a conference to develop strategies to ensure that some action would take place on implementing these 167 recommendations of the Report. It was from this event that a local feminist group started — the "Vancouver Status of Women Action

Coordinating Council". In retrospect, I met some very special women who were also Charter Members of this group.

There was Joan Wallace, who was the Council's first President and also a member of the first Canadian Advisory Council on the Status of Women. With her extensive experience in journalism and public relations, she was always thinking up ways to publicize the feminist cause. It was Joan, a real mentor to me, who urged me to enter the *Chatelaine* magazine's "Mrs. Chatelaine — Woman of the Year" contest. The idea was to put forward a feminist perspective and also to urge the magazine to change Mrs. to Ms. — such a "radical" idea at that time! What a shock when I was actually chosen as their winner for 1973. Well, I knew we had a long way to go when I read a letter to the editor in the magazine that said I was "taking advantage of my mother". Why? Because after eleven years at home raising five children, I decided it was time to resume my career outside the home, and it was my mother who helped out as a care-giver to the only grandchildren she had. You see, I was an only child because my parents, after living through the Great Depression, decided they could only support one child and were so pleased when grandchildren arrived.

In the 1970s, attitudes toward working mothers were not very sympathetic. I believe there has been some shift away from this negative stance since there has been such an increase in mothers working outside the home over the past twenty years. Then, of course, there was Rosemary Brown, who was the first volunteer "ombudswoman" of the Vancouver Status of Women Action Coordinating Council. We were all so proud and pleased when she was elected the first Black woman member of the British Columbia Legislature. I will never forget the time she told me of her trip to the supermarket (when she was already an MLA) and while shopping for vegetables, she was approached by another woman shopper who presumed that since Rosemary was Black, she must be a domestic. She asked Rosemary how to prepare a particular vegetable and then went on to ask her if she might have some "available days" to work at her house. Rosemary replied that she was already too busy and so was not available. We shared a good laugh thinking about how foolish that woman would feel when she at some point in the future saw Rosemary Brown, MLA, in the news. For me, Rosemary was such a role model and I learned so much from observing her work and deal with all the cases of discrimination that women brought to the Council.

And finally, I remember what I learned from Hattie Ferguson, the only Aboriginal woman on the Board of our Council. She told us how Canadian legislation — the *Indian Act* — took away the status of Indian women when they married either non-native or non-status Indian men. She never did live to see the day when that Act was finally changed so that Indian women could regain their status.

At times it seems that changes take so long, or gains made are lost and we must start the work all over again. But what makes me optimistic is that I do see a growing consciousness and increased actions of women from under-represented groups in striving for the improvement of women's status, not just for themselves but for all women. The feminist movement will see a new wave of energy from these women who have so much to offer, but who in the past have not been included. Some of this I attribute to attitudes of discrimination on the part of those who do not see just how much women of the under-represented groups have to contribute and want to contribute in the struggle for equality.

So as I end my letter, it seems as if things have come full circle. During 1990, I saw the culmination of the efforts of a number of Vancouver women as they went about organizing a meeting to review women's concerns of today as well as those outlined twenty years previously in the Royal Commission on the Status of Women in Canada report. This time I was not the only woman of colour involved in the organizing work. Now there was a wide mix of women who were interested and ready to put their energies into ensuring that the situation of women will continue to improve during the nineties and beyond. There is no doubt that women of colour will be key players in the years ahead.

From

Carole Anne Soong

CAROLE ANNE SOONG (née Wong)

I came from a pioneer family with roots in this country pre-dating Confederation. My great-grandparents came on a sailing ship across the Pacific Ocean from China. They were seeking the gold mountain of California and British Columbia. Grandmother Elizabeth Wun Chang was the first baby girl of Chinese ancestry born in British Columbia in 1871 (the year B.C. became a province of Canada). I was born in Montreal but grew up in Vancouver. I am the mother of five children and grandmother of three, a Social Work graduate of the University of British Columbia, a feminist, and an advocate on human rights issues. I have more than twenty years of employment in the federal government.

THEMATIC INDEX

Childhood Experience/Racial Hatred of Small Children

Asein
Haruko Okano
Althea Samuels
Marcia Crosby
Alice Masak French
Lee Maracle

Children's Aid Wardship

Haruko Okano

Creativity

Lee Maracle
Haruko Okano
Minnie Peters

Culture Imperialism

Mary Panegoosho Cousins
Alice Masak French

Cultural Transmission/Preservation and Teaching of Histories

Nipisha Lau Bracken
Marcia Crosby
Mayann Francis
Maya
Rhoda Tagaq
Anita Jennifer Wong
Althea Samuels
Minnie Peters
Camille Hernández-Ramdwar
Beryl Tsang

Curriculum

Marcia Crosby
Mayann Francis
Maya
Anita Jennifer Wong
Althea Samuels

Difference (Coping with Looking and Being Different; Denial of Difference)

Thao P.T. Vo
Sharda Vaidyanath
Haruko Okano
Irshad Manji
Anna Woo
Anita Jennifer Wong

Heritage (see Cultural Transmission/Preservation and
                Teaching of Histories)

Identity/Self-esteem
   Asein
   Maya
   Anna Woo
   Anita Jennifer Wong
   Irshad Manji
   Camille Hernández-Ramdwar
   Beryl Tsang
   Jaya Chauhan
   Evelyn Hamdon
   Monica Goulet

Immigrant Experience
   Sharda Vaidyanath
   Rajani E. Alexander
   Heather Crichlow
   Pham thi Quê
   Chanthala Phomtavong
   Aruna Isaac Papp
   Minnie Aodla Freeman
   Thao P.T. Vo
   Beryl Tsang
   Beatrice Archer Watson
   Rosemary Eng
   Naïma Bendris
   Mila
   Ann Haney

Incest/Sexual Abuse
   Marcia Crosby
   Asein

Indian Act
   Carole Anne Soong (née Wong)

Internment Camps for People of Japanese Descent during WW II
   Haruko Okano
   Carole Anne Soong (née Wong)

Intersection of Gender and Racial Oppression
   Jaya Chauhan
   Evelyn Hamdon
   Sunera Thobani

238

Language Issues
    Thao P.T. Vo
    Anna Woo
    Irshad Manji
    Marcia Crosby
    Alice Masak French
    Minnie Peters
    Chanthala Phomtavong
    Carole Anne Soong (née Wong)

Lesbian Experience
    Asein

Maternal Love
    Monica Goulet
    Irshad Manji
    Lee Maracle

Media
    Rosemary Eng
    Beatrice Archer Watson
    Evelyn Hamdon
    Naïma Bendris

Mother-Daughter Relationship
    Ann Haney
    Asein
    Rajani E. Alexander
    Haruko Okano
    Anna Woo
    Anita Jennifer Wong
    Monica Goulet
    Irshad Manji
    Beryl Tsang

New Reproductive Technologies (see Sex Selection)

Northern Education
    Mary Panegoosho Cousins

Peace
    Minnie Aodla Freeman

Police (reluctance to intervene in cases of violence against racial minority women)
    Aruna Isaac Papp

Racism in Canada (see Anger, Childhood Experience/Racial Hatred of
Small Children, Curriculum, Discrimination in Employment,
Exclusion, Identity\Self-esteem, Immigrant Experience,
Language Issues, Media, Police, Residential Schools
for Aboriginal Children, School Experience, Stress,
Unemployment, and Violence)

Residential Schools for Aboriginal Children
Minnie Peters
Mary Panegoosho Cousins
Minnie Aodla Freeman
Alice Masak French

Ritual/Spirituality
Beryl Tsang
Mayann Francis
Marcia Crosby

Royal Commission on the Status of Women in Canada
Carole Anne Soong (née Wong)

Satisfaction
Ann Haney
Minnie Peters
Carole Anne Soong (née Wong)
Thao P.T. Vo
Sharda Vaidyanath

School Experience (see Curriculum, and Education)
Asein
Heather Crichlow
Rosemary Eng
Mayann Francis
Alice Masak French
Evelyn Hamdon
Minnie Peters
Althea Samuels
Beryl Tsang
Anita Jennifer Wong

Science
Jaya Chauhan
Asein

Sex Selection (see New Reproductive Technologies)
Sunera Thobani